Threat & Risk Assessments needed in the 21st Century!

By

Jeremy T.T. Mallenby, BA, BSc

and

Patricia E.A. Mallenby, BA, BSc

References courtesy of the Fair Use Act, for research purposes, to clarify the author's point of view.

The 1961 Report of the Register of Copyrights on the General Revision of the U.S. Copyright Law cites examples of activities that courts have regarded as fair use: "quotation of excerpts in a review or criticism for purposes of illustration or comment; quotation of short passages in a scholarly or technical work, for illustration or clarification of the author's observations; use in a parody of some of the content of the work parodied; summary of an address or article, with brief quotations, in a news report; reproduction by a library of a portion of a work to replace part of a damaged copy; reproduction by a teacher or student of a small part of a work to illustrate a lesson; reproduction of a work in legislative or judicial proceedings or reports; incidental and fortuitous reproduction, in a newsreel or broadcast, of a work located in the scene of an event being reported."

Preface

There are some terrific courses out-there about Conflict Analysis, Conflict Management, Conflict Resolution, and some of the hazards of our 21st Century.

This little book is about some of them.

It also emphasizes the need, in such a world we find ourselves, it pays for everyone to take personal precautions for themselves, their families, and their loved ones.

Jeremy T.T. Mallenby, BA, BSc

and

Patricia E.A. Mallenby, BA, BSc

Index

Global Conflict & Homeland Security	Page 4
The Conflict in Kosovo	Page 8
Other Conflicts	Page 12
Injustice	Page 16
World Security	Page 19
The Root of All Evil	Page 27
Be Ever Vigilant	Page 30
Irrational Fears or the State of the World Today	Page 36
Identifying Subjects of Interest	Page 42
Surprising "Terrorist" Groups	Page 47
Terrorist Targets	Page 54
Nuclear, biological, and chemical weapons	Page 60
Religious Legitimacy	Page 65
Personal Protection Equipment and Officer Safety	Page 70
Risk Management	Page 77
Personal Precautions in These Dangerous Times	Page 82
Appendices	Page 85

Global Conflict & Homeland Security

As cited in the United States Institute of Peace Certificate Course in Conflict Analysis[1], it is cited:

"As the specter of nuclear confrontation began to fade, many held hope that this spirit of cooperation might set a precedent, that absent the context of superpower rivalry, nations of the world might find a new willingness to work together, as an international community, to resolve conflicts through peaceful negotiations and diplomacy."[2]

And, with "the end of the Cold War brought relief and optimism to people throughout the world. Former adversaries made major reductions in their conventional and nuclear arms. New leaders found ways to cooperate on a range of international issues."[3]

For example, as summarized by the Arms Control Association[4], "over the past four decades, American and Soviet/Russian leaders have used a progression of bilateral agreements and other measures to limit and reduce their substantial nuclear warhead and strategic missile and bomber arsenals."[5]

Specifically, "begun in November 1969, the Strategic Arms Limitation Talks (SALT) produced by May 1972 both the Anti-Ballistic Missile (ABM) Treaty, which limited strategic missile defenses to 200 (later 100) interceptors each, and the Interim Agreement, an executive agreement that capped U.S. and Soviet ICBM and SLBM forces."[6]

Continuing with, "the Strategic Arms Reduction Treaty (START I), first proposed in the early 1980s by President Ronald Reagan and finally signed in July 1991, required the United States and the Soviet Union to reduce their deployed strategic arsenals to 1,600 delivery vehicles, carrying no more than 6,000 warheads as counted using the agreement's rules."[7]

And, "in June 1992, Presidents George H. W. Bush and Boris Yeltsin agreed to pursue a follow-on accord, START II was signed in January 1993, called for reducing deployed strategic arsenals to 3,000-3,500 warheads and banned the deployment of destabilizing multiple-warhead land-based missiles."[8]

However, "START II was effectively shelved as a result of the 2002 U.S. withdrawal from the ABM treaty."[9]

And, "on April 8, 2010, the United States and Russia signed New START, a legally binding, verifiable agreement that limits each side's deployed strategic nuclear warheads to 1,550 and strategic delivery systems (ICBMs, SLBMs and heavy bombers) to 800 deployed and non-deployed, such as submarines in overhaul, with a sub limit of 700 deployed."[10]

With, "the U.S. Senate approved New START on Dec. 22, 2010. The approval process of the Russian parliament (passage by both the State Duma and Federation Council) was completed January 26, 2011. The treaty entered into force on February 5, 2011."[11]

Nonetheless, not all was well in many parts of the world.

Again, as cited in the United States Institute of Peace Certificate Course in Conflict Analysis[12]," the international community failed to provide a coherent response to the genocide in Rwanda [see Appendix 1]."[13]

As stated elsewhere, "the genocide was sparked by the death of the Rwandan President Juvenal Habyarimana, a Hutu, when his plane was shot down above Kigali airport on 6 April 1994 [see Appendix 2]."[14]

With a French judge blaming the current Rwandan President, Paul Kagame - at the time the leader of a Tutsi rebel group - and some of his close associates for carrying out the rocket attack."[15]

No matter, "whoever was responsible, within hours a campaign of violence spread from the capital throughout the country, and did not subside until three months later."[16]

Where, "in an attempt to eliminate Rwanda's Tutsi minority, the Hutu majority systematically slaughtered 800,000 individuals, most of them civilians, in just 100 days, a rate of killing that rivals the worst in human history."[17]

And, "armed with machetes, the killers were both vicious and organized, torturing their victims, murdering them in cold blood, and dumping their bodies in mass graves. In numerous cases, such killing took place while international peacekeepers stood by helplessly."[18]

As cited, "in the debates and soul-searching following the Rwandan genocide, there has been little agreement over what exactly could have been done when and by whom. However, on two points analysts generally concur: that individual nations, regional organizations and the international community need to be better prepared to prevent such catastrophes in the future, and that part of this preparation is attempting to understand what went wrong in Rwanda."[19]

Ethnic cleansing was the new term, where "the genocide in Rwanda was one of the worst cases of ethnic violence in world history. On a smaller but still substantial scale, ethnic violence cost lives in countries such as Burundi, Yemen and Ethiopia."[20]

As reported, "since 1993 approximately 150,000 Burundians—2.5% of the population in this tiny Central African country—have been slaughtered in ethnic-based massacres of civilians by the ruling Tutsi forces and insurgent Hutu militias [see Appendix 3]."[21]

Where it was cited, "this is only part of a wave of politically motivated genocides that have swept across Central Africa. During three months in 1994, a small Hutu ruling clique in neighboring Rwanda, fearing they would lose political power, unleashed the extermination of about 800,000 people, mainly minority Tutsis."[22]

In Ethiopia, as reported, "government troops have executed civilians and conducted ethnic cleansing in Ethiopia's Somali Region, a rebel group said on Friday. The Ogaden National Liberation Front (ONLF) said the bodies of a civil servant and a businessman were found dead in Kebridehar in eastern Ethiopia on January 17, a day after they and 17 other people were rounded up by security officials."[23]

With the government rejecting such allegations"[24], instead insisting "the ONLF is fighting for independence for the ethnic Somali-dominated Ogaden province. Ethiopia believes the Ogaden basin may contain 4 trillion cubic feet of gas reserves and major oil deposits, drawing interest from foreign firms."[25]

With respect to Yemen, as cited, head of the opposition coalition, the Joint Meeting Parties (JMP), Hassan Zaid Monday said "the war in Sadaa is initiated to obliterate the Zaydi ideology from Yemen and replace it with the Suni ideology," adding "the war in Sadaa began when the state insulted the Zaydis and Hashemites, kicked them out of their jobs, and took over their mosques," stressing "what is happening in Yemen is a war on behalf of other states." Zaid who was talking to Aylaf online magazine said "Zaydis in Yemen are treated as if they were foreigners or agents and as if they have no right to life and liberty."[26]

Footnotes

1 - 3. United States Institute of Peace
2301 Constitution Avenue, NW
Washington, DC 20037
http://www.usip.org/education-training/international/online-courses
Certificate Course in Conflict Analysis - Academics and professionals in the field of conflict management face extraordinary challenges in dealing with the various phases of conflict, whether it is rebuilding in the aftermath, stopping conflict in progress, or preventing conflict before it begins.

4 - 11. Arms Control Association
1313 L St, NW, Suite 130

Washington, DC 20005
U.S.-Russian Nuclear Arms Control Agreements at a Glance
http://www.armscontrol.org/factsheets/USRussiaNuclearAgreementsMarch2010

12 - 13. United States Institute of Peace
2301 Constitution Avenue, NW
Washington, DC 20037
Certificate Course in Conflict Analysis
http://www.usip.org/education-training/international/online-courses

14 - 16. Rwanda: How the genocide happened
BBC News Thursday, 18 December 2008
http://webcache.googleusercontent.com/search?q=cache:IZ_WnI801DEJ:www.bbc.co.uk/2/hi/1288230.stm+genocide+in+Rwanda+ends&cd=7&hl=en&ct=clnk&gl=ca&source=www.google.ca

17 - 20. United States Institute of Peace
2301 Constitution Avenue, NW
Washington, DC 20037
Certificate Course in Conflict Analysis
http://www.usip.org/education-training/international/online-courses

21 - 22. Burundi and the Crisis in Central Africa
Foreign Policy in Focus
By Stephen Weissman, January 1, 1997
http://webcache.googleusercontent.com/search?q=cache:biDEZ992HDIJ:www.fpif.org/reports/burundi_and_the_crisis_in_central_africa+ethnic+cleansing+Burundi&cd=1&hl=en&ct=clnk&gl=ca&source=www.google.ca

23 - 25. Rebels accuse Ethiopian army of ethnic cleansing
Reuters Fri Jan 21, 2011
By Aaron Maasho
http://af.reuters.com/article/topNews/idAFJOE70K0E320110121

26. Opposition Chief Says Yemen Seeking to Wipe out Zaydis
Posted by Mohammed Al-Amrani on Oct 6th, 2009
http://yementribune.com/blog/?p=720

The Conflict in Kosovo

In addition, as cited in the United States Institute of Peace Certificate Course in Conflict Analysis, it is mentioned: "in a number of former communist countries, the end of the Cold War acted to trigger conflict, as long-standing internal divisions boiled to the surface in the sudden absence of single-party rule."[1]

And, "for the most part, the countries of Eastern and Central Europe managed their transitions without violence"; however, "the one exception was Yugoslavia, which disintegrated in a series of violent conflicts, including conflicts in Croatia, Bosnia, and Kosovo."[2]

As further noted, "Ethnic Cleansing created more than two million refugees and displaced persons in former Yugoslavia during the war in Bosnia. This number increased with the expulsion of Serbs from Croatia and with the ferocious atrocities committed by Serbs against the Albanian majority in Kosovo, prior and during (in spite of) NATO air strikes."[3]

With, "although Serbs were by far the most successful "cleansers," all sides adopted this method in the course of war. Record ethnic cleansing operations were Serbian Operation Horseshoe in Kosovo and Croatian Operation Storm in Krajina."[4]

As cited, "Rudolf Scharping, Germany's Defence Minister, said: "the clear objective (of Operation Horseshoe) was to ethnically cleanse Kosovo and remove the whole civilian population [see Appendix 4]."[5]

The United States Institute of Peace Certificate Course in Conflict Analysis recorded "ethnic cleansing and other atrocities in Kosovo resulted in an estimated 10,000 civilian deaths, over 1.5 million internally displaced persons and refugees, burning of homes, use of human shields in combat, rape as an instrument of war, and summary executions [see Appendix 5 & 6]."[6]

Continuing, "on August 4, 1995, the Croatian Army launched 'Operation Storm', an offensive to retake the Krajina region, which had been controlled by separatist ethnic Serbs since early 1991. The offensive, which lasted a mere thirty-six hours, resulted in the death of an estimated 526 Serbs, 116 of whom were reportedly civilians, and in the displacement of an estimated 200,000 who fled in the immediate aftermath."[7]

With "while the Croatian military committed violations of humanitarian law during the course of the offensive such as the bombardment of a column of retreating Serbian civilians and soldiers which caused deaths among the civilians, the vast majority of the abuses committed by Croatian forces occurred after the area had been captured."[8]

And, "these abuses by Croatian government forces, which continued on a large scale even months after the area had been secured by Croatian authorities, included summary executions of elderly and infirm Serbs who remained behind and the wholesale burning and destruction of Serbian villages and property. In the months following the August offensive, at least 150 Serb civilians were summarily executed and another 110 persons forcibly disappeared."[9]

The after math, war-crime tribunals and trials:

As noted, "Ratko Mladic, the fugitive Bosnian Serb general considered Europe's most wanted war criminal, was captured in Serbia on Thursday after a decade and a half on the run from an indictment for genocide. Gen. Mladic, who is accused of directing the 1995 Srebrenica massacre of some 8,000 Muslim men, was the last of the major figures accused of war crimes in the 1992-95 Yugoslav wars to evade capture [see Appendix 7]."[10]

And, "Slobodan Milosevic, the former Yugoslav President, died of a heart attack in 2006 before his own trial was concluded [see Appendix 8]"[11], with "Former Bosnian Serb General Dragomir Milosevic was transferred on Tuesday (March 22nd) to Estonia to serve his 29-year sentence for crimes against civilians during the 44-month siege of Sarajevo in 1994-1995."[12]

As noted, "two former top Croatian generals were today convicted and sentenced to lengthy jail terms by a United Nations war crimes tribunal over atrocities carried out against ethnic Serb civilians during a military offensive in the Balkan conflicts of the 1990s. Judges serving on the ICTY trial chamber found Ante Gotovina and Mladen Markac guilty of various crimes against humanity, including murder, persecutions, deportation and plunder [see Appendix 9]."[13]

Continuing, "a commander hailed by Croats as a hero of the Balkan conflict was convicted of war crimes by a UN court Friday and sentenced to 24 years in prison for a campaign of shelling, shootings and expulsions aimed at driving Serbs out of a Croatian border region in 1995. The conviction of Gen. Ante Gotovina was a blow to the Croatian view of its wartime generals as national heroes who reclaimed Croatian land from a more powerful Serb force [see Appendix 10]."[14]

Footnotes

1 - 2. United States Institute of Peace
2301 Constitution Avenue, NW
Washington, DC 20037
Certificate Course in Conflict Analysis
http://www.usip.org/education-training/international/online-courses

3 - 4. Ethnic Cleansing in former Yugoslavia
http://webcache.googleusercontent.com/search?q=cache:fGHKqJsWQ4MJ:balkansnet.org/ethnicl.html+ethnic+cleansing+in+yugoslavia&cd=1&hl=en&ct=clnk&gl=ca&source=www.google.ca

5. "Operation Horseshoe", World: Europe, Did Nato miscalculate?
BBC News, Friday, April 23, 1999
http://webcache.googleusercontent.com/search?q=cache:UOMcnfVn9LMJ:news.bbc.co.uk/2/hi/europe/326864.stm+Serbian+Operation+Horseshoe+in+Kosovo&cd=11&hl=en&ct=clnk&gl=ca&source=www.google.ca

6. United States Institute of Peace
2301 Constitution Avenue, NW
Washington, DC 20037
Certificate Course in Conflict Analysis
http://www.usip.org/education-training/international/online-courses

7 - 9. Impunity for Abuses Committed During "Operation Storm" and the Denial of the Right of Refugees to Return to the Krajina
Publisher - Human Rights Watch
Publication Date - 1 August 1996
Citation / Document Symbol - D813
http://www.unhcr.org/refworld/country,,HRW,,HRV,,3ae6a7d70,0.html

10. Serbia Arrests Fugitive Gen. Mladic
EUROPE NEWS MAY 27, 2011
http://webcache.googleusercontent.com/search?q=cache:LcvrSKg6rKMJ:online.wsj.com/article/SB10001424052702304520804576346960916648594.html+serbian+general+war+crimes&cd=7&hl=en&ct=clnk&gl=ca&source=www.google.ca

11. Serbian war criminals: Slobodan Milosevic profile
By Victoria Ward
Wednesday 17 August 2011
http://www.telegraph.co.uk/news/worldnews/europe/serbia/8538575/Serbian-war-criminals-Slobodan-Milosevic-profile.html

12. Dragomir Milosevic to serve war crimes sentence in Estonia
The Southeast European Times Web site, 23/03/2011
http://www.setimes.com/cocoon/setimes/xhtml/en_GB/newsbriefs/setimes/newsbriefs/2011/03/23/nb-05

13. UN war crimes tribunal convicts two former Croatian generals over atrocities
ICTY courtroom, 15 April 2011 –
http://webcache.googleusercontent.com/search?q=cache:8YiyrQk4T8gJ:www.un.org/apps/news/story.asp%3FNewsID%3D38125%26Cr%3Dicty%26Cr1%3D+Croatian+Operation+Storm+in+Krajina&cd=10&hl=en&ct=clnk&gl=ca&source=www.google.ca

14. Croatian general convicted of war crimes
The Associated Press
Posted: Apr 15, 2011
http://www.cbc.ca/news/world/story/2011/04/15/croatia-serbia-war-crimes-un.html

Other Conflicts

As further cited in the United States Institute of Peace Certificate Course in Conflict Analysis, "other conflicts include Georgia, Armenia/Azerbaijan and Chechnya".[1]

As noted, the name of the region has its origin in the high mountains that cover the region from the Black Sea to the Caspian Sea. The Caucasus Mountains divides the region in two: South Caucasus (also called Trans Caucasus) and North Caucasus. North Caucasus consists of: Karatchaevo-Tcherkessia, Kabardino – Balkaria, North Ossetia, Inguschetia, Chechnya, and Dagestan. South Caucasus consists of Georgia, Armenia, Azerbaijan [see Appendix 11]."[2]

As further noted, "the conflict in Chechnya originated from a dispute between the former Chechnyan Autonomous Republic and Russia when the latter refused to acknowledge the self-proclaimed Chechnyan independence in 1993. In the first war against Russia (1994-1996), almost every Chechnyan group was involved. In the second war (1999 – onwards), it is the groups from Southern Chechnya who fought Russia. Whereas the first war was a war of independence, the second has the characteristics of a religious war."[3]

Continuing, "for more than 250 years, Chechnya's relations to Russia have been characterised by resistance and revolt. The Caucasian wars in the 18th century and Stalin's deportations of Chechnyans in 1994 caused strong anti-Russian sentiments among most Chechnyans. In the early 1980s, Moscow's Glasnost and Perestroika policies reinforced already existing nationalist feelings in Chechnya, and popular nationalist movements were created here as well as in the other Caucasian republics."[4]

And, "the conflict in Chechnya is the most important of the conflicts in the Caucasus, with nationalist as well as religious aspects, and it is also the deadliest. Since 1994, at least 150,000 people have died as a result of the conflict and another 300,000 has left the republic. Before the war, Chechnya had 1.1 million inhabitants, but today it is estimated that only 715,000 remain in the republic. Although Russia's President Putin has claimed for years that the war is over and supports a pro-Russian government in Chechnya, there are clashes occurring daily and the conflict is far from over. It remains one of the major destabilizing factors in the Caucasus."[5]

In terms of the Armenia-Azerbaijan conflict, Carol Migdalovitz (2003) cites, "a clash between the principles of territorial integrity and self-determination, is the longest interethnic dispute in the former Soviet Union. Ethnic Armenians, the majority in the Nagorno Karabakh region of Azerbaijan, have a different culture, religion, and language than Azeris. They seek to join Armenia or to become independent."[6]

While, "Azerbaijan seeks to preserve its national integrity. The dispute has produced violence, mutual expulsion of rival nationals, charges and counter-charges. After the December 1991 demise of the Soviet Union and subsequent dispersal of sophisticated Soviet weaponry, the Nagorno Karabakh conflict worsened, and thousands of deaths and 1.4 million refugees resulted."[7]

In an article by Anatol Lieven (2008) mentions, "many factors are involved in the present conflict but the central one is straightforward: the majority of the Ossetes living south of the main Caucasus range in Georgia wish to unite with the Ossetes living to the north, in an autonomous republic of the Russian Federation; and the Georgians, regarding South Ossetia as both a legal and an historic part of their national territory, refuse to accept this."[8]

Continuing, "twice in the past century, when the empire to the north weakened and Georgia declared its independence, the southern Ossetes revolted against Georgian rule. It happened in 1918-20, between the collapse of the Russian empire and the Soviet Union's conquest of Georgia in 1921; and it happened again in our own time with the fall of the Soviet Union [see Appendix 12]."[9]

As further noted Kırdar (2008), "conflict between Georgia and Russia remains unresolved after nearly a century."[10]

In explanation, "during the era of Soviet domination, major nationalities were granted political status within the Soviet state and were ranked in a hierarchical federal system. Their place in this hierarchy depended on population size, geographical location and political power with the Communist Party elite. In the Soviet hierarchical system, the highest status was the union republic, followed by the autonomous republic and the autonomous region in the third rank. 5 Each national group which had received the right to constitute one of these units was recognized as its 'titular nation'. For instance, Abkhazhia was the titular nation of the Autonomous Soviet Socialist Republic of Abkhazia and the Georgia was the titular nation of the Soviet Socialist Republic of Georgia."[11]

Continuing, "at the end of the 1980s with the disintegration of the Communist Party, institutional guarantees for minorities disappeared. With the democratization of the Soviet system and the collapse of centralized power, the legitimacy of the federal order and hierarchical relations between union republics, autonomous republics and autonomous regions became one of the main subjects of dispute."[12]

Finally, as cited by Jim Nichol (2008):

"ethnic conflicts have kept the South Caucasus states from fully partaking in peace, stability, and economic development since the Soviet collapse in 1991, some observers lament. The countries are faced with on-going budgetary burdens of arms races and caring for refugees and displaced persons. Other costs of ethnic conflict include threats to bordering states of widening conflict and the limited ability of the region or outside states to fully exploit energy resources or trade/transportation networks."[13]

And:

"U.S. and international efforts to foster peace and the continued independence of the South Caucasus states face daunting challenges. The region has been the most unstable part of the former Soviet Union in terms of the numbers, intensity, and length of its ethnic and civil conflicts. The ruling nationalities in the three states are culturally rather insular and harbor various grievances against each other. This is particularly the case between Armenia and Azerbaijan, where discord has led to the virtually complete displacement of ethnic Armenians from Azerbaijan and vice versa.

The main languages in the three states are dissimilar (also, those who generally consider themselves Georgians — Kartvelians, Mingrelians, and Svans — speak dissimilar languages). The borders of the countries do not coincide with eponymous ethnic populations. Attempts by ethnic minorities to secede are primary security concerns for all three states. The secessionist NK, Abkhazia, and South Ossetia have failed to gain international recognition. NK relies on economic support from Armenia, and Abkhazia and South Ossetia from Russia."[14]

Footnotes

1. United States Institute of Peace
2301 Constitution Avenue, NW
Washington, DC 20037
Certificate Course in Conflict Analysis
http://www.usip.org/education-training/international/online-courses

2 - 5. Caucasus
http://webcache.googleusercontent.com/search?q=cache:AbgB8rfQECYJ:www.forgottendiaries.org/en/diaries/caucasus/+Other+conflicts+include+Georgia,+Armenia/Azerbaijan+and+Chechnya.&cd=5&hl=en&ct=clnk&gl=ca&source=www.google.ca

6 - 7. Order Code IB92109
CRS Issue Brief for Congress
Received through the CRS Web
Armenia-Azerbaijan Conflict

Updated August 8, 2003
Carol Migdalovitz
Foreign Affairs, Defense, and Trade Division
http://docs.google.com/viewer?a=v&q=cache:t_0Ip27DWuEJ:www.au.af.mil/au/awc/awcgate/crs/ib92109.pdf+conflict+armenia+azerbaijan&hl=en&gl=ca&pid=bl&srcid=ADGEESgMdVCSD1CFbmGh_fEy9MmTApC_UrGImu_WQAPcrSAf-jdd8e6TyJH1vgHX_XFz9bHAxk8oY74oHixphOA09BW74_IiuBhT0LA95Y3DjSu3LvIOBQd26DCpPWQK0es-HkO-iS4T&sig=AHIEtbQ6GrKQodn0i5YU2ydsCDfEItrWpQ

8 - 9. Analysis: roots of the conflict between Georgia, South Ossetia and Russia
Anatol Lieven
From The Times, August 11, 2008
http://www.timesonline.co.uk/tol/news/world/europe/article4498709.ece

10 - 12. Conflict Resolution in Georgia: An analysis applying the intractable conflict theory and the governmental politics model.
Seda Kırdar, Perceptions, Winter 2008
http://docs.google.com/viewer?a=v&q=cache:jR_XSOs8UqgJ:www.sam.gov.tr/perceptions/volume13/winter/seda_kirdar.pdf+conflict+Georgia&hl=en&gl=ca&pid=bl&srcid=ADGEESgZTMX4dnGTMj2B9Gd8MXbbsHQdVtGk64VY23z51vurugX0geXdgFbYO2WgMFTiADMEOEWe7d1_QxOvTNdnhw0GxODDdeDO_D88LZGG016N7v1bKbajXh-PZze19e6CCEeSluP_&sig=AHIEtbRM0qNCrpsNxXgR_lVa7TyPHu2MeA

13 - 14. Order Code RL33453
Armenia, Azerbaijan, and Georgia:
Political Developments and Implications for U.S. Interests
Updated August 13, 2008
Jim Nichol
Specialist in Russian and Central Asian Affairs
Foreign Affairs, Defense, and Trade Division
http://docs.google.com/viewer?a=v&q=cache:Or2IpUAyGE0J:fpc.state.gov/documents/organization/109516.pdf+Other+conflicts+include+Georgia,+Armenia/Azerbaijan+and+Chechnya.&hl=en&gl=ca&pid=bl&srcid=ADGEESjeerGTqWjdJinHbSMCvJ0Bzn1mWcJY1s96j_2gcobj-918XxaUFYCngPDsZnSwXb6kPfo1Jd2jvniE6Kq7urvz9dHVMMpGjb9uqggKYVrWnAFdkNgNP0VKuOm6pYrbXRWLWGB3&sig=AHIEtbQajPft_tin9vx1V-yQ0N8Os_2a0Q

Injustice

As cited in my United States Institute of Peace Certificate Course in Negotiation and Conflict Management "on March 21, 1960, in the township of Sharpeville, South Africa, police opened fire on a large but peaceful protest, killing and wounding scores of unarmed demonstrators. The day marked a particularly tragic event in a long, bitter struggle against racial oppression. On the anniversary of this massacre, 25 years later, police opened fire once again, killing and wounding more unarmed protestors."[1]

"Like the generation before them, these desperate men and women were protesting apartheid, a brutal, comprehensive system that through a range of notorious laws and practices—including the Mixed Marriages Act, the Group Areas Act, the Bantu Education Act, and the Job Reservation Act —was designed to enforce racial privilege."[2]

"By 1986, in a determined attempt to hold on, the South African government declared a national state of emergency and launched a bloody crackdown. Tens of thousands of youths were detained without trial, and many were tortured and killed. In response, the Mass Democratic Movement, representing over 7,000 organizations and 2,000,000 individuals, called for general insurrection. The nation teetered on the edge of civil war."[3]

As noted, Apartheid was a "social and political policy of racial segregation and discrimination enforced by white minority governments in South Africa from 1948 to 1994." [4]

"The term apartheid (from the Afrikaans word for "apartness") was coined in the 1930s and used as a political slogan of the National Party in the early 1940s, but the policy itself extends back to the beginning of white settlement in South Africa in 1652. After the primarily Afrikaner Nationalists came to power in 1948, the social custom of apartheid was systematized under law."[5]

"The implementation of the policy, later referred to as "separate development," was made possible by the Population Registration Act of 1950, which put all South Africans into three racial categories: Bantu (black African), white, or Coloured (of mixed race). A fourth category, Asian (Indians and Pakistanis), was added later. The system of apartheid was enforced by a series of laws passed in the 1950s: the Group Areas Act of 1950 assigned races to different residential and business sections in urban areas, and the Land Acts of 1954 and 1955 restricted non-white residence to specific areas. These laws further restricted the already limited right of black Africans to own land, entrenching the white minority's control of over 80 percent of South African land. In addition, other laws prohibited most social contacts between the races; enforced the segregation of public facilities and the separation of educational standards; created race-specific job categories; restricted the powers of non-white unions; and curbed non-white participation in government."[6]

"Though the implementation and enforcement of apartheid was accompanied by tremendous suppression of opposition, continual resistance to apartheid existed within South Africa. A number of black political groups, often supported by sympathetic whites, opposed apartheid using a variety of tactics, including violence, strikes, demonstrations, and sabotage - strategies that often met with severe reprisals by the government. Apartheid was also denounced by the international community: in 1961 South Africa was forced to withdraw from the British Commonwealth by member states who were critical of the apartheid system, and in 1985 the governments of the United States and Great Britain imposed selective economic sanctions on South Africa in protest of its racial policy."[7]

"As antiapartheid pressure mounted within and outside South Africa, the South African government, led by President F. W. de Klerk, began to dismantle the apartheid system in the early 1990s. The year 1990 brought a National Party government dedicated to reform and also saw the legalization of formerly banned black congresses and the release of imprisoned black leaders. In 1994 the country's constitution was rewritten and free general elections were held for the first time in its history, and with Nelson Mandela's election as South Africa's first black president, the last vestiges of the apartheid system were finally outlawed."[8]

As further cited, "Nelson Mandela was released from prison on February 11, 1990 as South Africa prepared to move from apartheid to majority rule. He won the presidency in 1994 in South Africa's first democratic election."[9]

"Yet Mandela inherited a country that teetered on the edge of a civil war. Heavily armed right-wing militants threatened to revolt. People worried that the South African military would mutiny and many white South Africans were afraid to lose their jobs, farms, anthem, flag and even their lives."[10]

And, "while white right-wingers threatened bloody revolution, continuing political clashes between supporters of the ANC and the Zulu-dominated Inkatha Freedom Party threatened to turn parts of the country into a wasteland."[11]

"The new ANC-led government inherited a country in economic decline, fractured into numerous administrative bureaucracies fraught with corruption and racial divisions. Newly-appointed ministers were untested and inexperienced in governance."[12]

"Although the ANC is a party with a long tradition of consensual collective decision-making, President Mandela frequently took matters into his own hands as the quickest means to an end, demonstrating an authoritarian, disciplinary streak which stands in stark contrast to his public persona."[13]

Finally, "the South African example shows how courageous negotiations can curb violence within a state."[14]

Footnotes

1 - 3. United States Institute of Peace
2301 Constitution Avenue, NW
Washington, DC 20037
Certificate Course in Negotiation and Conflict Management
http://www.usip.org/education-training/international/online-courses

4 - 8. Alonford James Robinson, Jr., "Africa"
http://webcache.googleusercontent.com/search?q=cache:HYpCSh44epEJ:www.africanaencyclopedia.com/apartheid/apartheid.html+apartheid&cd=6&hl=en&ct=clnk&gl=ca

9 - 10. 'Invictus' hero recalls day Mandela transformed South Africa
December 10, 2009|By John Blake, CNN
http://webcache.googleusercontent.com/search?q=cache:VCvg-2_jgo0J:articles.cnn.com/2009-12-10/entertainment/invictus_1_francois-pienaar-afrikaners-nelson-mandela/3%3F_s%3DPM:SHOWBIZ+South+Africa+teetered+on+the+edge+of+civil+war&cd=2&hl=en&ct=clnk&gl=ca

11 - 13. "Profile: Mandela's magic touch"
Tuesday, 28 August, 2001 UK
http://webcache.googleusercontent.com/search?q=cache:eufcZmF25IgJ:news.bbc.co.uk/2/hi/africa/1513244.stm+South+Africa+teetered+on+the+edge+of+civil+war&cd=5&hl=en&ct=clnk&gl=ca

14. United States Institute of Peace
2301 Constitution Avenue, NW
Washington, DC 20037
Certificate Course in Negotiation and Conflict Management
http://www.usip.org/education-training/international/online-courses

World Security

In terms of between states, such organizations as the Organization for Security and Cooperation in Europe (OSCE) and its Rapid Expert Assistance and Cooperation Teams (REACT) in particular are available.

As cited in my United States Institute of Peace Certificate Course in Security and Cooperation in Europe, "the Organization for Security and Cooperation in Europe (OSCE) is a security organization whose 56 participating states span the geographical area from Vancouver to Vladivostok. It is an important instrument for early warning, conflict prevention, crisis management, and post conflict security building, as well as the promotion of democratic development and good governance, media freedom, human rights, and non-discrimination throughout the region."[1]

"Today's OSCE is the successor to the Conference on Security and Cooperation in Europe (CSCE) established in 1975. The CSCE was largely an arena for East-West debate until the collapse of communism in the Soviet Union and Eastern Europe. The changed environment in Europe in the 1990s made it possible for the Organization, renamed OSCE in 1995, to be used by participating states to deal with the conflicts and threats to regional security and stability resulting from the breakups of the Soviet Union and Yugoslavia, as well as other regional instability. As Russia and the West have moved away from cooperation in recent years, the challenges to OSCE playing an effective role in addressing regional problems have increased."[2]

As noted, "Cold War détente between the United States and the Soviet Union originated in the 1960s. President Richard Nixon's opening to China and the signing of the Strategic Arms Limitations Treaty (SALT) between the superpowers in 1972 were landmark events in easing tensions between the West and the communist world. Chancellor Willy Brandt's Ostpolitik and the Conference of Security and Cooperation in Europe (1973–1975) pursued better East-West relations in Europe."[3]

"Willy Brandt became Foreign Minister in the Federal Republic of Germany in 1966. He developed the policy of Ostpolitik (reconciliation between eastern and western Europe). This replaced the Hallstein Doctrine of the government led by Konrad Adenauer."[4]

"In 1969 Brandt became Chancellor of West Germany. He continued with his policy of Ostpolitik and in 1970 negotiated an agreement with the Soviet Union accepting the frontiers of Berlin. In 1971 an agreement was reached that made it easier for people in West Berlin to visit East Berlin."[5]

"As part of the policy of Ostpolitik, the Basic Treaty was signed in 1972. In this treaty the Federal Republic of Germany and German Democratic Republic committed themselves to developing normal relations on the 'basis of equality, guaranteeing their mutual territorial integrity as well as the border between them, and recognizing each other's independence and sovereignty'."[6]

"As a result of Ostpolitik the Federal Republic of Germany exchanged ambassadors with the Soviet Union, Poland, Czechoslovakia, Hungary and Bulgaria."[7]

As well, "neutrals like Austria played an important role in these negotiations. The Helsinki Final Act signed on August 1, 1975 by 35 nations represented the culmination of détente in Europe. The signatories for the first time accepted that treatment of citizens within their borders as a matter of legitimate international concern. This helped human rights in the Soviet sphere of influence and spawned dissident organizations like Charta 77 in Prague."[8]

"More importantly, the CSCE was not a one-time affair, but developed into a long-term process (eventually it became the "Organization of Security and Cooperation in Europe"). The CSCE-process with its follow-up conferences was later given credit for helping build democracy in the Soviet Union and Eastern Europe, thus contributing to the end of the Cold War. President Gerald R. Ford continued SALT negotiations with the USSR. Chairman Brezhnev and President Jimmy Carter signed the SALT II treaty in June 1979 in Vienna. Although it was never ratified by the U.S. Senate due to the Soviet invasion of Afghanistan during Christmas 1979, both superpowers adhered to the agreement. The Afghanistan invasion spelled the end of superpower détente for the early 1980s."[9]

"At the start of 2010, the OSCE employed about 450 persons in its primary institutions, as well as some 3,000 persons in its 17 field missions, including both direct hires and seconded personnel. Its 2010 budget was relatively modest, at 150,765 million Euros (about $230 million), almost 10% less than the previous year."[10]

"The OSCE's comprehensive view of security covers three "dimensions": the politico-military; the economic and environmental; and the human. The OSCE's activities cover all three of these areas, from "hard" security issues such as conflict prevention to fostering economic development, ensuring the sustainable use of natural resources, and promoting the full respect of human rights and fundamental freedoms."[11]

Today, the Organization of Security and Cooperation in Europe faces the following [see Appendix 13 & 14]:

- *"Arms control*
- *The OSCE helps to stop surplus weapons being available illegally and offers assistance with their destruction. The OSCE has also developed mechanisms to regulate the transfer of conventional arms, improve military transparency and build confidence between states.*

- *Border management*
- *The OSCE seeks to enhance border security while facilitating legitimate travel and commerce, protecting human rights and promoting human contacts.*

- *Combating human trafficking*
- *Human trafficking affects virtually all OSCE states, either as countries of origin or destination.*

- *Combating terrorism*
- *The OSCE contributes to world-wide efforts in combating terrorism through activities such as promoting more secure travel documents and training border staff, combating extremism on the internet, terrorist financing and protecting critical infrastructure from terrorist attacks.*

- *Conflict prevention and resolution*
- *The OSCE works to prevent conflicts from arising and to facilitate lasting comprehensive political settlements for existing conflicts. It also helps with the process of rehabilitation in post-conflict areas.*

- *Economic activities*
- *The OSCE undertakes numerous activities to support economic growth, including the strengthening of small- and medium-sized enterprises, monitoring the economic impact of trafficking and taking action against corruption and money laundering.*

- *Education*
- *Education programmes are an integral part of the Organization's efforts in conflict prevention and post-conflict rehabilitation. The OSCE's youth projects include human rights, environmental, tolerance, and gender education as well as support for minorities in education.*

- *Elections*

- *The OSCE is a leading organization in the field of election observation. It conducts election-related activities across the 56 participating States, including technical assistance and election observation missions.*

- *Environmental activities*
- *Recognizing the close connection between environmental issues and security, the OSCE assists participating States with the sustainable use and sound management of natural resources.*

- *Gender equality*
- *The OSCE aims to provide equal opportunities for women and men, as well as to integrate gender equality into policies and practices, both within participating States and the Organization itself.*

- *Good governance*
- *The OSCE assists OSCE participating States in fighting corruption and in building democratic, accountable state institutions.*

- *Human rights*
- *Respect for human rights and fundamental freedoms forms a key part of the OSCE's comprehensive security concept. The OSCE monitors the human rights situation in its 56 participating States.*

- *Media freedom and development*
- *Free and well-developed media are a cornerstone of democratic societies. The OSCE monitors media developments in its participating States for violations of freedom of expression. This includes reviewing legislation regulating the media, as well as monitoring cases where journalists are prosecuted for their professional activities or are the victims of harassment.*

- *Military reform and co-operation*
- *The Forum for Security Co-operation, which meets weekly in Vienna, provides a framework for dialogue between the OSCE participating States on military conduct, and on confidence- and security-building measures.*

- *Minority rights*
- *The OSCE identifies and seeks early resolution of ethnic tensions that might endanger peace or stability. It promotes the rights of national minorities and pays particular attention to the situation of Roma and Sinti.*

- *Policing*

- *OSCE police operations are an integral part of the Organization's efforts in conflict prevention and post-conflict rehabilitation.*

- *Roma and Sinti*
- *The OSCE promotes the rights of Roma and Sinti through projects on political participation, education, housing, civil registration, combating racism and discrimination, and protecting the rights of displaced persons.*

- *Rule of law*
- *The concept of rule of law forms a cornerstone of the OSCE's human rights and democratization activities. It not only describes formal legal frameworks, but also aims at justice based on the full acceptance of human dignity.*

- *Tolerance and non-discrimination*
- *The OSCE actively supports its 56 participating States in combating all forms of racism, xenophobia, and discrimination, including anti-Semitism, and discrimination against Christians and Muslims."*[12]

This included such events as: "the OSCE Chairperson-in-Office, Lithuanian Foreign Minister Audronius Ažubalis, today condemned the suicide bomb attack in Kabul that killed Afghanistan's former President and Head of the High Peace Council Burhanuddin Rabbani, and extended his condolences to the families of all those killed, and to the Afghan people."[13]

"Rabbani was a driving force in Afghanistan's efforts to achieve peace. His death is a great loss, but his mediation efforts must go on. Addressing security challenges in Afghanistan and the whole region requires co-ordination of international efforts. The OSCE will continue its engagement with Afghanistan to promote a stable, independent, prosperous and democratic country," Ažubalis said.[14]

In fact, the OSCE is looking at "enhancing early response to crises and emerging conflicts is the focus of a meeting in Vienna on 20 September 2011 hosted by the Lithuanian OSCE Chairmanship and the OSCE Conflict Prevention Centre. This is the fourth and final event in a series of meetings on early warning, conflict prevention, crisis management and post-conflict rehabilitation organized by the Lithuanian Chairmanship under the "V to V Dialogue" (Vancouver to Vladivostok via Vienna and Vilnius)."[15]

"This is the moment when we should collectively take stock of what has been proposed and discussed since our first informal meeting at the Ambassadors' level on 15 March. More importantly, we should take this opportunity to decide on a way forward," said Lithuanian Ambassador Renatas Norkus, the Chairperson of the OSCE Permanent Council, referring to the Chairmanship's proposal to adopt a relevant Ministerial Council Decision reflecting the collective commitment of 56 participating States to preserve and further strengthen the OSCE's role in preventing and managing crisis and conflict situations.[16]

"The need to respond to potential crisis situations before they evolve into conflict is clear. Now the time has come to demonstrate our political will," he added.[17]

As further mentioned, "the OSCE today occupies a unique place in international organizations in general and transatlantic security institutions in particular. It has also been experiencing a "mid-life crisis" in recent years that has raised some fundamental questions about itself, requiring a new set of adaptations if the organization is to continue to play a leading role in regional security and cooperation.[18]

However, "this crisis reflects a declining consensus about the normative foundations of the OSCE, especially of the human dimension documents adopted in the years immediately following the collapse of communism in Central and Eastern Europe; several renewed crises in the realm of security, especially between Russia and NATO countries; and the stalemate in the arms control regime and other political foundations of cooperation that had created a favorable context for the OSCE to develop in the decade of the 1990s."[19]

And, "the European Union has enlarged and now includes over half the OSCE participating states, and has developed independent security institutions that, at least in part, compete with those of the OSCE."[20]

Is this a problem, where "the OSCE's decision-making and negotiating bodies arrive at their decisions by consensus. Consensus is understood to mean the absence of any objection expressed by a participating state to the taking of the decision in question."[21]

"This principle reflects the Organization's cooperative approach to security, and the fact that all states participating in OSCE activities formally have equal status. In practice, state power and influence frequently drive the deliberations and decisions of the Organization. Consensus, however, means that no decision can be made that is strongly opposed by any of the participating states, even the smallest."[22]

"OSCE decisions are politically and not legally binding on the participating states. This results from the Organization itself being based on the political commitment of the participating states, rather than on an international treaty."[23]

"The EU recently proposed giving the OSCE a status as a legal entity, and Russia subsequently proposed replacing it with a new, legally-binding charter on security covering the entire OSCE region."[24]

As emphasized, "in spite of this largely positive track record, many international lawyers (including those involved with human rights) still dismiss the OSCE human dimension commitments due to their lack of legally binding status."[25]

In addition, "OSCE bodies, like the UN General Assembly, are currently not authorized to make decisions that are explicitly legally binding on its participating States. While there have been attempts to "legalize" the OSCE14 (and a working group is currently debating this matter, as discussed in the conclusion), the prevailing opinion, championed by the United States, is to maintain the Organization as an informal diplomatic discussion group, albeit with executive powers."[26]

However, "this ambiguous legal status has not stopped the OSCE from drafting legally binding treaties, such as the Convention on Conciliation and Arbitration within the OSCE, the Treaty on Conventional Armed Forces in Europe (CFE), and the Open Skies Treaty."[27]

In character with its strictly political, diplomatic origins, and its basis in the concepts of "co-operative security", "community of values", and "community of responsibility", it is emphasized that decisions within the OSCE even though made on a consensual basis, decision made by consensus means that decisions enter into force, and thus are binding, immediately – the "universality principle".[28]

Footnotes

1 - 2. United States Institute of Peace
2301 Constitution Avenue, NW
Washington, DC 20037
Certificate Course in Security and Cooperation in Europe (OSCE)
http://www.usip.org/education-training/international/online-courses

3. "1975 Conference on Security and Cooperation in Europe"
http://webcache.googleusercontent.com/search?q=cache:Klf9pGySgi8J:www.austria1989.org/index.php%3Foption%3Dcom_content%26view%3Darticle%26id%3D60%26Itemid%3D90+conference+on+security+and+cooperation+in+europe+1975&cd=4&hl=en&ct=clnk&gl=ca

4 - 7. "Ostpolitik"
http://webcache.googleusercontent.com/search?q=cache:THjD2y-VzKEJ:www.spartacus.schoolnet.co.uk/2WWostpolitic.htm+ostpolitik&cd=3&hl=en&ct=clnk&gl=ca

8 - 9. "1975 Conference on Security and Cooperation in Europe"
http://webcache.googleusercontent.com/search?q=cache:Klf9pGySgi8J:www.austria1989.org/index.php%3Foption%3Dcom_content%26view%3Darticle%26id%3D60%26Itemid%3D90+conference+on+security+and+cooperation+in+europe+1975&cd=4&hl=en&ct=clnk&gl=ca

10. United States Institute of Peace
 2301 Constitution Avenue, NW
 Washington, DC 20037
Certificate Course in Security and Cooperation in Europe (OSCE)
http://www.usip.org/education-training/international/online-courses

11 - 12. "Organization of Security and Cooperation in Europe"
http://www.osce.org/

13 - 14. "Press release - OSCE Chairperson condemns assassination of former Afghan President Rabbani"
http://www.osce.org/cio/82709

15 - 17. "News - Expert meeting seeks to strengthen OSCE crisis response"
http://www.osce.org/cio/82654

18 - 24. United States Institute of Peace
 2301 Constitution Avenue, NW
 Washington, DC 20037
Certificate Course in Security and Cooperation in Europe (OSCE)
http://www.usip.org/education-training/international/online-courses

25 - 28. Eric Manton, "The OSCE Human Dimension and Customary International Law Formation"
http://docs.google.com/viewer?a=v&q=cache:Oy7Rq28qbh0J:www.osce.org/odihr/36254+OSCE+decisions+legally-binding&hl=en&gl=ca&pid=bl&srcid=ADGEEShwXtjOzkhUuQErHvK9rutBgEIdv0Z-XLqF8vwzA7oB_7YZopipyGfUVvo7VJv2bRpdU8_eEJyBSEwJ_n92aLcQfT97oKRQmf3HtjSpIg4n_18bAp5dAMqxKZCV1kYtnqT6zu90&sig=AHIEtbRuk2nSycMQIgppE7Ecf3ZDQvUyiQ

The Root of All Evil

In my course, MCTFT Drugs in America: Lessons for Law Enforcement it is cited "this course provides an overview of drugs of abuse for narcotic law enforcement officers:

"The course features a comprehensive survey of basic drug terminology, the Controlled Substances Act and the Uniform Code of Military Justice application of this act. Drugs of abuse are grouped into depressants, stimulants, hallucinogens, cannabis, steroids, and inhalants. Each group of drugs are then described in terms of method of production, means of ingestion, effects, and signs of abuse for classes of drugs. Drugs covered in this course include in part, opiates (heroin, codeine, morphine, and analogs), cocaine, crack, methamphetamines, LSD, PCP, ketamine, peyote, MDMA, psilocybin, cannabis, hash, testosterone, and inhalants. Produced by MCTFT in partnership with the United States Army Military Police School, and the National Guard Bureau Counterdrug Directorate."[1]

As such, it's important to put drugs, drug trafficking into an international perspective [see Appendix 15 & 16].

As cited, "transnational organized crime is considered as one of the major threats to human security, impeding the social, economic, political and cultural development of societies worldwide. It is a multi-faceted phenomenon and has manifested itself in different activities, among others, drug trafficking, trafficking in human beings; trafficking in firearms; smuggling of migrants; money laundering; etc."[2]

As further noted, "on December 9th 1994, the General Assembly of the United Nations issued a Declaration on Measures to Eliminate International Terrorism wherein it expressed, inter alia, its concern 'at the growing and dangerous links between terrorist groups and drug traffickers and their paramilitary gangs, which have resorted to all types of violence, thus endangering the constitutional order of states and violating basic human rights."[3]

"Since then, much stronger and broader statements have been made, especially in Security Council resolution 1373 (2001) wherein the Council 'Notes with concern the close connection between international terrorism and transnational organized crime, illicit drugs, money-laundering, illegal arms-trafficking, and illegal movement of nuclear, chemical, biological and other potentially deadly materials'."[4]

"Of all the alleged and real links between terrorism and other forms of crime, the one between illicit drug trafficking and terrorist and guerrilla organizations seems to be the strongest. It certainly appears to be the best documented. Yet, while there are hundreds of terrorist organizations and at least as many drug trafficking organizations, the evidence, which is said to exist, is derived from relatively few cases."[5]

Also, with the United Nations came into existence in 1945 and membership now stands at 185 States its primary focus was human rights, however, the global drug problem and the involvement of organized crime has become an important concern:

"The mission of the United Nations International Drug Control Programme (UNDCP) is to work with the nations of the world to tackle the global drug problem and its consequences. Two of the ways it intends to achieve this is by strengthening international action against drug production, trafficking and drug-related crime and by providing information, analysis and expertise on the drug issue."[6]

As further cited, in America, it was recorded that 77 million or 35% of Americans 12 years and older have reported illicit drug use as least once during life", and where those 12 to 17 indicated 23.7% had used illicit drugs in their life, with 18.8% reporting they had used illicit drug in the past year, 11.4% reporting they had used illicit drugs in the past month![7]

The source "3/4ths of Cocaine as of 1999 was found in Colombia - cocaine bases from Bolivia and Peru had their product processed in Colombia, with trafficking - through Mexico and central America to staging sites in northern Mexico by land, sea, or air - there are bases in Caribbean, Bahamas, and south Florida. Primary importation sites include Arizona, south California, south Florida, and Texas - border crossings are done via vehicle or 'mules' [person bodies]."[8]

Footnotes

1. "The Multijurisdictional Counterdrug Task Force Training (MCTFT): Drugs in America: Lessons for Law Enforcement", National Terrorism Preparedness Institute , St. Petersburg College in St. Petersburg, Florida.
http://www.mctft.com/cdrom_training/view_course.aspx?cdID=CD002

2. "UNODC and organized crime"
http://webcache.googleusercontent.com/search?q=cache:dEb-wZEw_sMJ:www.unodc.org/unodc/en/organized-crime/index.html+drug+trafficking+into+an+international+perspective&cd=1&hl=en&ct=clnk&gl=ca

3 - 5. Alex Schmid, Links between Terrorism and Drug Trafficking: A Case of "Narco-terrorism"?
January 27, 2005
http://webcache.googleusercontent.com/search?q=cache:NJd9NY8dMXUJ:english.safe-democracy.org/causes/links-between-terrorism-and-drug-trafficking-a-case-of-narcoterrorism.html+drug+trafficking+into+an+international+perspective&cd=5&hl=en&ct=clnk&gl=ca

6. "In Depth Information - An International Perspective"
http://webcache.googleusercontent.com/search?q=cache:Q2TtxTvDW84J:what-when-how.com/forensic-sciences/an-international-perspective/+drug+trafficking+into+an+international+perspective&cd=14&hl=en&ct=clnk&gl=ca

7 - . "The Multijurisdictional Counterdrug Task Force Training (MCTFT): Drugs in America: Lessons for Law Enforcement", National Terrorism Preparedness Institute, St. Petersburg College in St. Petersburg, Florida.
http://www.mctft.com/cdrom_training/view_course.aspx?cdID=CD002

Be Ever Vigilant

Another essential concern is the release of any kind of weapons of mass destruction, including a "dirty bomb" [Appendix 17].

In fact, the National Terrorism Preparedness Institute (NTPI) at St. Petersburg College opened in 1998 as a result of the Nunn-Lugar-Domenici Act, commonly known as the Weapons of Mass Destruction Act. In my course at NTPI, we looked at "School Terror" [see Appendix 18 & 19].

As mentioned in the course, "September 11, 2001, ushered in a new era for the citizens of the United States. In an age of newly recognized vulnerability, Americans have been forced to accept a different kind of "normal" and must now think about keeping their communities safe and the homeland secure from terrorist threat and attack. While the mention of terrorism typically evokes images of international terrorists or domestic hate groups, it is critical for those involved in providing safe schools to understand the similarities between school violence and acts of terrorism."[1]

Continuing, "the National Center for School Safety defines terrorism in schools as a threat or criminal act against school personnel, students, or property that creates immediate or prolonged fear; manipulates the actions of others; causes primary and/or secondary victimization; and, may result or does result in death, bodily injury, or significant property damage. In comparing acts of international terrorism to acts of school terrorism, the National School Safety Center found that the two types of violence include similarities, such as the attackers' goals and hatred of others, the months of planning and rehearsal before an event, and several of the elements of the attacks. Because of events such as 9/11 and Columbine, both schools and law enforcement agencies now operate differently."[2]

As further mentioned, "Columbine high school was the site of the largest high school shooting in U.S. history, and it should have been a lot worse. Eric Harris, 18, and Dylan Klebold, 17, wandered the halls, cafeteria, and library of the school, shooting whoever they saw. The rampage lasted nearly an hour, left 12 students and one teacher dead and 23 injured, most critically. Finally, Klebold and Harris shot themselves in the library."[3]

"It should have been a lot worse. They had placed several bombs in the school building, and Harris was an expert bomb maker who had detonated several in practice (Brown & Merritt, 2002). Yet none of them exploded and surveillance cameras clearly show Klebold firing at one in frustration. Klebold and Harris had planned this incident for at least a year and had intended to kill at least 500 students, even expecting to be standing outside the school shooting people as they escaped."[4]

As further note, "in September of 2004, one of the most shocking events in the history of school violence took place in the Russian town of Beslan. A combined facility for grades 1 through 11, the Beslan Middle School housed just under 1,000 students from ages 6 to 17. At 8:45 a.m. in the wide plaza on the north side of the school, several thousand teachers, students, siblings, parents, and grandparents had gathered and were winding down the outdoor activities for the first day of classes when three military vehicles pulled up on the west side of the school."[5]

"More than a dozen terrorists leapt out. They came prepared, carrying automatic weapons, grenades, sniper rifles, night vision goggles, gas masks, explosives, and silenced weapons. Other terrorists, believed to be 49 in total, were already in the crowd at the school. Having been deposited in the town earlier, they simply walked to the school on that beautiful fall morning."[6]

"One group of terrorists immediately entered the school through the main entrance, moving quickly through the warren of corridors, driving anyone they found inside ahead of them and into the gym. The second group started to force the crowd of revelers into the adjacent courtyard to the east [and then] into the gym, through the door at its northeast corner on the far side of the courtyard. In addition to the lone security guard, one police officer happened to be in the crowd with a sidearm only. The two attempted to engage the terrorists. One managed to kill a terrorist, but outnumbered and outgunned, both died on the spot in the first seconds of what would become a 62-hour ordeal."[7]

"Though the number of casualties at Beslan has been debated, most sources put the death toll at 335 hostages, including 156 children, along with 26 hostage-takers and 10 Russian Special Forces soldiers."[8]

The lesson, "not only psychological preparation is important, but physical, tactical, and mental preparation of everyone. This means that every single person in America, including parents, teachers, students, police, and government officials, must be ready, must be alert, and must be able to respond to terrorism anywhere and everywhere, at all levels."[9]

As further emphasized, ""an Emergency Operations Plan (EOP) is a document describing how citizens and property will be protected in a disaster or emergency. Every community and school has a slightly different set of hazards, resources, response capabilities, and organizational structures. Despite these differences, the general response functions to an emergency event remain the same. Take time in the plan to describe each of these response functions, which agencies provide them, and how they will be incorporated in an overall community response to any emergency event."[10]

Including, "school emergency plans must be continually updated and revised to reflect a wide variety of threats, such as natural disasters, terrorist attacks, violent incidents on campuses and public health emergencies, including pandemic influenza."[11]

The course at the National Terrorism Preparedness Institute (NTPI) confirms that "once the Planning Team has been assembled, the Crisis Planning Process is broken into four steps:

Step 1—Hazard analysis is the process through which hazards that threaten the community are identified, researched, and ranked according to the risks they pose to vulnerable areas and infrastructure. The outcome of this step is a written hazard analysis that quantifies the overall risk to the community from each hazard.

Step 2—EOP development, including the basic plan, functional annexes, hazard-specific appendices, and implementing instructions. The outcome of this step is a completed plan, which is ready to be trained, exercised, and revised.

Step 3—Testing the plan through training and exercises. Exercises of different types and varying complexity illustrate what in the plan is unclear or not working. The outcomes of this step are lessons learned about weaknesses in the plan that can then be addressed in Step 4.

Step 4—Plan maintenance and revision are intended to revise the EOP based on current needs and resources (which may have changed since the development of the original EOP)."[12]

And, as mentioned, "the Risk Assessment Team should include a school-based law enforcement officer such as a School Resource Officer (SRO), if one is stationed at the school. School-based law enforcement officers typically have experience in responding to and managing manmade incidents and can assist the Risk Assessment Team in identifying such hazards within a school and in the surrounding community."[13]

And such plans should include, "a school EOP must equip personnel to address any possible crisis. In order to ensure that such a plan will work in all situations, the team must consider all potential hazards. Those conducting a Hazard

Assessment must address known hazards that have occurred in the past, such as storms, and must also consider potential hazards, such as terrorism. Determining the likelihood of specific incidents is a refinement that happens at the end of the hazard identification process."[14]

"Some examples of school hazards include bullying, fires, hazardous material spills, and violence. Safety experts suggest that risk assessment teams utilize site surveys to identify school hazards. During a school site survey, a risk assessment team inspects the building, facilities, and grounds for potential hazards. The National Clearinghouse for Educational Facilities provides a Safe Schools Checklist that can help teams to identify potential hazards during a school site survey."[15]

And to reduce tension and conflict, serious attention should be given "order maintenance involves attending to and reducing minor undesirable acts and providing measures that clearly state acceptable behavior. Expectations regarding behavior are clearly stated and consequences for unacceptable behavior are known and consistently applied. Examples of order maintenance include clarifying rules of behavior related to the cafeteria, lockers, backpacks, outside areas, parking lots, buses, parent pickup, emergency procedures and recreational events. The objective is to maintain and encourage behavior that is orderly and predictable, thereby preventing the escalation of tension and conflicts."[16]

As mentioned, "one additional consideration that cannot be overlooked is the perception of a lack of order on a school campus. If a school is perceived as unsafe (i.e., it appears that no adult authority prevails on a campus), then "undesirables" will come in, and the school will actually become unsafe. This is an embodiment of the broken window theory: one broken window left unrepaired will encourage additional windows to be broken. Seemingly small incidents or issues such as litter on a school campus can provide the groundwork for (or even just the reputation of) a problem school. Issues of vandalism and theft can be almost as harmful to a school as actual violence because they can create a fertile environment for loss of control and community confidence."[17]

"Issues contributing to a school's overall order maintenance must therefore be taken seriously, not unlike any other public facility. Reducing theft, deterring vandalism and graffiti, keeping outsiders off campus, keeping the facility in good repair, improving poor lighting, maintaining attractive landscaping, and getting rid of trash are all important to school security."[18]

"Technologies such as cameras, sensors, microdots (for identifying ownership), and antigraffiti sealers can contribute significantly in many (but not all) situations and are possible approaches to further support a school's order maintenance."[19]

As further reported, "the Safe School Initiative, begun in June 1999, was undertaken to explore the potential for adapting the threat assessment investigative process developed by the Secret Service to the problem of targeted school violence. Implemented through the Secret Service's National Threat Assessment Center and the Department of Education's Safe and Drug-Free Schools Program, the Safe School Initiative combines the Department of Education's expertise in helping schools facilitate learning the creation of safe environments for students, faculty, and staff, and the Secret Service's experience in studying and preventing targeted violence."[20]

"The Safe School Initiative concluded that most attackers did not threaten their targets directly but did engage in pre-attack behaviors that would have indicated a tendency toward or the potential for targeted violence had they been identified. Findings about the pre-attack behaviors of perpetrators of targeted violence validated the "fact-based" approach of the threat assessment process. This process relies primarily on an appraisal of behaviors rather than on stated threats or traits, as the basis for determining whether there is cause for concern. These findings argue favorably for adapting this threat assessment process for use by school administrators and law enforcement officials in responding to the problem of targeted school violence."[21]

"Students who engaged in school-based attacks typically did not "just snap" and engage in impulsive or random acts of targeted school violence. Instead, the attacks examined under the Safe School Initiative appeared to be the result of a comprehensible process of thinking and behavior—behavior that typically begins with an idea, progresses to the development of a plan, moves on to securing the means to carry out the plan, and culminates in an attack."[22]

Footnotes

1 – 2. "School Terror", National Terrorism Preparedness Institute, St. Petersburg College in St. Petersburg, Florida.
http://terrorism.spcollege.edu/Training/Courses/SchoolTerror.aspx

3 – 4. Brian T. Waterman, "Running Head: Terror in Our Schools: An Examination of the Recent School Shootings"
http://docs.google.com/viewer?a=v&q=cache:LEltOhdEm6oJ:www.bedrugfree.net/Terror.pdf+school+terror+drugs+in+schools&hl=en&gl=ca&pid=bl&srcid=

ADGEEShNI7ErGUvgoBmAKnF1XLzrONH7sFOOpanXBzWzym63g0reRKaSG3E3ulTkInUzn5N03uszZ2eHiz8HufzrHyYlYIy1ckUNcNw3zN6hkF_BH0lIqWP6ovrBox4EAYOWvQgkRpNH&sig=AHIEtbTF8iKyQzofAuTUoACO3rK1c70pOQ

5 – 10. "School Terror", National Terrorism Preparedness Institute, St. Petersburg College in St. Petersburg, Florida.
http://terrorism.spcollege.edu/Training/Courses/SchoolTerror.aspx

11. "School Safety Management and Emergency Operations Plans"
Posted on Tue, Sep 07, 2010
http://webcache.googleusercontent.com/search?q=cache:xCdvUtiFW9AJ:www.emergency-response-planning.com/blog/bid/29590/School-Safety-Management-and-Emergency-Operations-Plans+school+emergency+operations+plans&cd=2&hl=en&ct=clnk&gl=ca

12 – 16. "School Terror", National Terrorism Preparedness Institute, St. Petersburg College in St. Petersburg, Florida.
http://terrorism.spcollege.edu/Training/Courses/SchoolTerror.aspx

17 – 19. "Security Concepts and Operational Issues: The role of order maintenance"
http://webcache.googleusercontent.com/search?q=cache:-N-3wrrFveUJ:www.ncjrs.gov/school/ch1_10.html+school+%22Order+maintenance%22&cd=2&hl=en&ct=clnk&gl=ca

20 – 22. "School Terror", National Terrorism Preparedness Institute, St. Petersburg College in St. Petersburg, Florida.
http://terrorism.spcollege.edu/Training/Courses/SchoolTerror.aspx

Irrational Fears or the State of the World Today

In my course at National Terrorism Preparedness Institute, we also looked at "Force Protection / Anti-Terrorism", specifically Understanding Islamic Terrorism and Arabic Names where the course "provides law enforcement personnel and first responders with awareness level information on Islamic fundamentalist terrorism and Arabic names and culture in order to dispel misconceptions and assist with interactions between first responders and Muslims and Arabs."[1]

As emphasized, it's complicated: deciding who the terrorists are in any given country is complicated [see Appendix 20].

The anonymous quote—"one man's terrorist is another man's freedom fighter"—reveals that geo-political, socio-economic, and religious perspectives are used to justify extreme acts on either side of a conflict. For instance, a U.S. military action directed against a war criminal is justified from the United States' point of view, but it's likely perceived as a terrorist attack by the host country."[2]

Obviously, not all Muslims are terrorists.

Unfortunately, however, people like Osama bin Laden brought the most well-known militant organizations al-Qaeda to the forefront on everyone's' mind – especially America.

The result: an irrational fear of Muslims, or is it the state of the world today?

Obviously, there are now splinter groups:

"In recent years, many of the most horrific bombings attributed to al-Qaeda—most notably Bali, Madrid, London, and Algeria—are believed to have been carried out by terrorist groups linked more in spirit than in substance to al-Qaeda. Al-Zarqawi, the most active terrorist in recent years, for example, only officially joined al-Qaeda in the years after he initiated his reign of terror in Iraq. Al-Qaeda has been more than happy to take credit for the various bombings, but it is thought that it has offered philosophical motivation more than a direct support for the atrocities committed by these splinter groups. While al-Qaeda encourages its reputation as a vast global network, many experts believe that at this stage al-Qaeda itself has just a small core of adherents, but serves as the virulent inspiration to countless violent Islamic extremists."[3]

"While the war on terror has cost the United States some $1 trillion, al-Qeada remains a global threat. In fact, in August 2008, Ted Gistaro, the U.S. government's senior terrorism analyst, said in a report that by forging closer ties to Pakistani militants, al-Qaeda is more capable of launching an attack in the United States than it was in 2007. The Pakistani militants have given al-Qaeda leaders safe haven in remote areas to train recruits."[4]

John Brennan, President Barack Obama's senior adviser on counterterrorism and homeland security, said in August 2009 that although al-Qaeda "has been seriously damaged and forced to replace many of its top-tier leadership with less experienced and less capable individuals," the terrorist group remains the country's No. 1 threat.[5]

"In the wake of bin Laden's death, that threat may escalate. Analysts expressed concern that Al-Qaeda may seek retaliation. U.S. embassies throughout the world were put on high alert, and the U.S. State Department issued a warning for travelers visiting dangerous countries, instructing them "to limit their travel outside of their homes and hotels and avoid mass gatherings and demonstrations." Some Afghan officials expressed concern that bin Laden's death might be seen as a reason for the U.S. to withdraw from Afghanistan, saying terrorism continues to plague the country and the region."[6]

On the home-front, we also have "domestic terrorism involves groups or individuals whose terrorist activities are directed at elements of the U.S. government or population without foreign direction."[7]

The FBI defines domestic terrorism as: "…involving groups or individuals who are based and operate entirely within the United States and Puerto Rico without foreign direction and whose acts are directed at elements of the U.S. government or its population."[8]

"Domestic terrorists can act as a group, but some of the most dangerous domestic terrorists have acted as "lone wolf" types who may sympathize with extremist groups but carry out their acts of terror on their own. They may base their actions on the general philosophy of a group to which they belong or have a loose affiliation, but they act alone. They are the most difficult type of terrorist to defend against. Some of the more ill-famed lone wolf domestic terrorists include Timothy McVeigh, Ted Kaczynski, and Eric Robert Rudolph."[9]

And with the devastating bombing by Timothy McVeigh, it too was classed as a terrorist bomb: "the Oklahoma City bombing was a terrorist bomb attack on the Alfred P. Murrah Federal Building in downtown Oklahoma City on April 19, 1995. It was the most destructive act of terrorism on American soil until the

September 11, 2001 attacks. The Oklahoma blast claimed 168 lives, including 19 children under the age of 6, and injured more than 680 people. The blast destroyed or damaged 324 buildings within a sixteen-block radius, destroyed or burned 86 cars, and shattered glass in 258 nearby buildings. The bomb was estimated to have caused at least $652 million worth of damage."[10]

Little wonder, "the challenge for the U.S. government is to effectively protect America's critical infrastructure; specifically, the Nation's telecommunications systems, electrical power grids, transportation systems, gas/oil delivery and storage systems, water purification and delivery mechanisms, banking and finance centers, fire/police/EMS/disaster systems, and other government services."[11]

The USA Patriot Act defines critical infrastructure as "systems and assets, whether physical or virtual, so vital to the United States that incapacitating or destroying such systems and assets would have a debilitating impact on national security, national economic security, national public health or safety, or any combination of those matters."[12]

This becomes doubly important considering the terrorist attacks on 9 / 11:

"The September 11 attacks (also referred to as September 11, September 11th or 9/11) were a series of four coordinated suicide attacks upon the United States in New York City and the Washington, D.C., area on September 11, 2001. On that Tuesday morning, 19 terrorists from the Islamist militant group al-Qaeda hijacked four passenger jets.

The hijackers intentionally crashed two planes, American Airlines Flight 11 and United Airlines Flight 175, into the Twin Towers of the World Trade Center in New York City; both towers collapsed within two hours. Hijackers crashed American Airlines Flight 77 into the Pentagon in Arlington, Virginia. The fourth jet, United Airlines Flight 93, crashed into a field near Shanksville, Pennsylvania, after passengers attempted to take control before it could reach the hijacker's intended target in Washington, D.C. Nearly 3,000 died in the attacks."[13]

This led to a mistrust and actual hate crimes of retaliation: "numerous incidents of harassment and hate crimes against Muslims and South Asians were reported in the days following the 9/11 attacks. Sikhs were also targeted because Sikh males usually wear turbans, which are stereotypically associated with Muslims. There were reports of verbal abuse, attacks on mosques and other religious buildings (including the firebombing of a Hindu temple), and assaults on people, including one murder: Balbir Singh Sodhi, a Sikh mistaken for a Muslim, was fatally shot on September 15, 2001 in Mesa, Arizona."[14]

"According to an academic study, people perceived to be Middle Eastern were as likely to be victims of hate crimes as followers of Islam during this time. The study also found a similar increase in hate crimes against people who may have been perceived as Muslims, Arabs and others thought to be of Middle Eastern origin. A report by the South Asian American advocacy group known as South Asian Americans Leading Together, documented media coverage of 645 bias incidents against Americans of South Asian or Middle Eastern descent between September 11 and September 17. Various crimes such as vandalism, arson, assault, shootings, harassment, and threats in numerous places were documented."[15]

The course highlights things to look for, in order to thwart any attack:

- "Loitering in/around sensitive areas
- Muslim males living together
- Ample money and no regular job
- Repeated use of "God," not coupled with profanity
- Use of foreign terms/phrases, not in context
- Radical literature/materials
- Parking, standing, or loitering in the same areas over multiple days
- A pattern or series of false alarms requiring law enforcement and/or emergency response
- Reported thefts of military, law enforcement, or fire ID cards, license plates, uniforms, etc.
- Unscheduled maintenance work
- Deliveries that are not anticipated
- Evidence of vandalism or tampering
- Asking suspicious questions and taking notes regarding security procedures
- Allegedly getting lost during tours or visits to facilities
- "Mistakenly" entering nonpublic areas of sensitive sites
- Taking photos of security staff, security cameras, or various infrastructure or high-value target areas."[16]

As further reported, "a sample list of the types of tools a terrorist may need to plan and carry out an attack. Although these things may be insignificant individually, if an officer observes several of these items without a reasonable explanation for their existence, the officer should investigate potential links to terrorist activity:
- Global Positioning System (GPS)
- Maps/charts/diagrams
- Multiple forms of identification
- Numerous credit cards
- Backpacks/suitcases

- Blueprints
- One-way airline tickets
- Cameras or video recorders
- Unauthorized/stolen uniforms
- Indications of frequent travel
- Computer hardware/software
- Night vision equipment
- Binoculars/spotting scopes
- Explosives and/or components
  - Improvised explosive devices
  - Commercial explosives and detonators
  - Suicide bomber vests."[17]

No matter who the culprit, domestic or international, one has to be vigilant at all times.

Footnotes

1 – 2. "Law Enforcement Guide to Understanding Islamic Terrorism and Arabic Names: Force Protection / Anti-Terrorism" National Terrorism Preparedness Institute, St. Petersburg College in St. Petersburg, Florida.
http://terrorism.spcollege.edu/Training/Courses/LEGuidetoIslamicTerrorism.aspx

3 – 6. "Al-Qaeda: Osama bin Laden's Network of Terror, The Splintering and Proliferation of Al-Qaeda"
http://webcache.googleusercontent.com/search?q=cache:jZQRGKbwhsQJ:www.infoplease.com/spot/al-qaeda-terrorism.html+al-Qaeda+splinter+groups&cd=2&hl=en&ct=clnk&gl=ca

7 – 9. "Law Enforcement Guide to Understanding Islamic Terrorism and Arabic Names: Force Protection / Anti-Terrorism" National Terrorism Preparedness Institute, St. Petersburg College in St. Petersburg, Florida.
http://terrorism.spcollege.edu/Training/Courses/LEGuidetoIslamicTerrorism.aspx

10. "Oklahoma City bombing"
http://en.wikipedia.org/wiki/Oklahoma_City_bombing

11 – 12. "Law Enforcement Guide to Understanding Islamic Terrorism and Arabic Names: Force Protection / Anti-Terrorism" National Terrorism Preparedness Institute, St. Petersburg College in St. Petersburg, Florida.
http://terrorism.spcollege.edu/Training/Courses/LEGuidetoIslamicTerrorism.aspx

13 – 15. "September 11 attacks"

http://en.wikipedia.org/wiki/9-11_attack

16–17. "Law Enforcement Guide to Understanding Islamic Terrorism and Arabic Names: Force Protection / Anti-Terrorism" National Terrorism Preparedness Institute, St. Petersburg College in St. Petersburg, Florida. http://terrorism.spcollege.edu/Training/Courses/LEGuidetoIslamicTerrorism.aspx

Identifying Subjects of Interest

Another problem in Homeland Security as cited in the course is "identifying subjects of interest can be extremely challenging [see Appendix 21], especially if the subjects are being deceitful. Law enforcement officers should not ask, "what's your name?" or say, "first, middle, and last name." They must ask for a given name, the father's name, and so on."[1]

It's important to remember that "ibn/bin" is not a suspect's name, but simply means "son of." Similarly, "Abu" is not a name, nor is "Abdul"; these are titles meaning "father of" and "servant of," respectively, as noted above. When making new acquaintances or trying to identify individuals, law enforcement personnel should also ask suspects for their children's names. Because Islam has such a significant influence on Arabic culture, there are some very popular Islamic names that are repeatedly used. It is also customary to name male children after the grandfather on the father's side of the family. As a result, many Arabic names contain the same name twice [see Appendix 22 & 23].[2]

Similarly, "in the United States, there are many men named "Michael Patrick Callahan." To deal with this problem, U.S. officials rely on the social security number as a unique identifier to determine precise identity. Unfortunately, there is no social security number in the Arabic world, and people are frequently mistaken for others with the same name."[3]

As cited, the origin of the name Callahan, just as an example, is: "Callaghan - Ó Ceallacháin The derivation from ceallach, strife, which usually given, is questioned but no acceptable alternative has been suggested. The eponymous ancestor in this case was Ceallacháin, King of Munster (d. 952). The sept was important in the present Co. Cork until the seventeenth century and the name is still very numerous there. The chief family was transplanted under the Cromwellian regime to east Clare, where the village of O'Callghan's Mills is called after them" [see Appendix 24 & 25].

In fact, there are many cultural components to naming one's child [see Appendix 26]. As cited, "many Native Americans developed naming systems in which a person's individual name included the name of his or her clan. For example, all the members of a clan that has the bear as its totem animal have names relating to bears, such as Black-Bear Tracks and Black-Bear Flashing Eyes."[4]

Similarly, "in rural areas, many Chinese names still include a "generation name," a word or syllable that is the same for all children born in a family in the same generation. Three sisters, for example, might be named Yuan-Chun, Ying-

Chun, and Xi-Chun, which mean "First Spring," "Welcome Spring," and "Cherish Spring"."[5]

One possible solution to identifying a suspect is the new burgeoning technology in the field. As cited, "before September 11, the public viewed the technology with much more skepticism than it does today. Many people remain skeptical when it comes to widespread use of the technology in areas other than public safety and security" [see Appendix 27 & 28].

The course also looked at "the differences between basic crime and terrorist activities"[4], and, as cited: "according to the Department of Defense dictionary, the terms terrorism, terrorist, and terrorist group are defined as:

- *Terrorism - The calculated use of unlawful violence or threat of unlawful violence to inculcate fear; intended to coerce or to intimidate governments or societies in the pursuit of goals that are generally political or religious or ideological*

- *Terrorist - An individual who uses violence, terror and intimidation to achieve a result.*

- *Terrorist Group - Any element, regardless of size or espoused cause, that commits acts of violence or threatens violence in pursuit of its political, religious, or ideological objectives.*

- *National Terrorists — This term is used around the world to refer to individual terrorists or organizations that conduct all their operations within the territorial boundaries of a single nation. In the United States, the term "Domestic Terrorism" refers to National Terrorists operating within the territorial boundaries of the U.S. and its protectorates.*

- *Transnational Terrorist — This term is widely used to describe those terrorists and organizations that operate across the borders of countries. This is often confused with the term "International Terrorism," which will be defined later.*

- *Domestic Terrorism: Involves groups or individuals who are based and operate entirely within the United States and its protectorates without foreign direction, and whose acts are directed at elements of the U.S. Government or population."*[5]

With, "domestic terrorism is viewed by the United Nations as part of the internal sovereign affairs of a state, and refers to national or permanent residents of a given country committing or planning terrorist acts within the borders of that country, without external involvement. Domestic terrorism has directly accounted for an estimated 42 million victims worldwide during the 20th

Century (if genocide, ethnic cleansing or depopulation, and purges are included in the definition of terrorism). From the perspective of the United Nations, domestic terrorism is unlikely to result in war between nations, while international terrorism has that possibility."[6]

And, "the National Advisory Committee on Criminal Justice Standards and Goals was a Presidential Commission formed in 1976 that determined motivation for a crime was a key component in determining if an act was purely criminal or terrorism. The necessary element according to the Commission was whether the act was politically motivated."[7]

As noted, "according to the National Advisory Committee on Criminal Justice Standards and Goals, there are six distinct types of terrorism. All of them share the common traits of being violent acts that destroy property, invoke fear and attempt to harm the lives of civilians:

1. Civil disorder is a sometimes violent form of protest held by a group of individuals, usually in opposition to a political policy or action. They are intended to send a message to a political group that "the people" are unhappy and demand change. The protests are intended to be non-violent, but they do sometimes result in large riots in which private property is destroyed and civilians are injured or killed.

2. Political terrorism is used by one political faction to intimidate another. Although government leaders are the ones who are intended to receive the ultimate message, it is the citizens who are targeted with violent attacks.

3. Non-political terrorism is a terrorist act perpetrated by a group for any other purpose, most often of a religious nature. The desired goal is something other than a political objective, but the tactics involved are the same.

4. Quasi terrorism is a violent act that utilizes the same methods terrorists employ, but does not have the same motivating factors. Cases like this usually involve an armed criminal who is trying to escape from law enforcement utilizing civilians as hostages to help them escape. The law breaker is acting in a similar manner to a terrorist, but terrorism is not the goal.

5. Limited political terrorism acts are generally one time only plots to make a political or ideological statement. The goal is not to overthrow the government, but to protest a governmental policy or action.

6. State terrorism defines any violent action initiated by an existing government to achieve a particular goal. Most often this goal involves a conflict with another country."[8]

With, "every type of terrorism utilizes distinct methods of violence to get their message across. They can be anything from assault weapons or explosive devices to toxic chemicals that are released into the air. These attacks may occur at any time or place, which makes them an extremely effective method of instilling terror and uncertainty into the general public."[9]

A further distinction is made in the course where terrorists have or are:

- *"Organizational structure*
- *Team oriented*
- *Belief systems*
- *Motivational values*
- *Use of crime for a symbolic statement about a political cause"*.[10]

With the added information that, "even if terrorists are alone when they perform a violent act, they are still team oriented. Even suicide bombers do not act entirely alone; They are supported by an organization, and go on a mission that is assigned to them by the leaders of the organization."[11]

Whereas, criminals, on the other hand, are seen as:

- *"Economically opportunistic.*
- *Impulsive.*
- *Uncommitted.*
- *Self-centered and undisciplined.*
- *Use crime to obtain goods for self"*.[12]

With the emphasis on: "these distinctions are of greatest relevance to members of the law enforcement community. It is necessary for law enforcement personnel to make these distinctions between criminals and terrorists during investigations and attempts to locate possible perpetrators."[13]

"Typically, to be successful at finding criminals, law enforcement personnel question known associates of the suspect, and keep family and friends of the suspect under surveillance."[14]

"However, to be successful at investigating terrorism, law enforcement personnel must focus on the possible terrorist ideology, as well as group and individual behavior. It is also critical to share information over broad geographical areas to identify large-scale terrorist activity."[15]

Footnotes

1 – 3. "Law Enforcement Guide to Understanding Islamic Terrorism and Arabic Names: Force Protection / Anti-Terrorism" National Terrorism Preparedness Institute, St. Petersburg College in St. Petersburg, Florida.

http://terrorism.spcollege.edu/Training/Courses/LEGuidetoIslamicTerrorism.aspx

3. "Baby-Naming Trends"
by Cleveland Kent Evans
http://webcache.googleusercontent.com/search?q=cache:bcDShBaXaIAJ:tlc.howstuffworks.com/family/baby-name-trends-ga2.htm+cultural+naming+of+children&cd=1&hl=en&ct=clnk&gl=ca

4 – 7. "Introduction to Anti-Terrorism" National Terrorism Preparedness Institute, St. Petersburg College in St. Petersburg, Florida.
http://terrorism.spcollege.edu/Training/Courses/IntroductiontoAnti-Terrorism.aspx

8 - 9. "Types of Terrorism"
http://webcache.googleusercontent.com/search?q=cache:IqjTMTXEJN8J:www.crimemuseum.org/library/terrorism/typesOfTerrorism.html+national+advisory+committee+on+criminal+justice+standards+and+goals+-+terrorism&cd=1&hl=en&ct=clnk&gl=ca

10 – 15. "Introduction to Anti-Terrorism" National Terrorism Preparedness Institute, St. Petersburg College in St. Petersburg, Florida.
http://terrorism.spcollege.edu/Training/Courses/IntroductiontoAnti-Terrorism.aspx

Surprising "Terrorist" Groups

When people think of terrorism or terrorist acts, they immediately think of colossal and tragic events – such as 9/11 World Trade Center attack:

"These were a series of coordinated attacks by Al-Qaeda on America on September 11, 2001. Four commercial passenger jet airliners were hijacked by 19 Al-Qaeda members and they intentionally steered two of the planes towards the Twin Towers of World Trade Center, consequently bringing them down to earth.

The third airliner was crashed into The Pentagon in Arlington, Virginia, just outside Washington, D.C. and the fourth one crashed into a field near Shanksville in rural Pennsylvania. There were no survivors from any of the flights. This event triggered many changes in the world as a whole and was the beginning of a very horrendous film for the humans across the globe because humans had to pay a very heavy price of this terrorist attack and this fact is conspicuous from the current state of affairs."[1]

And, very likely, the Oklahoma City bombing comes to mind, where "this incident took place on April 19, 1995 and it was an attack on the Alfred P. Murrah Federal Building in downtown Oklahoma City. It was the most deadly terrorist attack on the American soil until 9/11, and it claimed 168 lives, including 19 children under the age of 6, and injured more than 680 people."[2]

Most likely too "the worst terrorist attack in British history and the deadliest attack on American civilians before 9/11" would most likely come to mind, when "Pan Am 103 exploded over Lockerbie, Scotland, killing all 259 passengers and crew, as well as 11 residents of the town below"[3] [see Appendix 29].

The London "Tube" bombings may also come to mind, where, "on the morning of Thursday, 7 July 2005, four terrorists detonated four bombs, three in quick succession aboard London Underground trains across the city and, later, a fourth on a double-decker bus in Tavistock Square. Fifty-two people, as well as the four bombers, were killed in the attacks, and over 700 more were injured. The explosions were caused by homemade organic peroxide-based devices packed into rucksacks. The bombings were followed exactly two weeks later by a series of attempted attacks."[4]

Depending on where you live in the world, or your country of origin, other terrorist acts may come to mind [see Appendices 31, 32, 33].

For example, the 2002 Bali bombings which "occurred on 12 October 2002 in the tourist district of Kuta on the Indonesian island of Bali. The attack was the deadliest act of terrorism in the history of Indonesia, killing 202 people, (including 88 Australians, and 38 Indonesian citizens). A further 240 people were injured. The attack involved the detonation of three bombs: a backpack-mounted device carried by a suicide bomber; a large car bomb, both of which were detonated in or near popular nightclubs in Kuta; and a third much smaller device detonated outside the United States consulate in Denpasar, causing only minor damage. Various members of Jemaah Islamiyah, a violent Islamist group, were convicted in relation to the bombings."[5]

Another was the 3 February 2007 Baghdad market bombing, which resulted from "the detonation of a large truck bomb in a busy market in the Iraqi capital of Baghdad on 3 February 2007. The suicide attack killed at least 135 people and injured 339 others. The bomb, estimated to be about one ton in weight, brought down at least 10 buildings and coffee shops and obliterated market stalls in a largely Shi'ite enclave less than a half mile from the Tigris River."[6]

Another example, the 2008 Mumbai attacks, "also referred to as November 26 or 26/11 and this terrorist attack targeted India's largest city Mumbai. It was actually a series of 10 coordinated shooting and bombing attacks across Mumbai by Islamic terrorists who are believed to have come from Pakistani Seawaters and backed by ISI, Pakistani secret service agency. It affected the Indo-Pak relation immensely and the bilateral relations were debilitated which have never returned to normalcy since."[7]

Again another market bombing, this time in the Peshawar market, where "a massive car bomb tore through the heart of a bustling marketplace in Peshawar, Pakistan, Wednesday, killing at least 100 people -- including many women and children -- and injuring at least 200 others, officials said. A vehicle packed with 150 kilograms (330 pounds) of explosives detonated at the Meena Bazaar, a labyrinth of shops popular with women. The impact destroyed buildings, burying people underneath the rubble, and sparked massive fires in the shops, mosques, and homes. In a year of seemingly endless militant attacks in Pakistan, this was the deadliest."[8]

However, is much thought given to other types of "terrorist" attacks, groups or lone individuals?

This course highlighted other examples of "terrorists", known as examples of Single Issue Terrorist Causes[9], and have included:

- *"Animal Rights Groups and Eco-Terrorists*

    This category includes eco-terrorist groups and animal rights groups who resort to violent means to attain goals and/or address concerns. They profess humanitarian motives for their actions, and several splinter groups strongly urge their members to be extremely careful not to harm humans physically, but to cause maximum property damage. Others intentionally target people, as do some members of the Animal Liberation Front (ALF). ALF is based in the United Kingdom and the United States, and members use explosives in the form of letter bombs, car bombs, and booby traps. These movements became popular in Europe in the 1960s, and have grown rapidly since the late 1980s in America. They continue to represent a serious threat to those individuals, groups, or businesses that they target.

There are many environmental protection groups around the world that have sincere concerns that they express in socially acceptable ways. There are a few, however, who use terrorism to force the issue. Examples include anti-logging groups who "spike" trees marked for harvesting so the cutting chain of the chainsaw will snap and injure the logger. The environmentalist group Green Peace has also been labeled a terrorist organization by some governments.

- *Anti-Abortion Groups*

Anti-abortion groups also claim humanitarian or social conviction as their motives. Not all are violent, but incidents of violence by anti-abortionists increased during the 1990s. In 1999, they were responsible for at least 7 murders, 16 attempted murders, 40 bombings, 161 arsons, and 3 kidnappings. In some cases, the rhetoric is a bit confused and the rationale comes across as though they believe so strongly in the right for human life that they are going to kill someone to make their point.

- *Anti-Tax Groups*

This is a common motive for "Patriot" groups who perform acts of terrorism. An example from 1995 is when four members of the Minnesota Patriots Council (an anti-tax group) were convicted of possession of Ricin (an extremely toxic biological agent) with intent to kill various federal and county officials.

- *Cults*

A cult is formed when a person convinces other people to become totally dependent on him or her for almost all major life decisions. The cult leader is able to imbue these followers with a belief that he or she has some special talent, gift, or knowledge.

Some of the more infamous cult leaders include Jim Jones and David Koresh. Jim Jones convinced more than 900 of his followers to kill their children and themselves by drinking Kool-Aid laced with cyanide. David Koresh of the Branch Davidians died in a fire, along with many of his followers in Waco Texas during a siege by American law enforcement agencies.

> *Another example of a cult is the Aum Shinrikyo, led by Shoko Asahara. This Armageddonist terrorist cult has used a variety of weapons of mass destruction against civilian targets in an effort to create mass casualties. Between 1990 and 1993, they used bioagents (Botulism and Anthrax), and in 1994 and 1995, they used chemical nerve agents (Sarin)."*[10]

In this latter incident, on March 20, 1995 "religious cultists release the toxic nerve gas sarin at multiple locations in the Tokyo subway [see Appendix 34]. A dozen people will die, and thousands suffer injuries ranging from mild to severe. Aum Shinrikyo was a Japanese cult combining bits of Buddhism, Hinduism, shamanism and end-of-days Christianity. The name combined the Buddhist mantra om with the Japanese for 'supreme truth'."[11]

"The cult also built a facility to manufacture biological and chemical weapons by the ton. Aum experimented with botulin toxin, anthrax, cholera, Q fever and the Ebola virus. Operatives tried to release botulin near the Diet in 1990, and near the imperial palace in 1993. An anthrax release from its Tokyo office building in 1993 caused foul smells, brown steam, pet deaths and stains on cars and sidewalks. None of these attacks is known to have caused death or injury."[12]

"Aum Shinrikyo managed to pull off its most audacious — and deadly — attack just nine months later. In the Monday morning rush hour of March 20, five cult members boarded different subway trains converging on central Tokyo. Four of them each carried two plastic bags loaded with sarin, and the fifth had three bags. At nearly the same moment, they each dropped the bags to the floor of the jam-packed train and punctured them with a specially sharpened umbrella tip. The cultists then quickly stepped off the trains as they pulled into the next station. Getaway drivers were waiting outside the station for each of them."[13]

"Estimates of the injured range from 3,800 up to 6,000. The sarin killed 12 people ... About 200 people were arrested. About 20 are either still in Japan's lengthy trial process standing trial or have already been convicted. At least eight Aum members, including the founder, have received death sentences for their roles in the attack."[14]

As cited, however, "contrary to depictions in Western media, and popular stereotypes, religious terrorism is not limited to radical Islamic groups in the Middle East, and the U.S. domestic terrorist threat may lie closer to home. A few new religious groups and movements may pose the greatest threat."[15]

For example, "in September 1984, 750 people became sick after eating in restaurants in The Dalles, Oregon. Investigators later learned that Bhagwan Shree Rajneesh, the leader of the nearby religious commune of Rajneeshpuram, had ordered followers to spread the salmonella bacteria in restaurants in order to influence local elections. The event was thought to only be a trial run for a larger attack, and "resulted in the largest outbreak of foodborne disease" in the U.S. that year."[16]

And, the "House of Yahweh, founded by 'Yisrayl' Hawkins, with branches in Odessa and Abilene, Texas. This group may have a large collection of weapons, they believe their group will play a major role in the coming War of Armageddon, and members of the group have been linked to Posse Comitatus, a radical, anti-government group connected to the racist Christian Identity movement."[17]

And, as warned, "Anders Behring Breivik defied the stereotype about who a terrorist is, and is yet another reminder that extremism knows no racial, religious, or ethnic boundaries."[18]

"Anders Behring Breivik, 32, is handsome, green-eyed, and blond—in other words, not a stereotypical terrorist. His good looks worked to his advantage, helping him gain access to the island of Utoya and allowing him to kill scores of people in one of the bloodiest attacks in Norwegian history. The assault that he carried out on Friday was not only horrific; it also exposed a weakness in counterterrorism strategy in Europe and the United States. The commonly held notion of who a terrorist is means people may lower their guard around Breivik and others who look not Arab, but Western, and the results can be devastating."[19]

Vigilance becomes doubly important in our world today?

What seemed like an "ordinary" guy, "Anders Behring Breivik is a Norwegian right-wing extremist, confessed perpetrator of the Norway attacks on 22 July 2011: the bombing of government buildings in Oslo that resulted in eight deaths, and the mass shooting at a camp of the Workers' Youth League (AUF) of the Labour Party on the island of Utøya where he killed 69 people, mostly teenagers."[20]

As cited, "the 32-year-old, previously unknown to police, was arrested on Friday after a bomb blast in central Oslo killed seven people and a shooting rampage at a youth camp near the capital left at least 85 dead and scores wounded. He explained that it was cruel but that he had to go through with these acts", where "the attacks were apparently planned over a long period of time."[21]

With, "many experts believe that the FBI's assessment was based on the color of Stack's skin (white) and on his non-Arabic-sounding name, rather than on the facts of the case. In other words, he [Anders Behring Breivik] had carried out an act of political violence, but officials refused to recognize him in this way because he did not fit their idea of what a terrorist looks like."[22]

So, behind that "innocent face" [Anders Behring Breivik's picture on his Facebook page shows a man with longish blonde hair and piercing eyes[23]], apparently lay the heart of a "monster", where his "far-right militant ideology" includes "Islamophobia, far-right Zionism, anti-feminism, right-wing populism, Serbian paramilitarism, and white nationalism. It regards Islam and "cultural Marxism" as the enemy, and argues for the violent annihilation of "Eurabia" and multiculturalism, to preserve a Christian Europe"[24] venting his ideology on over 70 innocent victims.

Footnotes

1 – 2. "10 Worst Terrorist Attacks"
Posted by Haider on June 9, 2011 in Crime, History, Life
http://www.tiptoptens.com/2011/06/09/10-worst-terrorist-attacks/

3. "20 Years Later, the Lockerbie Terror Attack Is Not as Solved as We Think"
By Nathan Thrall
January 2, 2009
http://webcache.googleusercontent.com/search?q=cache:vhl86yRlg2kJ:www.usnews.com/opinion/articles/2009/01/02/20-years-later-the-lockerbie-terror-attack-is-not-as-solved-as-we-think+terror+Lockerbie+Scotland&cd=3&hl=en&ct=clnk&gl=ca

4. "7 July 2005 London bombings"
http://webcache.googleusercontent.com/search?q=cache:5o2EQX_0f2cJ:en.wikipedia.org/wiki/7_July_2005_London_bombings+tube+bombing+in+london&cd=1&hl=en&ct=clnk&gl=ca

5. "2002 Bali bombings"
http://webcache.googleusercontent.com/search?q=cache:FD5GC8ncrD8J:en.wikipedia.org/wiki/2002_Bali_bombings+12+Oct+2002+car+bombing+outside+nightclub+in+Kuta,+Indonesia&cd=1&hl=en&ct=clnk&gl=ca

6. "3 February 2007 Baghdad market bombing"
http://en.wikipedia.org/wiki/3_February_2007_Baghdad_market_bombing

7. "10 Worst Terrorist Attacks"
Posted by Haider on June 9, 2011 in Crime, History, Life
http://www.tiptoptens.com/2011/06/09/10-worst-terrorist-attacks/

8. "Survivors recount narrow escape from deadly Peshawar market bombing"
October 28, 2009
http://webcache.googleusercontent.com/search?q=cache:X_Ug7FF2bgcJ:articles.cnn.com/2009-10-28/world/pakistan.blast_1_peshawar-car-bomb-militant%3F_s%3DPM:WORLD+28+Oct+2009+bombing+at+marketplace+in+Peshawar,+Pakistan&cd=1&hl=en&ct=clnk&gl=ca

9 – 10. "Introduction to Anti-Terrorism" National Terrorism Preparedness Institute, St. Petersburg College in St. Petersburg, Florida.

http://terrorism.spcollege.edu/Training/Courses/IntroductiontoAnti-Terrorism.aspx

11 - 14. "March 20, 1995: Poison Gas Wreaks Tokyo Subway Terror"
By Randy Alfred 03.20.09
http://webcache.googleusercontent.com/search?q=cache:kcYThoVV0NEJ:www.wired.com/science/discoveries/news/2009/03/dayintech_0320+20+Mar+1995+sarin+nerve+gas+attack+in+subway+in+Toyko,+Japan&cd=3&hl=en&ct=clnk&gl=ca

15 – 17. "Religious Terrorism: Apocalypse Now: Armageddon Enters the New Age of Terrorism"
by John W. Morehead, Associate Director, Watchman Fellowship of California
http://webcache.googleusercontent.com/search?q=cache:Tb2Ns_XAZ3kJ:www.apologeticsindex.org/t22.html+religious+terrorist+attacks&cd=8&hl=en&ct=clnk&gl=ca

18 - 19. "Norway's Terrorist in Disguise"
By Tara McKelvey, Jul 23, 2011
http://webcache.googleusercontent.com/search?q=cache:n7oUE_nIbN4J:www.thedailybeast.com/articles/2011/07/23/norway-terrorist-attack-christian-perpetrator-defied-stereotypes.html+The+Norway+terrorist+attacks+and+religious&cd=2&hl=en&ct=clnk&gl=ca

20. "Anders Behring Breivik"
http://en.wikipedia.org/wiki/Anders_Behring_Breivik

21. "Norway suspect admits responsibility"
Updated: 09:12, Sunday July 24, 2011
http://www.skynews.com.au/topstories/article.aspx?id=641833&vId=

22. "Norway's Terrorist in Disguise"
By Tara McKelvey, Jul 23, 2011
http://webcache.googleusercontent.com/search?q=cache:n7oUE_nIbN4J:www.thedailybeast.com/articles/2011/07/23/norway-terrorist-attack-christian-perpetrator-defied-stereotypes.html+The+Norway+terrorist+attacks+and+religious&cd=2&hl=en&ct=clnk&gl=ca

23. "Norway suspect admits responsibility"
Updated: 09:12, Sunday July 24, 2011
http://www.skynews.com.au/topstories/article.aspx?id=641833&vId=

24. "Anders Behring Breivik"
http://en.wikipedia.org/wiki/Anders_Behring_Breivik

Terrorist Targets

In my course at National Terrorism Preparedness Institute, it was also mentioned that "virtually any target may be acceptable to terrorists. Some have more value as terrorist targets, but any property or person whose destruction or death could negatively impact the terrorists "enemy" is acceptable. Osama bin Laden declared that the best thing his followers could do was to kill an American soldier, and the next best was to kill any American."[1]

And, "the more valuable or costly the target, the more attractive the target is to the terrorist wishing to make a statement. This is especially true when the publicity generated over the act of terrorism is greater. An example of this is the first terrorist bombing of the U.S. World Trade Center in 1993. Beside the six persons killed and many injured, there was 600 million dollars in structural damage, and the information about the event was immediately broadcast around the world."[2]

In helping to determine what target a terrorist group might choose, some have suggested the efficacy of mathematic modeling [see Appendix 35], where, as cited, in "A Terrorist Target Selection and Prioritization Model" (2003), the senior authors described a mathematical model they believed to be of the type used by al-Qaeda planners in selecting targets. By using this model, those responsible for safeguarding against acts of terrorism would have a heads-up as to which targets terrorists are likely to attack."[3]

This has also been suggested by others [see Appendix 36], where it is mentioned that "the choice of target for a terrorist organisations is far from random. What often defines a terrorist group as opposed to those who claim to be freedom fighters or a liberation movement is that a terrorist organisations will strike against non-military targets. There has been a radical change in the targeting policy of terrorist groups, traditional politically motivated terrorist groups often seen in the west such as the IRA or the Italian Red Brigades chose to strike at high profile political targets or against targets that would guarantee media attention like the bombing of commercial centres."[4]

As further cited in the course, "terrorist organizations choose targets based on what they hope to accomplish. For example, if the objective were to change political policy, then the target would generally be a specific government. In other cases, the target may be the assassination of an individual, which would make the target also the victim. Most terrorist organizations go through separate phases of target and victim selection. Objectives may include changing a law or political policy or the assassination of a victim, publicity, extortion of cash, military withdrawal, realization of ethnic or religious goals, or vengeance. Targets can be a government, government agencies and departments, commercial enterprises, or individual people."[5]

The course also mentioned "national infrastructure, transportation, telecommunications, energy, banking, public health, and water supply are becoming increasingly dependent on computerized systems and linkages. They are all prime candidates for attacks by cyberterrorism."[6]

In fact, Robert S. Mueller III, the Director of the Federal Bureau of Investigation emphasized this same point [see Appendix 37], where he said in 2005 "nearly 10 years ago, we joined forces with you to defend our critical national infrastructure. Our national infrastructure is a soft target, ranging from bridges and buildings to public utilities and power grids across the country. More than 90 percent of our infrastructure is owned and operated by private industry or state and local governments. And it is increasingly managed by computer networks and the Internet.

The Internet has opened the doors to a new world of communication and commerce. But technology is a double-edged sword. Entrepreneurs and engineers are not the only ones who recognize the vast potential of the Internet. Criminals and terrorists do, too."[7]

With, "terrorists who shun our way of life are more than willing to use our technology to carry out and publicize their attacks--from airplanes used as missiles, to coordinated attacks on mass transportation ... Al Qaeda and other criminal organizations are using that same technology to wreak havoc around the world. Criminals and terrorists no longer need to be in the same room, or even the same country, to plan, finance, and execute attacks."[8]

Our course also warned against too much information. For example, "government agencies openly and aggressively advertise information about their hours of operation, services, equipment, capabilities, and often details about personnel. This gives terrorists easy access to all the essential intelligence for making the most effective attack."[9]

For example, in 2003 "three American diplomats are killed by a roadside bomb targeting their convoy in Gaza. Palestine Resistance Committees, an umbrella organization has taken responsibility for the attack"[10] [see Appendix 38].

In, 2007 an American embassy was attacked in Athens, Greece and the next year US diplomat John Granville was assassinated in Khartoum, Sudan.[11]

In the following years, attacks on American consulates and embassies included:

- *"22 January 2002, Calcutta, Harkat-ul-Jihad al-Islami gunmen attack Consulate*
- *14 June 2002, Karachi, al-Qaeda truck bomb detonates outside Consulate*
- *12 October 2002, Denpasar, Consular Office bombed by Jemaah Islamiyah as part of the Bali bombings*
- *28 February 2003, Islamabad, Unknown gunmen attack Embassy*
- *30 June 2004, Tashkent, Islamic Movement of Uzbekistan suicide bomber attacks Embassy*
- *6 December 2004, Jeddah, al-Qaeda gunmen raid diplomatic compound*
- *2 March 2006, Karachi, Car bomb explodes outside Embassy*
- *12 September 2006, Damascus, Gunmen raid US Embassy*
- *12 January 2007, Athens, RPG Fired at Embassy by Revolutionary Struggle*
- *18 March 2008, Sana'a, Mortar attack against US Embassy*
- *9 July 2008, Istanbul, Armed attack against Consulate*
- *17 September 2008, Sana'a, Two car bombs outside US embassy in Yemeni capital*
- *5 April 2010, Peshawar, An attack near the U.S. Consulate in Peshawar, Pakistan".*[12]

The State Department has parroted this warning [see Appendix 39; also see an earlier warning in Appendix 40], by saying "the State Department is warning Americans that al Qaeda and affiliated organizations continue to plan terrorist attacks against U.S. interests around the world, including Europe, Asia, Africa, and the Middle East. These attacks may employ a wide variety of tactics including suicide operations, assassinations, kidnappings, hijackings, and bombings …"[13]

A similar warning for British interests abroad also mentioned "the UK has long-standing commercial, political and military links with many countries in the Muslim world. Our involvement in the region is strongly opposed by Al Qaida and other extremist groups. This has resulted in British interests and citizens abroad repeatedly being targeted by international terrorists."[14]

The article also listed these events, "a number of significant terrorist attacks have been carried out or attempted against British targets in the Mediterranean and Middle East region over the last five years:

•*June 2002 - A planned terrorist attack on US and UK naval ships in the Straits of Gibraltar was thwarted.*

•*November 2003 - Al Qaida suicide bombers carried out attacks against the British Consulate and HSBC building in Istanbul, Turkey, killing 27 people including three British citizens.*

•June 2004 - A BBC news crew was attacked by Al Qaida gunmen in Riyadh, killing the cameraman and severely injuring the reporter.

•September 2004 - A British national living in Saudi Arabia was shot and killed in a Riyadh shopping centre by Al Qaida gunmen.

•October 2004 - British engineer Kenneth Bigley was murdered by the Al Qaida in Iraq (AQI) group.

•March 2005 - A British teacher was killed in a car bomb explosion in Doha, Qatar."[15]

The course also mentions "commercial oil exploration is also becoming a common target because of the lax security in remote areas of drilling and pipelines. These companies are consequently more vulnerable to localized terrorist organizations that seek to extort resources or cash from them."[16]

As further cited, "major oil producing regions in the world are politically unstable, where political unrest, civil war and revolution poses great threats to the stability of international energy market. The threat of terrorist attacks on oil fields or principal transit routes also present serious challenges to energy security" [see Appendix 41].[17]

With, "today, the U.S. is more dependent on foreign oil than ever before, any shocks or disruptions from oil exporting countries would have a worse impact on the economy. Secondly, the terrorists' attacks are more diversified and unpredictable. Oil fields and principal transit routes are their potential targets, which could seriously disrupt the global market. Further, inappropriate dealing with political conflicts in oil producing regions could result in direct confrontation and revenge attacks in the United States."[18]

This threat occurs all over the world [see Appendix 42 & 43]. For example, "the Australian Strategic Policy Institute has identified petroleum facilities in Western Australia, including offshore platforms, ports, processing plants and pipelines as potential targets of military or terrorist attack. Offshore structures and floating production and storage vessels have few defences against attack. In a 2005 report on maritime security threats, the Institute noted that the general trend in Australian petroleum production from onshore to offshore and from Bass Strait to the Northwest Shelf posed increasing risks for the Western Australian petroleum industry."[19]

Another included, "the Joint Revolutionary Council, a coalition of militants and community leaders not previously known for such strikes, said in a statement emailed to the media it had blown up Agip's Tura manifold ... We demand the immediate vacation of all the international oil companies operating in the Niger Delta territory pending future negotiations (with the authorities)," it said.[20]

And, as cited, "according to the US State Department, between 1996 and 2004 there were at least 80 terrorist attacks against oil companies world-wide, that resulted in kidnappings, casualties, damages and large monetary losses."[21]

Footnotes

1 – 2. "Introduction to Anti-Terrorism" National Terrorism Preparedness Institute, St. Petersburg College in St. Petersburg, Florida.
http://terrorism.spcollege.edu/Training/Courses/IntroductiontoAnti-Terrorism.aspx

3. "A Prescription for Safeguarding Against Terrorist Attacks"
July 2006
http://www.homelandsecurity.org/journal/Default.aspx?oid=146&ocat=1

4. Dugdale-Pointon, TDP. (26 May 2005), "Terrorist Targets"
http://www.historyofwar.org/articles/concepts_terrortargets.html

5 - 6. "Introduction to Anti-Terrorism" National Terrorism Preparedness Institute, St. Petersburg College in St. Petersburg, Florida.
http://terrorism.spcollege.edu/Training/Courses/IntroductiontoAnti-Terrorism.aspx

7 - 8. Robert S. Mueller III, Director, Federal Bureau of Investigation
InfraGard 2005 National Conference, Washington, D.C. August 09, 2005
http://www.fbi.gov/news/speeches/working-together-to-protect-national-infrastructure-from-crime-and-terrorism

9. "Introduction to Anti-Terrorism" National Terrorism Preparedness Institute, St. Petersburg College in St. Petersburg, Florida.
http://terrorism.spcollege.edu/Training/Courses/IntroductiontoAnti-Terrorism.aspx

10 - 11. "List of assassinations and acts of terrorism against Americans"
http://en.wikipedia.org/wiki/List_of_assassinations_and_acts_of_terrorism_against_Americans

12. "Terrorist attacks on U.S. diplomatic facilities"
http://en.wikipedia.org/wiki/Terrorist_attacks_on_U.S._diplomatic_facilities

13. "State Department updates warning to Americans overseas"
July 26, 2011, By Jill Dougherty, CNN Foreign Affairs Correspondent
http://articles.cnn.com/2011-07-26/us/state.department.caution_1_islamic-maghreb-target-both-official-qaeda?_s=PM:US

14 - 15. "Attacks on UK citizens and interests abroad: Aftermath of terrorist attack on the British Consulate in Istanbul, November 2003", Lynsey Addario
https://www.mi5.gov.uk/output/attacks-on-uk-citizens-and-interests-abroad.html

16. "Introduction to Anti-Terrorism" National Terrorism Preparedness Institute, St. Petersburg College in St. Petersburg, Florida.
http://terrorism.spcollege.edu/Training/Courses/IntroductiontoAnti-Terrorism.aspx

17 - 18. "Oil - Political Impact"
http://climate.org/climatelab/Oil

19. "Petroleum industry in Western Australia"
http://en.wikipedia.org/wiki/Petroleum_industry_in_Western_Australia

20. "Nigeria rebel faction says attacks Agip oil facility"
By Nick Tattersall and Joe Brock
Thu Mar 4, 2010
http://grendelreport.posterous.com/terrorists-attack-western-oil-facilities-in-n

21. "Targeting Energy Infrastructure: Examining the Terrorist Threat in North Africa and its Broader Implications (ARI)"
Jennifer Giroux
ARI 25/2009 - 13/2/2009
http://www.realinstitutoelcano.org/wps/portal/rielcano_eng/Content?WCM_GLOBAL_CONTEXT=/elcano/elcano_in/zonas_in/international+terrorism/ari25-2009

Nuclear, biological, and chemical weapons

The most frightening terrorist attack would probably be that using nuclear, biological, and chemical weapons. In fact, as cited, "a study prepared for Nuclear Control Institute by five former U.S. nuclear weapons designers concluded that a sophisticated terrorist group would be capable of designing and building a workable nuclear bomb from stolen plutonium or highly enriched uranium, with potential yields in the kiloton range. This risk must be taken seriously, particularly in light of documented attempts by al Qaeda to acquire nuclear material and nuclear-weapon design information. Despite claims to the contrary from plutonium-fuel advocates in the nuclear power industry, effective and devastating weapons could be made using 'reactor-grade' plutonium, hundreds of tons of which are processed, stored and circulated around the world in civilian nuclear commerce"[1] [see Appendix 44].

As further cited, "the consequences of a biological attack are almost beyond comprehension. It would be 9/11 times 10 or a hundred in terms of the number of people who would be killed," former Sen. Bob Graham said. Graham said a biological attack was more likely than a nuclear one because it would be easier to carry out.

Biological weapons "are more available," he said. "Anthrax is a natural product of dead animals. Other serious pathogens are available in equally accessible forms." "There are so many scientists who have the skills to convert a pathogen from benign, helpful purposes into an illicit, very harmful weapon."[2]

That has actually occurred on more than one occasion. For example, the 2001 anthrax attacks in America come to mind, where "… one week after the September 11 attacks. Letters containing anthrax spores were mailed to several news media offices and two Democratic U.S. Senators, killing five people and infecting 17 others."[3]

"Bruce Edwards Ivins, became a focus of investigation around April 4, 2005. Ivins was a scientist who worked at the government's biodefense labs at Fort Detrick in Frederick, Maryland ... On August 6, 2008, despite having no direct evidence of his involvement, federal prosecutors declared Ivins to be the sole culprit of the crime."[4]

However, "a review of the scientific methods used in the investigation at the National Academy of Sciences, published in February 2011, cast doubt on the US government's conclusion that Ivins was the perpetrator. The review found that, although the type of anthrax used in the letters was correctly identified as the Ames strain of the bacterium, there was insufficient scientific evidence for the FBI's assertion that it originated from Ivins' laboratory."[5]

The Halabja poison gas attack was another, which "was a genocidal massacre against the Kurdish people that took place on March 16, 1988, during the closing days of the Iran–Iraq War, when chemical weapons were used by the Iraqi government forces in the Kurdish town of Halabja in Iraqi Kurdistan. The attack killed between 3,200 and 5,000 people, and injured around 7,000 to 10,000 more, most of them civilians; thousands more died of complications, diseases, and birth defects in the years after the attack."[6]

As cited in my course, "many military and police agencies define weapons of mass destruction as 'NBC' weapons, or nuclear, biological, and chemical weapons. However, explosives and fire are also used as weapons that generate mass destruction and casualties, so other authoritative sources include them as weapons of mass destruction. The acronym used to remember these five categories of WMD is 'B-NICE,' for biological, nuclear, incendiary, chemical and explosive."[7]

The poor soldiers and civilians injured, maimed or killed by incendiary bombs / devices in recent times bears this to be a true terrorist weapon [see just a few examples, Appendices 45 to 48].

As cited, "the Taliban know that in pitched battles they will lose against coalition forces, so have resorted to increasingly sophisticated terrorist warfare. While many of the devices use old munitions for the explosive component - such as artillery shells, rockets and even mortar bombs - the method of detonation has become steadily more technical. The Taliban have also used command wire devices and pressure plates, the latter often constructed from the simple but effective use of two saw blades held apart by a piece of wood and encased in a car tyre inner tube. A vehicle passing over the buried device connects the saw blades and triggers the device."[8]

Like many incidents, this brave soldier tells his tale: "I joined the NDNG when I was 17 years old, B Company 164th Engineers out of Williston. I was attending the local community college in 2003 when my unit was activated shortly before Thanksgiving. My company, B Company 164, along with C Company 164 was combined to make up A Co 141st Engineers because the original A Co 141 was on airport security. The 141st Engineers mobilized out of Fort Carson Colorado. We spent a month and a half there then went to Iraq."[9]

Continuing, "we were given a job called Taskforce Trailblazer, which entails finding bombs alongside the road. I was in Iraq for 8 and half months when a roadside bomb went off next the Humvee I was driving. It consisted of four 155-artillery rounds and three incendiary grenades. I lost my left leg below the knee and sustained injuries to my left hand. The passenger escaped the attack with a bruise on his arm. The gunner, who was my best friend Cody Wentz, was killed on November 4th, 2004 from injuries sustained to the head. He was 21 years of age."[10]

In addition, as cited [see Appendix 49], "between 1991 and 2000, 93 terrorist attacks worldwide produced more than 30 casualties, with 885 of these incidents involving explosions. The 2005 London subway bombings, the 1995 bombing of the Murrah Federal Building in Oklahoma City, and the catastrophic explosions of aircraft into 3 buildings on September 11, 2001 in New York City and Washington DC reminded health care workers of the magnitude of injuries and death that can result from a blast mechanism."[11]

With, "approximately 25,000 US and coalition forces and 100,000 Iraqis were estimated to have been injured or killed by explosions in the Global War on Terrorism as of early 2009."[12]

And finally, "a roadside bomb killed three NATO service members in southern Afghanistan on Thursday, while a bomb targeting Afghan policewomen killed three people in the west, officials said. The coalition did not disclose further details about the deaths of the three NATO troops. So far this year, 447 international service member have been killed in Afghanistan. The bomb targeting the policewomen was planted on a motorbike parked on a road leading to the airport in Herat, said Sayd Sharif Mohammadi, the police commander for the airport. When five Afghan policewomen rode by in their vehicle, the remote-controlled device was detonated, killing one policewoman and two civilians. Mohammadi said the explosion also wounded 10 people — the other four female police officers riding in the police vehicle, its driver and five civilians who were near the blast."[13]

Another factor cited by the course is the suicide terrorist, with the definition of a Suicide Terrorism as the "operational method in which the very definition of the attack is dependent upon the death of the perpetrator."[14]

How does one protect themselves when the terrorist has no expectation to survive?

We saw that in the Kamikaze pilots of WWII [see Appendix 50], where a paragraph from the Kamikaze pilot's manual, located in their cockpits read:

> *"Transcend life and death. When you eliminate all thoughts about life and death, you will be able to totally disregard your earthly life. This will also enable you to concentrate your attention on eradicating the enemy with unwavering determination, meanwhile reinforcing your excellence in flight skills."*[15]

Similarly, the terrorists who flew into the World Trade Centre on 09/11 fully expected to die, as did the other hijackers involved in the 09/11 madness. Are such people insane or defective in some way? Apparently, not really, "the emerging understanding contradicts the notion that suicide bombers are deranged fanatics. The evidence is just the opposite: They tend to be free of obvious mental illness. Many are competent, successful, even loving and loved"[16] [see Appendix 51].

They are, however, somewhat vulnerable to pressure, where "most have fallen under the influence of an extreme group, whether it be Al Qaeda, Hamas or the Tamil Tigers of Sri Lanka, experts say. Like a cult, the group demands absolute obedience and promises immortality to the most devoted."[17]

"They believe there's a higher purpose, that in some way they are bringing about a purification, a perfection. They are destroying the world to save it."[18]

However, "to the leaders of some terrorist organizations, a suicide bomber is just another weapon in their arsenal. This type of terrorist is able to strike more target types, because they only have to gain access; they do not have to escape. There is little that security forces can do to protect against suicide bombers."[19]

Hard to protect against, definitely because:

- *"The terrorist himself chooses the time and place of action, according to the prevailing circumstances.*

- *The operation is simple and low cost, requiring no escape routes or complicated rescue operations.*

- *There is no danger of the terrorist being captured and giving away important information."*[20]

Again, vigilance is essential in our world today.

Footnotes

1. "Nuclear Terrorism: How To Prevent It"
http://www.nci.org/nci-nt.htm

2. "Report: Nuclear or Biological Terrorist Attack By 2013"
http://www.terroristplanet.com/2013.htm

3 - 5. "2001 anthrax attacks"
http://en.wikipedia.org/wiki/2001_anthrax_attacks

6. "Halabja poison gas attack"
http://en.wikipedia.org/wiki/Halabja_poison_gas_attack

7. "Introduction to Anti-Terrorism" National Terrorism Preparedness Institute, St. Petersburg College in St. Petersburg, Florida.

http://terrorism.spcollege.edu/Training/Courses/IntroductiontoAnti-Terrorism.aspx

8. "The increasing sophistication of Taliban roadside bombs"
By Caroline Gammell and Tom Coghlan, 18 Jun 2008
http://www.telegraph.co.uk/news/2150789/The-increasing-sophistication-of-Taliban-roadside-bombs.html

9 - 10. "Taskforce Trailblazer"
http://www.operationsecondchance.org/heroes/sorenson.php

11 - 12. "Blast Injuries"
Author: Andre Pennardt, MD, FACEP, FAAEM, FAWM
http://emedicine.medscape.com/article/822587-overview

13. "NATO: 3 troops killed in bombing in Afghanistan"
http://www.mail.com/int/news/world/727048-nato-3-troops-killed-bombing-afghanistan.html#.1272-stage-hero1-2

14. "Introduction to Anti-Terrorism" National Terrorism Preparedness Institute, St. Petersburg College in St. Petersburg, Florida.
http://terrorism.spcollege.edu/Training/Courses/IntroductiontoAnti-Terrorism.aspx

15. "Wars and Battles, 1944-1945 Japan's Suicide Pilots of World War II"
http://www.u-s-history.com/pages/h1740.html

16 - 18. "Method Without Madness?"
Suicide bombers are not deranged, psychiatrists say. Under group pressure, they see logic and a 'higher purpose' in their actions.
By Benedict Carey
Los Angeles Times/July 30, 2002
http://www.rickross.com/reference/brainwashing/brainwashing22.html

19 - 20. "Introduction to Anti-Terrorism" National Terrorism Preparedness Institute, St. Petersburg College in St. Petersburg, Florida.
http://terrorism.spcollege.edu/Training/Courses/IntroductiontoAnti-Terrorism.aspx

Religious Legitimacy

As cited in my course, "mainly found in religious-based terrorism, the spiritual leader is someone who regularly reinforces the group's cause and political teachings, which may come from a sponsoring government. This person motivates the terrorist organization by instilling religious legitimacy into their actions."[1]

"Sheikh Muhammad Hussein Fadlallah, a member of Hizbollah in Lebanon, is one example of a spiritual leader"[2] [see Appendix 52].

"Another is cleric Omar Abdel Rahman, who encouraged terrorists to blow up the United Nations building, the FBI headquarters, two New York traffic tunnels and a bridge, and assassinate the Egyptian president, all in the name of religion."[3]

As cited, "Abdel-Rahman was accused of being the leader of Al-Gama'a al-Islamiyya (also known as "The Islamic Group"), a militant Islamist movement in Egypt that is considered a terrorist organization by the United States and Egyptian governments. The group is responsible for many acts of violence, including the November 1997 Luxor massacre, in which 58 foreign tourists and four Egyptians were killed."[4]

"Sheikh Omar Abdel-Rahman, commonly known in the United States as "The Blind Sheikh", is a blind Egyptian Muslim leader who is currently serving a life sentence at the Butner Medical Center which is part of the Butner Federal Correctional Institution in Butner, North Carolina, United States. Formerly a resident of New York City, Abdel-Rahman and nine others were convicted of seditious conspiracy, which requires only that a crime be planned, not that it necessarily be attempted"[5] [see Appendix 53].

As further cited in my course, "one instance that shows the extreme influence spiritual leaders can have on members is the Sarin nerve agent attack on a Tokyo railway station that killed 12 people in 1995. The spiritual leader Shoko Asahara, of the Armageddonist cult Aum Shinrikyo, by-passed top leaders to command this attack."[6]

"Sometimes this type of by-pass in leadership leads to the terrorist organization splitting into two or more separate groups. Disputes between the leadership about how aggressive or hard-line they will be often initiates these splits."[7]

"For example, the Jewish Palestinian Haganah group split in 1931, leaving the original group and a splinter group called Haganah B"[8] [see Appendix 54].

"From this group, an additional splinter group emerged in 1936 called Irgun

Zwei Leumi. Again in 1940, a smaller group took shape called Lochamei Herut Israel (the Stern Gang). As the groups divided they became increasingly fanatical"[9] [see Appendix 55].

The course also mentioned "terrorist organizations increase confusion by naming different groups or units of a single organization. In some cases, each cell has its own 'organizational' name. The goal is to confuse security forces into thinking there are more or larger groups then there actually are. This causes security forces to waste resources or to scatter forces instead of targeting one group. This strategy of misdirection was successful in the war against Soviet occupation in Afghanistan from 1979 to 1989 and in the present day conflict in Jammu and Kashmir, which has more than 100 named terrorist organizations involved."[10]

This was actually the topic of one thesis, where it was stated "in October 2001, over 10 years after the withdrawal of Soviet troops from across the Friendship Bridge, American forces launched Operation Enduring Freedom in Afghanistan. As a result, there has been increased focus in the ensuing years both on Afghanistan and on counterinsurgency. As U.S. and coalition forces find themselves conducting counterinsurgencies in both Iraq and in Afghanistan, historical examples of similar operations have renewed relevance for current policy. While it is problematic to attempt to draw parallels between Soviet and U.S. experiences in Afghanistan, the Soviet experience is useful for understanding general themes that recur for large powers facing insurgencies."[11]

Also, "it is undeniable that flaws in Soviet counterinsurgency strategy and deficiencies in Soviet military capabilities seriously hindered operations against the mujahedeen."[12]

With, "Soviet leaders also lacked a doctrine and a military force suited for counterinsurgency. This was partly a result of focusing on conventional threats in the context of the Cold War."[13]

And, "Soviet ideology at the time cultivated a perception that actions in Afghanistan were in support of workers and peasants, which promoted the underlying assumption that counterinsurgency was not all that needed, because Soviet policies aligned with the desires of the 'people'. Therefore, due to distractions of the Cold war and ideological bias, Soviet leadership initially did not pay necessary attention to the requirements of conducting an effective counterinsurgency in Afghanistan."[14]

However, as mentioned, "history has shown that military intervention has rarely been successful in stopping or preventing terrorism.[dubious – discuss] Although military action can disrupt a terrorist group's operations temporarily, it rarely ends the threat."[15]

"Thus repression by the military in itself (particularly if it is not accompanied by other measures) usually leads to short term victories, but tend to be unsuccessful in the long run (e.g. the French's doctrine described in Roger Trinquier's book Modern War used in Indochina and Algeria). However, new methods (see the new Counterinsurgency Field Manual) such as those taken in Iraq have yet to be seen as beneficial or ineffectual."[16]

As further cited in our course, "Domestic terrorist organizations can be placed in six categories. National/Ethnic Separatists are the most popular cause for terrorism around the world. Left Wing Social Revolutionaries seek to overthrow "Imperialism," while Right Wing Extremist groups follow anti-government or racist ideologies. Paramilitary groups are characterized by a military style of training members. These are followed by Special Interest Groups, such as anti-abortion or animal rights, and Cults, which will be discussed at length at the end of this module."[17]

In the wake of 9/11, however, the following is mentioned:

> *"there was a potential for a passive jurisdictional fight: the FBI has jurisdiction in domestic terrorism cases, NYPD had jurisdiction under local murder statutes, the National Transportation Safety Board has jurisdiction in the event of an accident, and while the Department of Defense and intelligence apparatus formally have no jurisdiction any international response is within their purview. The myriad of government agencies with jurisdiction is broadly representative of US policy with respect to terrorism in the pre-9/11 world, with the typical result being other agencies acting as support to the FBI (as in the Oklahoma City bombing). Though this may seem disorganized, in practice there is one clear tend: any organization with statutory jurisdiction is a civilian organization. This is indicative of a fundamental view point that combating terrorism is fundamentally an operation for police. Indeed as a result of these jurisdiction the United States military is barred from performing any functions, with US borders, as it would constitute law enforcement functionality which is strictly prohibited under the Posse Comitatus Act (1878)"*[18] [see Appendix 56].

However, "the last nine years have seen a radical shift in these policies. The most striking evidence for this is in the name given to these operations, 'War on Terror', designating these operations as a war is already a violent change in direction. The Central Intelligence Agency has largely been re-purposed to the point where it's primary function is obtaining and processing evidence on terrorism."[19]

Where "Hoffman argues that a new Global Counterinsurgency (GCOIN) strategy is needed to combat this international terrorist threat. This approach would include: vital information operations to counter the radical narratives;

separating the enemy from its support base to deny it sanctuaries and freedom of movement; continuing to detect and defuse the enemy domestically and internationally; and a commitment to build legitimate civil governance which could counter the underlying causes of terrorism and insurgency"[20] [see Appendix 57].

Nonetheless, "just because an organization such as Al-Qaeda may use terrorism on an international scale and dabble in domestic insurgencies does not make it subject to the same respective counter strategies."[21]

Footnotes

1 - 3. "Introduction to Anti-Terrorism" National Terrorism Preparedness Institute, St. Petersburg College in St. Petersburg, Florida.
http://terrorism.spcollege.edu/Training/Courses/IntroductiontoAnti-Terrorism.aspx

4 - 5. "Omar Abdel-Rahman"
http://en.wikipedia.org/wiki/Omar_Abdel-Rahman

6 - 10. "Introduction to Anti-Terrorism" National Terrorism Preparedness Institute, St. Petersburg College in St. Petersburg, Florida.
http://terrorism.spcollege.edu/Training/Courses/IntroductiontoAnti-Terrorism.aspx

11 - 14. "Soviet Counterinsurgency in the Soviet Afghan War Revisited: Analyzing the Effective Aspects of the Counterinsurgency Effort: A thesis presented"
by Andrei A. Doohovskoy
to the Standing Committee on the A.M. in Regional Studies – Russia, Eastern Europe, and Central Asia in partial fulfillment of the requirements for the degree of Master of the Arts in the subject of Regional Studies – Russia Eastern Europe, and Central Asia
http://docs.google.com/viewer?a=v&q=cache:xH-LYhSVGT0J:www.boekje-pienter.nl/images/coin-soviet-afghanwar.pdf+misdirection+successful+in+Soviet+occupation+in+Afghanistan&hl=en&gl=ca&pid=bl&srcid=ADGEESjzhEw2KRol0Qp7H4pCG-mekcdffIb9o6b5Zm-GVYYzd3-IUBmr-KG1IzUTeGgQpgrG5TsC3n9EUih3Isa6HuNxh7prW9bBqXvach2plyEeJaN_tlqFREAXsojc_9Glb5Nr-waB&sig=AHIEtbRxlZaTAHr1L_ffBUZyBTf6HiFmzw

15 - 16. "Counter-terrorism"
http://en.wikipedia.org/wiki/Counter-terrorism

17. "Introduction to Anti-Terrorism" National Terrorism Preparedness Institute, St. Petersburg College in St. Petersburg, Florida.

http://terrorism.spcollege.edu/Training/Courses/IntroductiontoAnti-Terrorism.aspx

18 - 19. "US Counterinsurgency and Terrorism Policy"
Posted September 26th, 2010.
http://alexgaynor.net/2010/sep/26/us-counterinsurgency-and-terrorism-policy/

20 - 21. "Counterterrorism and Counterinsurgency"
by Jason Rineheart
http://www.terrorismanalysts.com/pt/index.php/pot/article/view/122/html

Personal Protection Equipment and Officer Safety

In my next course, it was cited "as an asymmetric form of conflict, terrorism confers coercive power, with many of the advantages of military force, at a fraction of the cost. Due to the secretive nature and small size of terrorist organizations, they often offer opponents no clear organization to defend against or to deter. Methods may vary from incident to incident but, in reviewing terrorist acts during the last two centuries, they appear strikingly similar in concept"[1] [see Appendix 58].

For example, the Australian Federal Police reported:

"While strikingly similar to 21st century terrorist attacks, this is a description of a bombing that happened 30 years ago in Australia. The attack on the Sydney Hilton Hotel in 1978 was the catalyst for the formation of the Australian Federal Police (AFP)."[2]

"In 1980, the Turkish Consul-General to Australia and his bodyguard were shot dead on a Sydney street. The same obscure terrorist organisation which claimed responsibility for the attack struck again in 1986 when it bombed the Turkish Consulate in Melbourne."[3]

"In 1982, a bomb was detonated near the Israeli Consulate in Sydney and, within hours, another blast had rocked a nearby Jewish community building."[4]

"Since the September 11 terrorist attacks, the AFP has been involved in several successful counter terrorism operations. The organisation's determination and expertise was put to the test in October 2002, when three bombs exploded in a busy tourist area on the resort island of Bali. In all, 202 people were killed, including 88 Australians."[5]

In 2006, it was reported that:

"They are second-generation immigrants allegedly trained in the violent art of jihad. They are suburban young people accused of renting a storage facility to keep ammonium-nitrate fertilizer to be used to make a spectacular hit against the Western society they despise."[6]

"Those are some of the striking similarities between the suspected Canadian terrorist cell, caught up in a Toronto-area sweep last week, and seven British men aged 21 to 34 who are on trial on charges of conspiring to attack British targets."[7]

In addition, one can consider:

"The attacks in Kashgar on July 30-31, 2011 have the signature of previous terrorist attacks in Xinjiang, notably in Kashgar in 2008 and Aksu in 2010. While the details of the latest attack in Kashgar are hard to corroborate, what is clear is that the attackers chose a purely civilian target: Han Chinese diners and pedestrians."[8]

"The attack began on the evening of July 30 when a car bomb detonated on a street lined with pedestrians and food stalls frequented by Han Chinese. Shortly after, two Uighur men hijacked a truck, killed its driver, and then steered the truck onto the sidewalk and into the food stalls and then stabbed people at random."[9]

"On July 31, another attack occurred on a popular dining and shopping street for Han Chinese. After two blasts at one restaurant, as many as 10 Uighur men shot and stabbed people indiscriminately, including the firefighters who came to the rescue. Overall, more than 10 civilians and eight attackers were killed and more than 40 others wounded in the two days."[10]

"The attacks coincided with the two days prior to the start of Ramadan and are strikingly similar to an attack in Kashgar in August 2008. In that attack, two Uighur men from Kashgar armed with explosives, machetes, and a gun rammed a dump truck into a line of 70 Chinese police officers jogging near a police compound and then attacked the officers with machetes. The two men were arrested during the fight after killing 16 officers."[11]

And, finally, "in fact many of the causes and motivations remain strikingly similar to what could be called traditional modern terrorism. What is different is the religious ideological foundation, the broad definition of adversaries, the evolution in terrorist tactics and the desire and potential for devastating levels of destruction. Islamist extremists appear willing to ignore taboos against killing innocents and able to rationalize their actions by distorting Islamic teachings."[12]

As further reported in the course, and not mentioning the most horrific of all the 9 / 11 bombing of the World Trade Centre, "the following terrorist attacks in the 20th century have had a dramatic effect on American lives and sense of security:

> *1. September 16, 1920: Mario Buda kills 33 people by exploding a horse-drawn wagon filled with dynamite on Wall Street in New York City.*
>
> *2. July 22, 1946: Pushing for the creation of a Jewish state, Jewish terrorists blow up the King David Hotel (headquarters for the British Army in Palestine) in Jerusalem, killing 90 people.*
>
> *3. July 22, 1968: PLO terrorists conduct the first major airplane hijacking when they commandeer an El Al flight in hopes of forcing the*

release of Palestinian political prisoners.

4. September 5-6, 1972: Black September terrorists take over the Israeli Compound at the Olympic Games in Munich, resulting in the deaths of 11 athletes, 5 terrorists, and a German policeman.

5. November 4, 1979: Islamic students storm the U.S. Embassy in Tehran, Iran, and hold 52 Americans hostage for 444 days.

6. April 18, 1983: A suicide car-bomber blows up the U.S. embassy in Beirut, Lebanon, killing 17 Americans.

7. October 23, 1983: A Muslim suicide truck-bomber attacks the U.S. Marine barracks in Beirut, killing 241 U.S. Marines and sailors.

8. June 23, 1985: In an incident thought to be the work of Sikh separatists, an Air India flight explodes midair, killing 328.

9. December 21, 1988: A bomb, attributed to Libyan terrorists, explodes aboard a Pan Am airliner over Lockerbie, Scotland, killing all 259 passengers, as well as 11 others on the ground.

10. February 26, 1993: Six people are killed and more than 1,000 injured when Islamic militants detonate a truck bomb at the World Trade Center in New York City.

11. March 20, 1995: Aum Shinrikyo, a Japanese cult, releases sarin nerve agent on the Tokyo subway system, killing 12 and injuring up to 5,000.

12. April 19, 1995: American Timothy McVeigh, using a bomb concealed in a rental truck, destroys the federal building in Oklahoma City, killing 168 civilians.

13. November 13, 1995: A car bomb kills five Americans at a U.S. military headquarters in Riyadh, Saudi Arabia.

14. June 25, 1996: Nineteen U.S. Air Force personnel are killed, and more than 500 Americans and Saudis are injured, when a truck bomb explodes outside the Khobar Towers in Saudi Arabia.

15. November 17, 1997: Muslim militants massacre 58 tourists in the Temple of Hatshepsut in southern Egypt.

16. August 7, 1998: Truck bombings at the U.S. embassies in Kenya and Tanzania kill 224 people, including 12 Americans. A retaliatory cruise missile attack on a terrorist training camp in Afghanistan fails to kill its intended target, Osama Bin Laden.

17. August 15, 1998: IRA dissidents kill 29 people with a car bomb in Omagh, Northern Ireland.

18. October 12, 2000: Seventeen American service personnel are killed and dozens are injured after a small, explosives-laden boat crashes into the Navy destroyer USS Cole in the port of Aden, Yemen.

19. September 11, 2001: In an attack of unprecedented magnitude, hijacked planes are flown into the World Trade Center and the Pentagon, killing more than 2,700.

20. March 11, 2004: Ten bombs explode on commuter trains in Madrid, Spain, killing 191 people and injuring 1,800.

21. July 7, 2005: Three bombs explode on underground trains in London, England, killing 52 people and injuring 770.

22. June 30, 2007: A jeep loaded with gas cylinders is driven into the main terminal at Glasgow International Airport in Glasgow, Scotland, injuring five people."[13]

As further cited in the course, "the information below is excerpted from the seized Al Qaeda Manual and is provided to help give law enforcement officers an awareness of how the Al Qaeda organization views targets and conducts operational analysis: 'The strikes must be strong and have a wide impact on the population of that nation. Four targets must be simultaneously hit in any of those nations so that the government there knows that we are serious'."[14]

Hence, "simultaneous strikes are part of the Al Qaeda strategy, as evidenced in the 9/11 attacks on the World Trade Center and the Pentagon, as well as the London bus bombings."[15]

With such concerns, as cited in the course, "hazard assessment is a critical role of first responders. Assessment enables decisions to be made about the proper level of Personal Protection Equipment [PPE] needed. The risk benefit for entry and rescue is also determined from this hazard assessment. Standard tactical decisions must be made about rescuing victims and securing hazards. It is important for first responders to be aware of potential evidence upon arriving at a scene. If hazards are present, responders, evidence, and victims will need to be decontaminated. In many cases, these operations run concurrently, requiring good communication and coordination. In assessing the scene for hazards, the first responder must also evaluate the risks to self and others."[16]

As we now know, those brave first responders who weren't killed in the 9 / 11 attack, have gone onto suffer horrendous diseases from their searching the rubble for survivors.

For example:

"On November 28, 2006, the Village Voice reported that several dozen recovery personnel have developed cancer – as opposed to having contracted respiratory ailments, and that doctors have argued that some of these cancers developed as a result of the exposure to toxins at the Ground Zero site: "To date, 75 recovery workers at ground zero have been diagnosed with blood cell cancers that a half-dozen top doctors and epidemiologists have confirmed as having been likely caused by that exposure."[17]

"Dr. Larry Norton of Memorial Sloan-Kettering Hospital said 'Why isn't the whole nation mobilizing to take care of the chronic health impact of this disaster?'. Dr. Norton cited the 70 percent illness rate among first responders as 'a wakeup call.' Dr. Nathaniel Hupert of Weill Cornell Medical College, quoted by Jill Gardiner of the October 4, 2006 issue of the New York Sun said that premature deaths and other ailments of dogs in the area are 'our canary in the coalmine.' Richard Clapp and David Ozonoff, professors of environmental health at Boston University School of Public Health; Michael Thun, director of epidemiological research at the American Cancer Society; Francine Laden, assistant professor of environmental epidemiology at Harvard School of Public Health; Jonathan Samet, chairman of the epidemiology department at Johns Hopkins Bloomberg School of Public Health; and Charles Hesdorffer, associate professor of oncology at Johns Hopkins School of Medicine argue that the cancer incidence among monitored individuals cannot be called a coincidence. They assert that the Ground Zero cloud was likely the cause of the illnesses. The American College of Preventative Medicine is concerned that malignant mesothelioma will develop among persons exposed to Ground Zero air."[18]

"A study of 5000 rescue workers published in April 2010 by Dr. David J. Prezant the chief medical officer for the Office of Medical Affairs at the New York City Fire Department found that all the workers studied had impaired lung functions with an average impairment of 10 percent. The study found the impairments presented itself in the first year of after the attack with little or no improvements in the ensuing six years. 30 to 40 percent of workers were reporting persistent symptoms and 1000 of the group studied were on 'permanent respiratory disability'. Dr. Prezant noted the medications that are being given ease symptoms but are not a cure. Dr. Byron Thomashow, medical director of the Center for Chest Disease and Respiratory Failure at New York–Presbyterian/Columbia hospital said that the drop-off in lung function initially is really quite significant and doesn't get better. That's not what we've generally come to expect in people with fire and smoke exposure. They usually recover"[19] [see Appendix 59].

The importance of Personal Protection Equipment [PPE] becomes critically important under such circumstances, especially where "in the five months following the attacks, dust from the pulverized buildings continued to fill the air of the World Trade Center site."[20]

"The dust from the collapsed towers was 'wildly toxic', according to air pollution expert and University of California Davis Professor Emeritus Thomas Cahill. The thousands of tons of toxic debris resulting from the collapse of the Twin Towers consisted of more than 2,500 contaminants, more specifically: 50% non-fibrous material and construction debris; 40% glass and other fibers; 9.2% cellulose; and 0.8% of the extremely toxic carcinogen asbestos, as well as detectable amounts of lead, and mercury. There were also unprecedented levels of dioxin and PAHs from the fires which burned for three months. Many of the dispersed substances (asbestos, crystalline silica, lead, cadmium, polycyclic aromatic hydrocarbons) are carcinogenic; other substances can trigger kidney, heart, liver and nervous system deterioration. This was well known by the EPA at the time of collapse."[21]

But how do you immediately protect from such hazards, during a disaster or terrorist attack, where many of the first responders in the 9 / 11 attack after-math discarded their face masks as they were too restrictive or cumbersome to wear?

In the heat-of-the-moment, personal protection became secondary to finding possible buried victims?

That's human nature, in such brave souls!

Footnotes

1. "Terrorism Awareness for Law Enforcement" National Terrorism Preparedness Institute, St. Petersburg College in St. Petersburg, Florida.
http://terrorism.spcollege.edu/Training/Courses/TerrorismAwarenessforLE.aspx

2 - 5. "Countering Terrorism"
http://docs.google.com/viewer?a=v&q=cache:WS4rB8hbnDwJ:www.afp.gov.au/about-the-afp/our-organisation/~/media/afp/pdf/c/countering-terrorism.ashx+terrorist+acts+strikingly+similar&hl=en&gl=ca&pid=bl&srcid=ADGEESiq7fqbB5etdLFYHWgRkCxkTQB_300fvDEt7kNDQ57c47z4XCJF-MerJ6AXUK2CXT1L9nu5MWgSIzBidtafNaybN8ntANxuSuLbFMAb5zsYax-er_6JLZ6dBI5dca3VP6HwYeId&sig=AHIEtbTQ0dLT3W84SiN1gsLD2xMTYQw8BQ

6 - 7. "Terrorism cases strikingly similar"
By Hamida Ghafour,
Globe and Mail Update, June 10, 2006

http://limewoody.wordpress.com/2006/06/10/terrorism-cases-strikingly-similar/

8 - 11. "Violence Escalates in China's Xinjiang Province"
Sep 26, 2011
http://www.ctc.usma.edu/posts/violence-escalates-in-china%E2%80%99s-xinjiang-province

12. "International Terrorism"
Cause, Effect, and the Search for Solutions
http://www.globalfocus.org/GF-Terrorism.htm

13 - 16. "Terrorism Awareness for Law Enforcement" National Terrorism Preparedness Institute, St. Petersburg College in St. Petersburg, Florida.
http://terrorism.spcollege.edu/Training/Courses/TerrorismAwarenessforLE.aspx

17 - 21. "Health effects arising from the September 11 attacks"
http://en.wikipedia.org/wiki/Health_effects_arising_from_the_September_11_attacks

Risk Management

Another very useful topic covered in my course was Risk Management, where "the term risk management means any activity that involves the evaluation or comparison of risks and the development of approaches that change the probability or the consequences of a harmful action. Risk management determines if the risk is worth the benefit."[1]

In general, in terms of financial matters, Risk Management includes:

"The process of identification, analysis and either acceptance or mitigation of uncertainty in investment decision-making. Essentially, risk management occurs anytime an investor or fund manager analyzes and attempts to quantify the potential for losses in an investment and then takes the appropriate action (or inaction) given their investment objectives and risk tolerance. Inadequate risk management can result in severe consequences for companies as well as individuals."[2]

Operational Risk Management is a bit different, as described:

"An operational risk is, as the name suggests, a risk arising from execution of a company's business functions. It is a very broad concept which focuses on the risks arising from the people, systems and processes through which a company operates. It also includes other categories such as fraud risks, legal risks, physical or environmental risks."[3]

"A widely used definition of operational risk is the one contained in the Basel II regulations. This definition states that operational risk is the risk of loss resulting from inadequate or failed internal processes, people and systems, or from external events."[4]

In law enforcement or any kind of counter-terrorism situation, Operational Risk Management as cited in the course is:

"Operational risk management refers primarily to the risk of death or injury to first responders while they perform their duties at an emergency scene, such as a WMD crime scene. Managing risk is a fundamental responsibility of every first responder and is performed at every level of the incident management process."[5]

In so doing, one always considers the following:

- "Is the risk worth the benefit?
- Risk of death/injury to first responder
- Responsibility of every first responder"[6]

For example, in "Navy Doctrine for antiterrorism / force protection"[7], it cites in Chapter 6 the following preparation:

"Successful antiterrorism / force protection (ATFP) programs have two things in common across the spectrum from pre-incident responses through post-incident management: deliberate preparations and deliberate actions."[8]

It also lists the following protocols:

"ATFP operations are defensive operations: Terrorists choose the place, the method and the time to attack. Therefore, planners and the Antiterrorism Officer (ATO) at each command must:

1. Analyze the threat specific to a command's situation
2. Conduct risk assessments to determine the criticality and vulnerability of assets
3. Develop and execute an effective ATFP plan
4. Establish a baseline security posture
5. Implement random antiterrorism measures (RAM)
6. Conduct post-mission / deployment assessments to improve future performance."[9]

As well, "ATFP planners define what needs to be protected and to what level. Assessment tools that assist with quantifying tasks include:

1. Operational risk management
2. Criticality assessment
3. Vulnerability assessment
4. Planning assessment
5. Response element assessment
6. Vulnerability Assessment Management Program (VAMP)."[10]

My course also emphasized the importance of recognizing "Pre-Incident Indicators of Terrorist Activities"[11], where:

"History has shown that terrorist attacks do not occur in a vacuum; attacks are organized and planned weeks, months, or sometimes years in advance. The planning stage is law enforcement's best opportunity to prevent attacks. A number of activities are mandatory for terrorist organization members to conduct preparatory actions such as travel, communications with other terrorist group members, and disposable funds. Law enforcement may be able to prevent an attack during the planning phase by looking at these preliminary planning actions."[12]

"Terrorists, by nature, are secretive and do not make themselves obvious in our communities. In fact, they make every effort to disguise themselves and their intentions. Due to this fact, the law enforcement officer must develop an awareness of, and an ability to critically observe, all potential indicators of terrorist activity—no matter how subtle they might be."[13]

Various studies and divisions have examined "Pre-Incident Indicators of Terrorist Activities", with these as possible indicators [see Appendix 60]:

- "Surveillance
- Elicitation
- Test of Security
- Acquiring Supplies
- Suspicious People Who Don't Belong
- Dry Runs
- Deploying Assets/Getting Into Position"[14]

One of the most important aspects to guard against is an individual or group Testing Security, where:

"Tests of security is another area in which terrorists would attempt to gather data. This is usually conducted by driving by the target, moving into sensitive areas and observing security or law enforcement response. Terrorists would be interested in the time in which it takes to respond to an incident and/or the routes taken to a specific location. They may also try to penetrate physical security barriers or procedures in order to assess strengths and weaknesses. They often gain legitimate employment at key locations in order to monitor day-to-day activities. In any event, they may try to gain this knowledge in order to make their mission or scheme more effective" [see Appendix 60].[15]

Noor Razzaq (2007) in an excellent article entitled "The Detection and Prevention of Preparatory Terrorist Acts"[16], mentioned several "Pre-Incident Indicators of Terrorist Activities" including "some terrorist organizations have been known to go to the extent of infiltrating government contracting agencies in both information-sensitive roles and non-information-sensitive roles (e.g., janitors, mail room workers, etc), thereby allowing their own personnel to be in key positions to more easily elicit information on potential targets (Razzaq, 2003; SCN, 2005)."[17]

My course did cite some suspicious activities to watch for, with "deliveries are a common method for terrorists to carry out attacks. Be vigilant of the following activities:

- A vehicle with hazardous material parked or driving in an inappropriate area
- Unusual deliveries of chemicals or fertilizer
- Unattended bags or boxes in a public access place

- Unusual or unexpected mail."[18]

Britain's M15, for example, also cites this method:

"Explosive devices - These can be delivered to their targets in vehicles, by post or by a person. Currently an explosive device within a vehicle is the most prevalent means of attack ... Al Qaida networks often seek to ensure that their target is hit by employing a suicide operative within the vehicle to detonate the device at the required moment."[19]

"Suicide bombers are also deployed to carry an explosive device into the vicinity of a target individual or location. On some occasions the terrorists decide, as they did in the Madrid commuter train attacks in March 2004, to detonate their devices remotely, so that they can go on to perpetrate further attacks."[20]

"Other examples of terrorist explosive devices include the suicide attacks using vehicle-borne devices against the British Consulate and HSBC bank in Istanbul in November 2003 and Richard Reid's thwarted attempt in December 2001 to bring down an airliner with a small improvised explosive device concealed in his shoes. Al Qaida has also carried out two suicide attacks against ships using explosives packed into small boats (both off the coast of Yemen, in 2000 and 2002)."[21]

Continuing, one of the "scariest" prospects include chemical, biological and radiological (CBR) devices, with M15 listing these comments:

"It is possible that Al Qaida and some other associated networks may seek to use chemical, biological or radiological material against the West."[22]

In a June 2002 article, Al Qaida spokesman Sulaiman Abu Gaith also said "it is our right to fight [the Americans] with chemical and biological weapons"[23]

"In April 2005, Kamel Bourgass, an Algerian with known links to Al Qaida, was convicted of plotting to manufacture and spread poisons, including ricin, in the UK."[24]

Footnotes

1. "Terrorism Awareness for Law Enforcement" National Terrorism Preparedness Institute, St. Petersburg College in St. Petersburg, Florida. http://terrorism.spcollege.edu/Training/Courses/TerrorismAwarenessforLE.aspx

2. "Risk Management" http://www.investopedia.com/terms/r/riskmanagement.asp#axzz1b8bAuPVP

3 - 4. "Operational risk" http://en.wikipedia.org/wiki/Operational_risk

5 - 6. "Terrorism Awareness for Law Enforcement" National Terrorism Preparedness Institute, St. Petersburg College in St. Petersburg, Florida.
http://terrorism.spcollege.edu/Training/Courses/TerrorismAwarenessforLE.aspx

7 - 10. "NAVY DOCTRINE FOR ANTITERRORISM / FORCE PROTECTION"
NAVY WARFARE PUBLICATION NWP 3-07.2 (REV. A)
DEPARTMENT OF THE NAVY
OFFICE OF THE CHIEF OF NAVAL OPERATIONS
http://docs.google.com/viewer?a=v&q=cache:F3JBPnLF0fwJ:pmkuniversity.com/pmkReferences/3-07-2RevANWP.pdf+operational+risk+management+terrorism&hl=en&gl=ca&pid=bl&srcid=ADGEEShCELI6-6nOiVhlZb9EmPqXJB3_BC-H5mRVOkGjwr1xdzPFZsSR3VQFop_XuA6BcrZgSWaZl-DEPZv4AMkFC6uNN0TpARrfIE8Dvt9qOzwBuOdBa6lz3dzyQHX8ef5wWWHJHTC7&sig=AHIEtbQBpen8ChnY05aDET4UpFlug7a6xw

11 - 13. "Terrorism Awareness for Law Enforcement" National Terrorism Preparedness Institute, St. Petersburg College in St. Petersburg, Florida.
http://terrorism.spcollege.edu/Training/Courses/TerrorismAwarenessforLE.aspx

14 - 15. "Seven Signs of Terrorist Activity"
http://www.scnus.org/page.aspx?id=101218

16 - 17. "The Detection and Prevention of Preparatory Terrorist Acts"
Noor Razzaq (2007)
http://policelink.monster.com/training/articles/42681-the-detection-and-prevention-of-preparatory-terrorist-acts

18. "Terrorism Awareness for Law Enforcement" National Terrorism Preparedness Institute, St. Petersburg College in St. Petersburg, Florida.
http://terrorism.spcollege.edu/Training/Courses/TerrorismAwarenessforLE.aspx

19. "Terrorist Methods"
https://www.mi5.gov.uk/output/terrorist-methods.html

Personal Precautions in These Dangerous Times

In such a world we find ourselves, with fanatics like Osama bin Laden [see Appendix 61], it pays for everyone to take personal precautions for themselves, their families, and their loved ones.

In fact, as cited, "top federal officials on Monday issued their most pointed advice since Sept. 11, 2001, on precautions the public should take against terrorist attacks, warning that every home should be stocked with three days' worth of water and food in case of a strike with chemical, biological or radiological weapons."[1]

"They also recommended that families consider designating a room where they will gather in the event of such an attack and have on hand duct tape and heavy plastic sheeting to seal it, as well as scissors, a manual can opener, blankets, flashlights, radios and spare batteries. The officials said they believe the al-Qaida terrorist network is particularly targeting New York and Washington."[2]

"Ranking officials of the Department of Homeland Security told reporters at a briefing that Americans must take some personal responsibility for protecting themselves, but stressed that people should not feel panicked or abandoned by government."[3]

"We see information on citizen preparedness as prudent planning," said Gordon Johndroe, the department's spokesman. But given al-Qaida's interest in obtaining weapons of mass destruction, he added, "it's appropriate for citizens to be informed about how to respond to a terrorist attack, much as people have prepared for years to be ready for tornadoes, hurricanes or floods."[4]

"You have to talk to your family, and plan how you're going to communicate with each other" after a devastating terrorist attack, said David Paulison, the U.S. Fire Administrator, who is a top civil defense planner for the new department. For example, he said, families could designate a third party with whom telephone messages can be left.[5]

Another detailed article[6] [see Appendix 62], lists some very comprehensive plans for one's protection including, but not exclusively, the following:

"*At All Times -*

(1) Encourage security awareness in your family and discuss what to do if there is a security threat.

(2) Be alert for surveillance attempts or suspicious persons or activities, and report them to the proper authorities. Trust your gut feelings.

(3) Vary personal routines whenever possible.

(4) Get into the habit of checking in to let your friends and family know where you are or when to expect you.

(5) Know how to use the local phone system. Always carry telephone change. Know the emergency numbers for local police, fire, ambulance, and hospital.

(6) Know the locations of civilian police, military police, government agencies, US Embassy, and other safe locations where you can find refuge or assistance.

(7) Avoid public disputes or confrontations. Report any trouble to the proper authorities.

Know certain key phrases in the native language such as "I need a policeman," "Take me to a doctor," "Where is the hospital?," and "Where is the police station?"

(9) Set up simple signal systems to alert family members or associates that there is a danger. Do not share this information with anyone not involved in your signal system.

(10) Carry identification showing your blood type and any special medical conditions. Keep a minimum of a 1-week supply of essential medication on hand at all times.

(11) Keep a low profile. Shun publicity. Do not flash large sums of money.

(12) Do not unnecessarily divulge your home address, phone number, or family information.

(13) Watch for unexplained absences of local citizens as an early warning of possible terrorist actions.

(14) Keep your personal affairs in good order. Keep wills current, have powers of attorney drawn up, take measures to ensure family's financial security, and develop a plan for family actions in the event you are taken hostage.

(15) Do not carry sensitive or potentially embarrassing items."[7]

As one of my courses said, "stay low and keep moving"!

Should the reader ever find themselves in a desperate situation, maybe they are good words to follow?

Footnotes

1 - 5. "Officials Urge Public Precautions Against Potential Terrorist Attack"
By John Mintz
THE WASHINGTON POST -- washington
http://tech.mit.edu/V123/N3/terror.3w.html

6 - 5. "21st THEATER SUPPORT COMMAND"
Deputy G2 (Intelligence)
http://c21.maxwell.af.mil/terrorism/protective_measures.htm

Appendix 1

Cited from a terrific course:
United States Institute of Peace
2301 Constitution Avenue, NW
Washington, DC 20037
http://www.usip.org/education-training/international/online-courses
Certificate Course in Conflict Analysis - Academics and professionals in the field of conflict management face extraordinary challenges in dealing with the various phases of conflict, whether it is rebuilding in the aftermath, stopping conflict in progress, or preventing conflict before it begins.

The Nation of Rwanda
Rwanda is situated in the Great Lakes region of Africa, so named for the area's many magnificent bodies of water, including Lake Victoria, Lake Kivu, Lake Tanganyika and others.

The region was originally inhabited by the Twa, who lived in the forests as hunters and gatherers. The Twa were forced deeper into the forests upon the arrival of the Hutu, who felled trees, raised crops, and introduced more complex forms of social organization centered around clans. The Hutu were followed by the Tutsi, who through their ownership of cattle came to enjoy a position of prominence in the region.

Over time, Hutu and Tutsi intermarried and came to share the same language, Kinyarwanda. Through a feudal system known as ubuhake, those who tilled the soil, who were mostly Hutu, pledged their services to the cattle-owning aristocracy, who were mostly Tutsi.

When German colonists arrived in the region at the end of the 19th century, they found a highly-organized society, ruled by a Tutsi king, or mwami, and a hierarchy of chiefs, both Hutu and Tutsi. With the acquiescence of the mwami, the Germans established a protectorate in 1899, but the Germans would not be in Rwanda for long.

During the First World War, Germany lost the territory that would eventually become Rwanda. The territory was placed under Belgian administration by the League of Nations. With its substantial technical and military superiority, Belgium easily ruled over the native population, and the region enjoyed a long period of peace.

Yet practitioners in conflict analysis do not describe this period as a durable peace. Although there was little challenge to Belgian rule, and thus a period of general stability, the peace was not based on what Lund calls "shared values, goals, and institutions."

Rather, the stable peace was enforced through Belgium's vastly superior technical and military capability. Moreover, policies and actions taken by the European power during this period fueled the animosities and distrust that would eventually shake the foundations of this peace and ignite substantial violence, including the 1994 genocide.

Sharpening Ethnic Distinctions
In reports in the media in 1994, the Rwandan genocide was often portrayed as a conflict based on ancient hatreds, between peoples who had been killing each other in such a manner for hundreds of years. These reports were greatly misleading. Throughout its history, the Great Lakes region had not been free from conflict; however, there was no pattern of inter-communal violence between Hutu and Tutsi, and nothing approached or even suggested the level of violence of the 1994 genocide.

In pre-colonial Rwanda, the terms "Hutu" and "Tutsi" had, after centuries of intermarriage, come more closely to represent distinctions of economic class rather than ethnic origin. A Hutu who gained in wealth could become a "Tutsi," and conversely, a Tutsi could fall in economic stature and become a "Hutu." In 1926, however, the Belgians established policies to sharpen distinctions between Hutu and Tutsi. Those who owned more than 10 cows were designated as Tutsi and all others as Hutu, with no possibility of movement between the two groups. What had been a fluid distinction, developed over time and custom, was abruptly replaced by an inflexible, permanent categorization. In addition, the Belgians greatly favored the upper echelon of Tutsi, offering the wealthiest among them superior opportunities for education and economic advancement, and using them as administrators to enforce Belgian colonial rule.

Identity Cards
As part of their system of codifying ethnic distinction, the Belgians issued identity cards to all Rwandans. Modeled after similar cards used in Belgium, which helped to codify the distinction between the Dutch-speaking Flemish and the French-speaking Walloons, the Rwandan identity cards made clear into which ethnic group each individual had been classified.

Forced Labor
Along with the identity cards, the Belgians continued to carry out policies that alienated Hutu and Tutsi from one another, including a system of forced labor where selected Tutsi overseers were tasked with physically punishing slower workers.

In this system, Hutu agriculturalists no longer grew produce for their own consumption but were forced to grow cash crops for the benefit of the colonial administration. Following European models of social organization, a substantial divide in wealth and power was created, with the Belgians and a small number of Tutsi as the beneficiaries at the expense of other Tutsi and Hutu.

As tensions increased, unstable peace gave way to crisis in the late 1950s. The Belgians, who had favored the Tutsi throughout the colonial period, switched sides in 1959. They withdrew their support from Tutsi administrators, replacing them in all but a few cases with Hutu, and made little effort to stop outbreaks of violence.

Periodic political violence began in 1959 in the form of clashes between members of newly formed, ethnically-based political parties, or in the form of attacks on Tutsi orchestrated by newly appointed Hutu administrators.

This violence left hundreds of Tutsi dead and tens of thousands more displaced. Each violent incident prompted scores of Tutsi to flee the country. By 1961, some of the refugees had formed commando groups and launched the first of several, mostly ineffective, incursions into Rwanda.

Hutu-led political forces succeeded in abolishing the Tutsi monarchy in 1961, and a new colonial administrator, in concert with Hutu politicians, guided Rwanda to independence by July 1, 1962. With this victory, the Hutu proclaimed a republic and drafted a constitution. At independence, the Belgians transferred power to the Hutu, who proceeded to exercise a monopoly over political, economic and social affairs.

Hutu authorities used each attack as an excuse to strengthen their authority by massacring Tutsi civilians, causing more Tutsi flight. Following a particularly well-organized Tutsi raid in late 1963, rampaging Hutu killed an estimated 10,000 Tutsi civilians and drove another 200,000 into exile. By the end of 1964, 336,000 Rwandan Tutsi, nearly half the Tutsi population at that time, had officially become refugees in neighboring Tanzania (then Tanganyika), Burundi, the Congo, and Uganda.

Tutsi commando incursions and Hutu reprisals ended for the most part in 1967. Crisis prevailed until mid-1972, when large-scale massacres occurred in Burundi. There, minority Tutsi army units and their supporters killed an estimated 80,000 Hutu. This exacerbated Rwandan mistrust of Tutsi. In early 1973 various Hutu groups in Rwanda began a campaign of intimidation and assaults on Tutsi to enforce a newly-introduced ethnic quota system in education and the workforce. This triggered another wave of Tutsi flight, including university students who feared they were targeted for death.

Coup d'Etat
In 1973, Army Chief of Staff Juvenal Habyarimana, a Hutu, carried out a bloodless coup d'etat and declared himself president of Rwanda. While promising to improve conditions for Tutsi in Rwanda, he quickly consolidated

power, banning all political parties but his own and quashing political dissent. Through heavy-handed methods, he contained the violence in the region, with unstable peace prevailing throughout much of his rule. But the reduced tension came at significant cost.

In public service employment, the new president continued to enforce a strict policy of ethnic quotas. The Tutsi still living in Rwanda, who like all Rwandans still carried their identity cards, were restricted to 9% of available jobs in the public sector and to places in the schools and universities.

Throughout the 1970s and 1980s, Tutsi in Rwanda suffered through a growing number of policies that amounted to official discrimination. They became a favorite target of rising Hutu politicians, who blamed them for any number of the new nation's woes, and they continued to fear for their physical safety as convenient targets of military reprisal.

The Tutsi had come to represent a significant component of Museveni's army. However, the tide of public opinion in Uganda soon turned against the Rwandan Tutsi and they became a liability for Museveni. So, in 1987, the refugees formed the Rwandan Patriotic Front (RPF), an organization dedicated to the democratization of Rwandan society and the return of Rwandan refugees.

The organization was officially committed to achieving this repatriation through peaceful means; however, the Rwandan President insisted that the country had no room for the return of Tutsi exiles, and clashes between the Government and the RPF were inevitable. In 1988, massacres of Hutu occurred again in Burundi. Following Hutu attacks on Tutsi civilians, the Tutsi-dominated army killed up to 50,000 Hutu in retaliation. This heightened Rwandan anxiety about the return of exiled Tutsi.

Eventually, the Rwandan Patriotic Front formed the Rwandan Patriotic Army (RPA), which, in a surprise move, invaded Rwanda in October 1990. Although it was initially pushed back into Uganda, the RPA continued to wage a low-intensity war at the Rwandan-Ugandan border until the two sides agreed to a cease-fire and began peace negotiations in July 1992. By then, there were about 600,000 displaced persons inside Rwanda as a result of the conflict.

Planning and Preparation
When the killing began, it seemed sudden and spontaneous. Only later did the world at large become aware of the extensive planning and preparation that took place in advance of the genocide.

Presidential Assassination
In April 1994, the Presidents of Rwanda and Burundi were both killed when their plane was shot down with a surface-to-air missile as it approached the airport in Kigali. Many have come to suspect Hutu extremists of committing the

attack, either out of fear that Habyarimana would finally implement the Arusha Accords, or for the express purpose of touching off the genocide. Whatever the case, over the radio and in newspapers extremists in Rwanda blamed Tutsi for the murder and urged Hutu throughout the country to take swift revenge.

Mass Killing

In response, the Presidential Guard in Kigali, the Rwandan Army and the Interahamwe militias began systematic and unrelenting attacks on Tutsi civilians. In a carefully-orchestrated set of maneuvers, specific groups set up road blocks to close off escape routes, while others went from door to door to flush the victims out. Extremist radio stations not only cheered the killers on, but in some cases also directed their movements. Those bearing identity cards that said "Tutsi" were killed. Those without identity cards were assumed to be Tutsi and killed. Politically-moderate Hutu, those supporting power-sharing with the Tutsi, were singled out and killed along with them, as were Hutu who refused to participate in the killing, creating a climate of terror among Hutu and Tutsi alike.

The Withdrawal of the International Community

Still, many Tutsi felt safe in Rwanda due to the presence of United Nations peacekeepers. However, in spite of some advance warning, the UN did nothing to avert the catastrophe. The UN force there was relatively small. When authorizing its mandate and rules of engagement, the Security Council had not envisaged such an intervention.

As deaths continued to mount, local UN commanders warned their superiors in New York of the nature and extent of the killing; however, member nations on the Security Council decided to reduce the UN force to a bare minimum. The United States, stung by recent military casualties in Somalia, was among those nations that advocated the reduction. As UN peacekeepers pulled out, thousands of civilians who had taken shelter in UN compounds were massacred.

Victory of the RPF

Without support from the international community, the Rwandan Patriotic Army was on its own in trying to stop the genocide. To save innocent civilians—in many cases, friends and family members—soldiers in the RPF fought furiously, cutting rapidly through Government lines. By mid-July, the RPF had taken control of the country and installed itself as the new authority in Kigali.

Although isolated killings continued, the genocide was over. In just 100 days, an estimated 800,000 Rwandan civilians, almost all Tutsi, had been killed.
On September 1, 1996, the government passed a law designed to help expedite the process. The new law divided the accused into four categories: 1) organizers and notorious killers; 2) murderers; 3) those who committed assaults that did not result in death; and, 4) those who committed property crimes — such as looting. The new law also introduced the idea of plea-bargaining with the hope that some

suspects would provide information in exchange for leniency to assist the prosecution of those who had committed greater crimes. Even with the new law, court officials have been forced by limited resources to dispense with the highly standardized processes and rigorous rules of evidence used in formal court proceedings, and have been criticized by both accused and victim alike.

By contrast, the United Nations' International Criminal Tribunal for Rwanda (ICTR), set up in Arusha, Tanzania, has received millions of dollars in funding to prosecute fewer than seventy accused. With a fraction of those resources, the domestic courts of Rwanda had by 2003 conducted over 6,000 trials, an impressive number but one that still represented only a small percentage of the detainees awaiting trial. With far too many people to prosecute through usual channels, officials have instituted a new system, known as gacaca, based on traditional community hearings used to resolve disputes.
In the sprawling camps, international organizations had little success separating killers, or genocidaires, from innocents, creating conditions where true refugees have in many instances been held virtually as hostages. There has been insecurity along Rwanda's borders, along with incursions into the country's northwest provinces by genocidaires intent on killing surviving witnesses to the genocide.

The security problems posed by the camps led the Rwandan Patriotic Front to take a leading role in the rebellion in neighboring Zaire. By May 1997, with the assistance of Rwanda, Laurent Kabila replaced Mobutu Sese Seko as the new leader of the country, which was then renamed as the Democratic Republic of the Congo (DRC). In August of 1998, the fighting in the DRC evolved into a wider conflict involving several African nations and costing countless lives.

Over time, millions of refugees, both Hutu and Tutsi, have returned to Rwanda. There have been very few revenge killings. Some hard-core groups of genocidaires remain in the Congo, but as of early 2004, the Rwandan Government was negotiating with them and the Congo for their return.

Appendix 2

Rwanda: How the genocide happened
BBC News Thursday, 18 December 2008
http://webcache.googleusercontent.com/search?q=cache:IZ_WnI801DEJ:www.bbc.co.uk/2/hi/1288230.stm+genocide+in+Rwanda+ends&cd=7&hl=en&ct=clnk&gl=ca&source=www.google.ca

Between April and June 1994, an estimated 800,000 Rwandans were killed in the space of 100 days.

Most of the dead were Tutsis - and most of those who perpetrated the violence were Hutus.

Even for a country with such a turbulent history as Rwanda, the scale and speed of the slaughter left its people reeling.

The genocide was sparked by the death of the Rwandan President Juvenal Habyarimana, a Hutu, when his plane was shot down above Kigali airport on 6 April 1994.

A French judge has blamed current Rwandan President, Paul Kagame - at the time the leader of a Tutsi rebel group - and some of his close associates for carrying out the rocket attack.

Mr Kagame vehemently denies this and says it was the work of Hutu extremists, in order to provide a pretext to carry out their well-laid plans to exterminate the Tutsi community.

Whoever was responsible, within hours a campaign of violence spread from the capital throughout the country, and did not subside until three months later.

But the death of the president was by no means the only cause of Africa's largest genocide in modern times.

History of violence

Ethnic tension in Rwanda is nothing new. There have been always been disagreements between the majority Hutus and minority Tutsis, but the animosity between them has grown substantially since the colonial period.

The two ethnic groups are actually very similar - they speak the same language, inhabit the same areas and follow the same traditions.

However, Tutsis are often taller and thinner than Hutus, with some saying their origins lie in Ethiopia.

During the genocide, the bodies of Tutsis were thrown into rivers, with their killers saying they were being sent back to Ethiopia.

When the Belgian colonists arrived in 1916, they produced identity cards classifying people according to their ethnicity.

The Belgians considered the Tutsis to be superior to the Hutus. Not surprisingly, the Tutsis welcomed this idea, and for the next 20 years they enjoyed better jobs and educational opportunities than their neighbours.

Resentment among the Hutus gradually built up, culminating in a series of riots in 1959. More than 20,000 Tutsis were killed, and many more fled to the neighbouring countries of Burundi, Tanzania and Uganda.

When Belgium relinquished power and granted Rwanda independence in 1962, the Hutus took their place. Over subsequent decades, the Tutsis were portrayed as the scapegoats for every crisis.

Building up to genocide

This was still the case in the years before the genocide. The economic situation worsened and the incumbent president, Juvenal Habyarimana, began losing popularity.

President Kagame (l) and his officials have denied claims they shot down the president's plane
At the same time, Tutsi refugees in Uganda - supported by some moderate Hutus - were forming the Rwandan Patriotic Front (RPF), led by Mr Kagame. Their aim was to overthrow Habyarimana and secure their right to return to their homeland.

Habyarimana chose to exploit this threat as a way to bring dissident Hutus back to his side, and Tutsis inside Rwanda were accused of being RPF collaborators.

In August 1993, after several attacks and months of negotiation, a peace accord was signed between Habyarimana and the RPF, but it did little to stop the continued unrest.

When Habyarimana's plane was shot down at the beginning of April 1994, it was the final nail in the coffin.

Exactly who killed the president - and with him the president of Burundi and many chief members of staff - has not been established.

Whoever was behind the killing its effect was both instantaneous and catastrophic.

Mass murder

In Kigali, the presidential guard immediately initiated a campaign of retribution. Leaders of the political opposition were murdered, and almost immediately, the slaughter of Tutsis and moderate Hutus began.

Within hours, recruits were dispatched all over the country to carry out a wave of slaughter.

Some Tutsis managed to escape to refugee camps

The early organisers included military officials, politicians and businessmen, but soon many others joined in the mayhem.

Encouraged by the presidential guard and radio propaganda, an unofficial militia group called the Interahamwe (meaning those who attack together) was mobilised. At its peak, this group was 30,000-strong.

Soldiers and police officers encouraged ordinary citizens to take part. In some cases, Hutu civilians were forced to murder their Tutsi neighbours by military personnel.

Participants were often given incentives, such as money or food, and some were even told they could appropriate the land of the Tutsis they killed.

On the ground at least, the Rwandans were largely left alone by the international community. UN troops withdrew after the murder of 10 soldiers.

The day after Habyarimana's death, the RPF renewed their assault on government forces, and numerous attempts by the UN to negotiate a ceasefire came to nothing.

Aftermath

Finally, in July, the RPF captured Kigali. The government collapsed and the RPF declared a ceasefire.

As soon as it became apparent that the RPF was victorious, an estimated two million Hutus fled to Zaire (now the Democratic Republic of Congo).

These refugees include many who have since been implicated in the massacres.

At first, a multi-ethnic government was set up, with a Hutu, Pasteur Bizimungu as president and Mr Kagame as his deputy.

But the pair later fell out and Bizimungu was jailed on charges of inciting ethnic violence, while Mr Kagame became president.

Although the killing in Rwanda was over, the presence of Hutu militias in DR Congo has led to years of conflict there, causing up to five million deaths.

Rwanda's now Tutsi-led government has twice invaded its much larger neighbour, saying it wants to wipe out the Hutu forces.

And a Congolese Tutsi rebel group remains active, refusing to lay down arms, saying otherwise its community would be at risk of genocide.

The world's largest peacekeeping force has been unable to end the fighting.

Appendix 3

Burundi and the Crisis in Central Africa
Foreign Policy in Focus
By Stephen Weissman, January 1, 1997
http://webcache.googleusercontent.com/search?q=cache:biDEZ992HDIJ:www.f
pif.org/reports/burundi_and_the_crisis_in_central_africa+ethnic+cleansing+Bur
undi&cd=1&hl=en&ct=clnk&gl=ca&source=www.google.ca

Key Problems

Colonial-induced animosities and subsequent competition among ethnic elites have fueled a three-decade-long political conflict in Burundi, turning the country into a powder keg primed by fears for personal security.
Since 1993 some 150,000 Burundian civilians have been murdered in spreading genocidal conflicts in Central Africa.

The international community, which failed to act when the crisis began, now faces a major challenge in Burundi and, more widely, in Central Africa.
Since 1993 approximately 150,000 Burundians—2.5% of the population in this tiny Central African country—have been slaughtered in ethnic-based massacres of civilians by the ruling Tutsi forces and insurgent Hutu militias. This is only part of a wave of politically motivated genocides that have swept across Central Africa. During three months in 1994, a small Hutu ruling clique in neighboring Rwanda, fearing they would lose political power, unleashed the extermination of about 800,000 people, mainly minority Tutsis. Chased from Rwanda by a Tutsi exile army, the "genocidaires" used refugee camps in Zaire as bases for murderous forays into Rwanda to commit more genocide, incursions into Burundi to aid Hutu guerrillas fighting the minority Tutsi regime, and for "ethnic cleansing" in Zaire's Kivu Province. Rwanda (and, reportedly, also Burundi) retaliated by supporting Zairian Tutsi attacks on the Hutu refugee camps. The regional crisis and the continuing political disintegration in Zaire are now major challenges to the international community.

The current violence in Burundi is not a continuation of ancient tribal hatreds. It is the culmination of Belgium's colonial discrimination against the Hutu majority, subsequent political competition between Tutsi and Hutu elites, and the fear spawned by escalating cycles of political retaliation in Rwanda as well as Burundi. Through military-backed, one-party governments, a ruling clique from Burundi's 15% Tutsi minority has maintained political domination since shortly after independence in 1962. Armed Hutu challenges resulted in major massacres of Hutu civilians in 1965, 1972 (when 100,000 to 200,000, including almost the entire Hutu educated elite were murdered), 1988 (20,000 victims), and 1991. Thus even before the current wave of violence, the ethnic-based contest for political power had been enormously complicated by overwhelming fears for personal security and survival. As Central African expert Rene Lemarchand writes, "the conviction held by both Tutsi and Hutu [is] that unless the other's crimes are retaliated against by retribution, planned annihilation will inevitably follow."

A moment of hope appeared in 1992 when Tutsi President Pierre Buyoya, under heavy international pressure, agreed to allow a transition to multiparty democracy. His experiment, however, was short lived. Despite his ruling UPRONA party's efforts to co-opt Hutu support, the Hutu-led FRODEBU opposition party swept the June 1993 elections. But four months later, President Melchior Ndadaye was assassinated by a hardline faction of the Tutsi-dominated military, precipitating ethnic massacres on both sides. The violence also increased insecurity in Rwanda, contributing to the April 1994 genocide there.

From 1993 to the present, Burundi has experienced what many call a "creeping coup." Tutsi hardliners manipulated the judicial system, assassinated key Hutu opponents, and used the army to intimidate Hutu civilians and parliamentarians. This forced FRODEBU moderates to accept a series of increasingly disadvantageous powersharing agreements that eroded their 1993 election victory. By 1995 political power had largely reverted to the Tutsi-dominated army, UPRONA , and paramilitary militias.

This undercut the political legitimacy of those Hutu moderates committed to peaceful change. Former FRODEBU Minister Leonard Nyangoma responded by organizing the CNDD, a Hutu-led political movement-cum-rebel-army, which called for restoration of democracy. Using Zairian bases and supply channels and supported by many FRODEBU members inside Burundi, the CNDD fielded thousands of insurgents. Along with two smaller groups, it won control of much of Burundi's increasingly mono-ethnic rural countryside. The army concentrated on defending the largely Tutsi-dominated cities, towns, and displaced persons camps. As dramatic massacres by both sides prove, civilians have been the main victims. The late-1996 conflict in eastern Zaire eliminated CNDD base camps, but this is likely to prove a temporary setback rather than a strategic defeat.

Problems with Current U.S. Policy - Key Problems

Although the U.S. has become active in both planning for possible international military intervention and in facilitating negotiations among Burundi's warring parties, it has not developed a fully coherent approach to the conflict.
A U.S.-proposed, all-African force falls short of what is necessary either to prevent imminent genocide or to promote a political settlement.
The U.S. failed to adequately support regional economic sanctions against the Buyoya regime and to exert diplomatic pressure on insurgents to limit military escalation and civilian casualties.

The U.S. has neglected to confront the culture of impunity for human rights violations that prevails in Burundi.

During 1995 and early 1996, the UN, African states, and the U.S. launched more intensive efforts to reduce the carnage and coax the two warring sides into peace negotiations.

Initially, the Clinton administration did not play a major role in addressing the crisis. It was UN Secretary-General Boutros Boutros-Ghali who first lobbied leading nations to create a multilateral intervention force to deter the massacres. In early 1996, regional "Great Lakes States" (Tanzania, Uganda, Rwanda, Zaire, and Kenya), through former Tanzanian President Julius Nyerere, launched their own initiatives to mediate the conflict.

Concerned with swelling refugee numbers and threats of political instability, this African coalition pressed Burundi to follow through on its acceptance of a regional military force to guarantee security and move forward the process of negotiations (as part of the so-called Arusha Peace Plan). These efforts were interrupted in July 1996 when the military reinstalled former President Buyoya. The coalition retaliated with regional economic sanctions, to be lifted only if Buyoya restores Parliament, unbans political parties, and enters into unconditional negotiations with all factions to seek a political solution.

To its credit, the Clinton administration, since early 1996, has become more engaged in the deepening Burundi crisis. Clinton named former Congressman Howard Wolpe, a leading figure in African policymaking, as a special presidential envoy instructed to work toward a political solution in Burundi. The administration has joined the European Union (EU) in ending aid to the Burundi government and has partially supported the regional political, military, and economic policies toward Burundi. Despite Republican-led reservations about U.S. involvement in UN peacekeeping following the Somali debacle, the U.S. emerged as the principal Security Council supporter of contingency planning for humanitarian intervention.

Yet, the U.S. still lacks a fully coherent policy that can provide effective leadership to help resolve the conflict and prevent a slide toward more genocide. It failed to fully back UN Secretary-General Boutros-Ghali's plan for a 25,000 to 50,000-person international force that could be deployed to deter massacres without the consent of the warring parties. While Washington supported regional African leaders' call for a Western-funded regional force to provide security for Burundian peace negotiations, this became moot when the post-coup government backed out of the agreement to accept the force.

Washington's alternative September 1996 proposal for a Western financed and trained African Crisis Responses Force (ACRF) for Burundian and other emergencies is too little, too late. The ACRF's all-African 5-10,000 troop force would require at least six months training, enter Burundi only with the "acquiescence" of all parties, and be limited to assuring distribution of humanitarian assistance to displaced and vulnerable persons in a few "safe areas." Regrettably, the plan was introduced without adequate advance consultation with potential African participants, the Organization of African Unity (OAU), and the UN.

While Washington has had some success in promoting informal talks between the Buyoya regime and CNDD insurgents, it lacks an adequate strategy to promote a political settlement. In October 1996, Secretary of State Warren Christopher unsuccessfully lobbied the regional African leaders to relax economic sanctions, arguing that Burundi had partially met the political conditions required for lifting them. This was intended to bolster Buyoya against Tutsi extremist hardliners, even though the Burundian leader had not yet addressed the major substantive issues for political negotiations. While failing to mobilize effective international pressure on the CNDD to reach a political settlement, Washington has also been unable to curb external arms supplies flowing into Central Africa.

Finally, the U.S. has not specifically addressed the need to find ways to deal with the culture of impunity for human rights violators that enhances the risk of further genocide.

Toward a New Foreign Policy - Key Recommendations

The crisis challenges the post-cold war world to raise the priority of human rights and establish international norms and procedures to stop genocide. The U.S. should support early introduction into Burundi of a UN-authorized, international military force in order to advance peace negotiations and deter further massacres.

The U.S. should reinforce regional economic sanctions against the illegal Buyoya regime and diplomatically press the insurgents to move toward a political solution rather than military victory.
Burundi cannot be viewed in isolation. A strong and coherent U.S. regional policy toward Burundi, Rwanda, and a now rapidly deteriorating situation in Zaire is urgently needed to avoid new rounds of reciprocal ethnic violence, further refugee flows, and the spread of economic and social chaos in Central Africa.

In Burundi itself, a strengthened U.S. policy could help prevent further expansion of genocide, a flow of hundreds of thousands of new refugees, and possible mass starvation in Tutsi urban centers and displaced persons camps now surrounded by insurgent Hutu forces.

The spreading violence raises issues that reach far beyond the traditional confines of Africa policy. Is the post-cold war world ready to raise the priority of human rights by intervening to prevent genocide, i.e., the intentional destruction of racial, religious, and ethnic groups? Can the U.S. and other governments establish, even in an economically and strategically peripheral region, international norms and processes for limiting violent ethnic conflict that can be applied to other areas?

The first objective of an enhanced U.S. policy on Burundi must be to work with the parties to the conflict, regional African leaders, the OAU, and the UN to achieve a long-term political solution based on majority rule, protection of minority rights, and national reconciliation. Such a policy should include the following major components:

* Articulation by high-level U.S. policy makers, including the President, of America's and the world's moral and political interest in finding ways to cooperatively address the genocidal political conflicts in Central Africa.

* The urgent introduction into Burundi of a strong international military force with the dual mission of providing a secure atmosphere for peace negotiations and preventing further massacres.

The lesson of Rwanda in 1994 (and Bosnia in 1995) is that a successful political negotiation cannot be achieved in an intense conflict over national identity unless political extremists are controlled by a strong international military force. A top U.S. priority should be to persuade the parties to accept a multilateral force as quickly as possible. The fallback option, given the scale of the violence and rapid onset of past genocides, should be robust intervention, even without the consent of the conflicting parties.

The force should be authorized and guided by the UN and the OAU. But due to its ambitious mandate for peace enforcement rather than simply peacekeeping, it must be logistically supported by the U.S. and leading European powers (as in Haiti and Bosnia). Ground troops should come from interested regional actors (e.g., Tanzania, Ethiopia, and Uganda) and other third world countries with less local political baggage and greater relevant military experience (e.g., South Africa, Zimbabwe, India, Pakistan, Egypt).

* Concomitant, intensified pressures on the opposing parties to negotiate a political solution. Washington should stop calling for relaxed economic sanctions against the Burundi government in return for partial concessions. Further, the U.S. should offer to help monitor and publicize leakages of the embargo such as those occurring through Rwanda. New conditions for a permanent lifting of sanctions should be established in accordance with the OAU secretary-general's statement calling for "genuinely constructive dialogue" in the requisite political negotiations.

* U.S. support to help establish and monitor an international arms embargo against Burundi's military government and to assist with interception of illegal arms flows into the region. The U.S. should also diplomatically pressure CNDD insurgents to limit military escalation and support a fair political solution. Before military supply lines to the insurgents were disrupted by fighting in Zaire in late 1996, the U.S. and other countries repeatedly failed to take steps to limit the arms flows. Restricting the arms pipeline is a necessary prerequisite for any negotiated solution to the Burundi conflict.

A comprehensive and enduring approach to the intertwined ethnic conflicts of the region will, of course, have to go well beyond these urgent priorities. Postwar Burundi and Rwanda will require creative social healing policies aimed both at defining a new political system based on democracy and power-sharing rather than ethnicity and devising measures to deal with the prevailing culture of impunity. In Zaire, the decline of current ruler Mobutu Sese Seko will hopefully usher in a legitimate and public-spirited transitional government able to halt the slide toward national disintegration and further cross-border ethnic violence in the region as a whole.

Appendix 4

Did Nato miscalculate?
World: Europe
BBC News, Friday, April 23, 1999
Operation Horseshoe
http://webcache.googleusercontent.com/search?q=cache:UOMcnfVn9LMJ:news.bbc.co.uk/2/hi/europe/326864.stm+Serbian+Operation+Horseshoe+in+Kosovo&cd=11&hl=en&ct=clnk&gl=ca&source=www.google.ca

Operation Horseshoe: Panorama asks how much Nato knew
In January, international monitors accused Serb forces of the massacre of more than 40 civilians in the village of Recak, an atrocity that hastened the pace towards air strikes.

While Nato sent envoys to Belgrade to try to restore the October ceasefire, evidence gathered by Panorama reveals that the West had obtained knowledge of a plan of systematic ethnic cleansing, known as Operation Horseshoe.

Rudolf Scharping, Germany's Defence Minister, said: "The clear objective (of Operation Horseshoe) was to ethnically cleanse Kosovo and remove the whole civilian population.

Rambouillet: 'Milosevic treated it as theatre'

"The operation was prepared by President Milosevic and his regime. It was organised at November 1998, started during the Rambouillet negotiations and intensified after the talks ended."

While General Wesley Clark, Nato's supreme commander of European forces, has denied knowing of Operation Horseshoe, John Scanlon, former US ambassador to Belgrade, said that President Milosevic regarded the talks as nothing more than political theatre.

"President Milosevic's behaviour throughout was that he did not take it seriously," he said.

"I don't think that he even intended singing the agreement."

Military hamstrung

While second-guessing Belgrade presented its own problems, critics say military plans were seriously compromised when leaders ruled out using ground forces.

Paddy Ashdown: 'You have to keep your enemy guessing'

"In my view it was wrong," said Paddy Ashdown, leader of the UK's Liberal Democrats and a former British army Special Forces officer.

"It could not be done without ground troops. I suspect that Nato planners knew this.

"One of the things you do not do when you have an enemy in war is exclude any possibility. You keep them guessing.

"But Milosevic could then say, well this is something that is not going to happen.

Paddy Ashdown: "This cannot be done without ground troops"
"That left him room to manoeuvre for the terrible ferocity we saw."

General William Nash, a former US commander of Bosnia forces, added: "The lack of ground options gave Milosevic a view of the limit of our determination.

"But operationally, it allowed him to disperse his forces and make it much more difficult for the air forces to find and attack them."

US politicians have been among the more vocal critics of the policy of gradual escalation in air strikes.

One described the campaign as "bombing-lite" and both President Bill Clinton and Secretary of State Madeleine Albright have come under scrutiny.

The President, mired in the impeachment hearings, missed a crucial meeting in January when Mrs Albright put forward her proposals for limited Kosovo autonomy backed by troops - the basis of Rambouillet.

The Secretary of State has also been accused, most notably by "diplomatic insiders" in the Washington Post, of prosecuting a personal conflict born out of childhood experiences as a refugee.

Endgame

Nato leaders deny that they are attempting to fight a "painless war" to try and keep the wide alliance together.

Infrastructure targeted: Fears for Serbian stability

But while there are signs that some Nato leaders are moving towards ground intervention, questions remain over what the endgame will be.

US Senator Pat Roberts, member of the intelligence and armed forces committees, said: "Gen Clark needs to be given full authority to run this war.

"The tactics are not being dictated by the intelligence.

There will be no peace until Milosevic is removed from power."

While some leaders are calling for President Milosevic to go, others believe that he should still be negotiated with.

Analysts also say that as the bombs continue to destroy Serbia's infrastructure there are serious implications for the country's long-term stability.

"The question is being asked, what if the bombing does not work," said Porter Goss. "The answer has always been blurred."

Whatever the future of the region, a judgement has to be made soon about ground troops, said Paddy Ashdown.

"I have been at the other end of the line as a soldier," he said. "Politicians should not be taking these decisions."

"Nato believed it could bomb President Milosevic into submission. I have always thought that unlikely. We should be planning for Plan B - to use ground troops - when it is possible to do so.

"I do not know of anyone who believes that you can have a casualty-less war."

Appendix 5

Milosevic and Operation Horseshoe
By Peter Beaumont and Patrick Wintour with reporting by Chris Bird in Pristina, John Henley in Paris, John Hooper in Rome
The Observer, Sunday 18 July 1999 00.59 BST
http://webcache.googleusercontent.com/search?q=cache:7Vb2P0-ubmEJ:www.guardian.co.uk/world/1999/jul/18/balkans8+Serbian+Operation+Horseshoe+in+Kosovo&cd=5&hl=en&ct=clnk&gl=ca&source=www.google.ca

Article history

If the planes had been flying lower - as they did later in the war - they would have seen close-up the unfolding of the most appalling humanitarian disaster in Europe in half a century. Down on the ground Operation Horseshoe, Milosevic's final solution to the Kosovo problem, was under way.
The operation's title was strictly descriptive. The Serb military and police would squeeze the KLA and civilians in an attack launched from three sides, destroying the KLA's bases and fighters and driving out the population as refugees fled through the open southwestern end of the horseshoe into Macedonia and Albania.

The game had been given away to Western intelligence in a number of statements that should have been impossible to ignore. Most chillingly its purpose had been described to western diplomats last September by General Sreten Lukic, the same man who commanded the Racak operation and also - as intelligence intercepts would latter make clear - its cover-up.

Lukic had described it as a massive 'clockwise' sweep across the country that would finally destroy the KLA. He had said he hoped to complete the KLA's annihilation by October.

Despite the ceasefire, Operation Horseshoe - as was clear to all of those on the ground - was never far from the minds of the Serb leadership. Even as the Rambouillet talks went on it had been reactivated. Serb forces were building up in Kosovo. Columns of armour were scouring the countryside, training aggressively for all to see.

At times they did more than train. As the first round of peace talks ran down, Serbs forces launched a series of actions, described to OSCE monitors as 'winter live fire exercises', beginning with a large scale attack on KLA positions above the town of Vucitrn, reducing whole villages with tank, artillery and rocket fire.

But it was Vojislav Seselj, the rabidly nationalist Serb Deputy Prime Minister, who was clearest about what was in Serb minds in the event of a less than whole-hearted attack by Nato forces. Speaking at a rally he had warned that any bombs would be met by a Serb attack on Kosovo, and that 'not a single Albanian would remain if Nato bombed'.

Four days before the Nato raids the Yugoslav military reiterated its warning. On March 20, Lt Gen Nebojsa Pavkovic, commander of the Yugoslav Third Army in Kosovo, warned that if attacked: 'Yugoslavia will deal with the remaining terrorists in Kosovo.'

The message had not gone unnoticed by the CIA and the European intelligence agencies. But in Washington the CIA had chosen to produce two contradictory assessments of the risk of Milosevic turning on the Kosovan civilians. And once again the US crossed its fingers and counted on the most optimistic gloss.

As Nato's raids began, Milosevic's forces moved into position. As darkness fell in the largely ethnic Albanian town of Djakovica on the night of 24 March, black balaclava'ed paramilitaries were scouring the old town, firing at random and attacking selected houses that had been associated with the work of the OSCE monitors who had left in a five-mile convoy a few days prior to the start of the campaign.

In Pec, 22 miles north-west, and Prizren, 15 miles south-east, Serbian forces began firing wildly and burning Albanian-owned shops. In the capital Pristina, Serbs set fire to Albanian-owned property.

It was the beginning of an operation - meticulously planned - that within weeks would drive over one million people from their homes and out of the country, amid appalling massacres and the deliberate destruction of Albanian property.

The purpose of the Nato military action, as laid out in the capitals of the participating nations, had opened a new chapter in international law. It was - as Defence Secretary George Robertson made clear in the first few hours of the war 'a humanitarian intervention' against a 'genocidal' power.

And as Operation Horseshoe cranked up on the ground in Kosovo, sending vast columns of weary, dehydrated and beaten civilians across international borders, even many of those who had questioned the legality of a Nato operation, conducted without the mandate of a UN resolution, were shocked by the ferocity of Milosevic's campaign.

But even as the world's first 'anti-genocidal' war was launched, the military judgements over the 'demonstrative' opening to Nato's campaign, and Milosevic's intentions on the ground, were crystalising into one of the most disturbing episodes of the war. As hundreds of thousands of desperate ethnic Albanians poured out of Kosovo, stripped of their money, homes, identity cards and even car licence plates, the forces of 'humanitarian intervention' were not ready for them.

And as the people came they brought with them details of what was happening inside Kosovo. For the first time the world heard of villages like Velika Krushe, the mine works at Trepca, the streets of Djakovica - places to which the war crimes investigators would rush following the eventual entry of Nato troops.

In London, the ferocity of Operation Horseshoe was not anticipated. 'The speed with which he unleashed the ethnic cleansing took us all by surprise,' says Tebbitt. 'We did not foresee he would move so thoroughly and so fast. I have asked myself since whether we should have predicted more precisely.'

Neither had Hubert Vedrine's government anticipated the scale of crisis. 'We knew about the massacres, of course,' he told the Observer. 'Massacres by Serbs, terrorism by KLA. Everyone knew they would continue. But one had to act, in spite of that. But the mass expulsions had not been foreseen by anyone - KLA, Rugova, Macedonians, Albanians, no one foresaw it.

What we had expected was the Serb army to attack all KLA positions, and for the KLA to launch a guerrilla war. That's what we thought. And most experts thought the KLA would have held out for longer. What most experts underestimated was that the collective memory of massacres in the Balkans was such as to unleash mass migrations.'

Appendix 6

Cited from a terrific course:
United States Institute of Peace
2301 Constitution Avenue, NW
Washington, DC 20037
http://www.usip.org/education-training/international/online-courses
Certificate Course in Conflict Analysis - Academics and professionals in the field of conflict management face extraordinary challenges in dealing with the various phases of conflict, whether it is rebuilding in the aftermath, stopping conflict in progress, or preventing conflict before it begins.

The Battle of Kosovo

On June 28, 1389, on the plains of Kosovo Polje, Serbia fought the most famous battle of its history. Exactly 600 years later, at an outdoor assembly on the same battlefield, Serbian nationalist Slobodan Milosevic stirred up this memory, rallying Serbs behind his move to end the limited autonomy enjoyed by Kosovo's Albanians. Milosevic's rhetoric was based on a long tradition. In their struggles against the Albanians, Serbian nationalists often conjured up the memory of the Battle of Kosovo.

Both Orthodox Serbs and Muslim Albanians have lived in Kosovo since before 1389, and for this reason both have developed strong attachments to the land. In the early centuries, Serbs outnumbered Albanians; however, over time Serbs in search of a better life tended to move inward toward Belgrade, while Albanians tended to move northward into Kosovo. As a result, although Serbs still have greater numbers in the region as a whole, Albanians have since the end of the 18th Century been the majority in Kosovo. In a small region with limited resources, the two communities have often struggled against one another, either on their own or as a part of wider events, such as the fighting in World Wars I and II.

Tito maintained a complex balance among the country's various nationalities. Serbs, as the largest group, enjoyed a position of prominence. Albanians, more numerous as a people than Macedonians, Montenegrins and Slovenians (each of whom had their own republic within the SFRY, as did the more numerous Croats), were categorized as a "nationality" or narodnost. A rationale for this was that unlike other peoples of Yugoslavia, Albanians constituted the majority in a neighboring nation-state, Albania. Thus, they already had a separate independent republic "of their own."

Within Yugoslavia, the Albanian population was actually divided among three republics (Serbia, Montenegro, and Macedonia) and constituted a linguistic and cultural minority in all three. The largest number lived in the province of Kosovo within Serbia, where they constituted a local majority, and where Albanian cultural and political activism was most intense.

In 1948, Tito broke with the Soviet Union. He helped found the Non-Aligned Movement and made Yugoslavia one of the new movement's leaders. Within Yugoslavia, his countrymen took pride in the nation's enhanced international profile, and this pride helped strengthen the country's internal cohesion. Most groups, whatever their differences, shared Tito's desire to limit Soviet influence over the country. Under Tito's leadership, the country experienced an extended period of stable peace.

Still, underlying problems between the various nationalities were only stifled, not resolved. Meanwhile, Yugoslavia's anti-Soviet stance led the West not to focus on human rights there, or on the nationalities problem. Moreover, to discourage a Soviet invasion, Tito built a relatively strong army and encouraged a well-armed citizenry to be prepared for the sort of guerrilla resistance he had led in World War II. When confrontations within Yugoslavia turned violent in the 1990s, the antagonists had ready access to weapons and were well prepared to fight.

Death of Tito

Tito never designated a successor. After his death in 1980, an eight-member presidency exercised power. It was composed of representatives from the six republics and the two autonomous provinces, Vojvodina and Kosovo. These representatives rotated as President, ensuring discontinuous and, eventually, highly sectarian and factional leadership.

The Soviet invasion of Afghanistan, along with confrontation between the United States and the Soviet Union in Central America and over nuclear issues, raised Cold War tensions throughout the world and prompted increased militarization of Yugoslavian society. To some extent, continued resistance to the Soviet threat provided the last agreed-upon basis for central authority among the republics and provinces that made up Yugoslavia.

With such a limited foundation, central authority became increasingly ineffective, and internal problems worsened. As the most powerful republic, and the seat of the national capital (Belgrade), Serbia benefited most from what remained of central power structures, to the detriment and resentment of the other republics and provinces. Throughout the 1980s, the economy continued to deteriorate.

Problems in Kosovo

In Kosovo, Albanians pressed for formal recognition as a republic, a move seen in Belgrade as an unacceptable step in a secessionist agenda. Territorial integrity remained vital to the regime. Its importance only increased when the extent of foreign debt built up during the last years of Tito's rule came to be known. As unrest in Kosovo continued to rise, the peace became increasingly less stable. The province was placed under martial law in 1981.

Kosovo's Albanian political leaders continued to resist. In December 1989, Ibrahim Rugova founded the Democratic League of Kosovo (or LDK, by its Albanian initials). In July 1990, with wide support from Kosovar Albanians, Rugova declared Kosovo a republic. This initiated a period of parallel administration or a "shadow state" in Kosovo.

Rugova's parallel administration organized an "underground referendum" in September 1991, which indicated overwhelming support for independence, and then elections, in which the LDK dominated the new parliament, and Rugova became president. While there was no international monitoring and the central government did not recognize the results, these votes, flawed as they were, gave focus to Albanian nationalist aspirations. The shadow state offered employment and services to Kosovo's Albanians who had lost their jobs and who were increasingly treated as second-class citizens by the Serbian authorities.

Kosovo's fragile peace became ever less stable; however, the region was not yet in a state of crisis. Repression intensified, but under Rugova's leadership, Kosovo's Albanian population preached and largely practiced non-violence. Meanwhile, tension in the rest of Yugoslavia, and the issue of the future status of Serbs in Croatia and in Bosnia-Herzegovina, diverted the attention of the Belgrade leadership. The two sectors of Kosovo, a Serb-dominated official administration, and a rival Albanian society, did not clash often, and so little violence occurred even though there were frequent demonstrations.

Wars in Slovenia, Croatia and Bosnia

The end of the Cold War had also taken its toll on the legitimacy of the federal regime in Belgrade and its ability to maneuver effectively internationally. In June of 1991, Slovenia and Croatia officially declared independence from the Yugoslavian Federation. The Serb-dominated federal army soon gave up on Slovenia, which did not share a border with Serbia and whose population was overwhelmingly Slovene. Federal forces were out of the republic by October of 1991. By contrast, Milosevic sought to hold Croatia, which is adjacent to Serbia and whose Serb population stood at approximately 12%. For a time, Serb forces held on to almost a third of the Republic's territory, but by 1995 Croatia had regained all but a thin slice of its lands.

Bosnia-Herzegovina also declared independence, but with its mix of Orthodox Serbs, Catholic Croats, and Bosnian Muslims, was split along ethnic lines. In the war that followed, Milosevic actively intervened to support the Serb side, as the new Croatian Government did to support the Croat side. The savagery of the fighting, which included rape as a weapon of war and the murder of civilians, generated enormous hate, fear and mistrust.

Efforts by the international community to halt the violence were ineffective during most of the war, as demonstrated most tragically in the 1995 Serb massacre of thousands of Bosnian Muslims in the village of Srebrenica, which was supposedly under UN protection. Finally, after concerted international intervention and pressure, the Bosnian war ended with the formal signing of the Dayton Peace Accords in December, 1995.

Formation of the Kosovo Liberation Army

For Kosovo, these events spelled the end of unstable peace and the onset of a rapidly escalating crisis. Having lost Slovenia and Croatia, and ultimately abandoning the Serbs in Bosnia, Milosevic stepped up his repression in Kosovo as a new "last stand" for Serbian nationalism. He cast his hard line against Kosovar Albanians as dictated by the imperative of protecting Serbia's territorial integrity. Serbian military resources shifted for action in Kosovo. At the same time, Albanians in Kosovo saw the Croats and Slovenes gain independence and, in spite of the violence, took encouragement. A new guerrilla force had appeared in Kosovo, calling itself the Kosovo Liberation Army, or KLA (in Albanian, UCK). Members of the KLA openly advocated Kosovo's unification with Albania and escalated their campaign of violence against the Serbian presence in the province.

Collapse of Albania

By 1996, the new Democratic Party in Albania had overseen the rapid termination of perhaps the most dysfunctional communist economy in the world, followed by a generally unsuccessful effort to a introduce a free-market economy.

Instead of productive investment and capital formation, pyramid schemes of investment, which promised large and swift returns on capital investment by private individuals, were numerous.

In early 1997, a number of these schemes collapsed (as they were bound to), enriching a handful at the expense of many other, smaller investors, who reportedly lost over a billion dollars.

This prompted a virtual collapse of the Albanian state. Huge quantities of weapons were looted from barracks and armories, many of which fell into the hands of the KLA. As Albanian instability threatened to spread across borders, international efforts to help Albania highlighted the need for similar efforts in Kosovo.

Final Phases of the War

Over half a million people were internally displaced by the fighting, in which federal forces experienced major successes. In October, the threat of peacemaking by NATO air strikes finally forced Milosevic to cease all-out offensives, withdraw some forces, and permit international observers.

But NATO's intervention was insufficient to end the conflict, and military activity continued on both sides. A turning point was reached in January of 1999, when international observers reported that Serbian security forces killed over 40 Albanian civilians in the village of Racak. The international community undertook efforts at diplomatic conflict management, backed by the prospect of peacemaking by military force.

NATO again threatened air strikes to get the Belgrade government to attend a peace conference held in Rambouillet, France, in February. The two sides were presented with a draft of a political settlement, along with an authorization for a NATO-led international force to guarantee the Kosovars' security.

After resisting the settlement proposal for over two weeks, the Kosovar Albanian delegation finally signed the agreement — but only after they knew it would not take effect because the Serb delegation had refused to sign it.

In the face of widespread ethnic cleansing of Kosovar Albanians by Serbian security forces, and amid international determination not to permit mass murder of civilians as had occurred in Bosnia, a NATO air campaign was launched against Yugoslavia on March 24, 1999 and continued for almost three months.

As the scale of Serb military operations against the Kosovar Albanian civilian population increased, Serbian paramilitaries also began to operate in the province. Mass killings of at least 2,000 Kosovar Albanians occurred in the province, and hundreds of thousands of people were forced from their homes. Fearing for their own safety from government forces and the paramilitaries, over half of Kosovo's Albanian population sought refuge outside Yugoslavia, either in Albania or Macedonia. While a majority of the refugees were sheltered privately by family or friends, many were housed in camps. The KLA, meanwhile, continued to fight against Yugoslav forces.

The NATO air campaign did serious damage to infrastructure within Serbia. In June of 1999, Milosevic signed an agreement to withdraw Serbian military and paramilitary forces from Kosovo and allow NATO forces to enter. Peace making had finally succeeded, and the stage was set for peace enforcement and peacekeeping operations.

Primary actors are normally thought of as those directly involved in the conflict. In Kosovo, primary actors included the Serb side led by Slobodan Milosevic, the Democratic League of Kosovo and its "shadow government" led by Ibrahim Rugova, and the Kosovo Liberation Army. In Rwanda, primary actors included the multi-party government led by moderate Hutu, the hard-line Hutu Power leadership, the Hutu-led Rwandan Armed Forces, and the Tutsi-led Rwandan Patriotic Front.

Secondary actors are not actual parties to the conflict but nevertheless have a high degree of interest in and influence over it, often due to their proximity. In Kosovo, secondary actors included the Republic of Albania and the ex-Yugoslavian Republics, particularly Macedonia and Montenegro with their large Albanian populations. In Rwanda, one very important secondary actor was Radio Television Libre des Milles Collines (RTLM), the station that urged the killing of Tutsi and moderate Hutu over the airwaves.

In addition to primary and secondary actors, analysts consider other parties with interests in and influence over events, including regional and global players. In Rwanda, regional actors included Uganda and Tanzania. International actors with influence included the United Nations, the United States, Belgium and France. In Kosovo, the United States, the United Kingdom, Russia, Germany, France, and Italy formed the Contact Group, which had considerable influence over events. International organizations with influence included the United Nations, the Organization for Security and Cooperation in Europe, the European Union and NATO.

For more immediate causes, analysts note the refugee crisis that resulted from the massacres of Tutsi beginning in the late 1950s, the desire of the Tutsi refugees to return to Rwanda, Hutu fears of the return of the refugees, and the willingness of the Hutu establishment to exploit those fears to remain in power.

In Kosovo, analysts point to the strong attachment that both Serbs and Albanians have for the land; the scarcity of resources and generally poor economic conditions in the region; the long-running desire of the Albanians, who form the local majority in Kosovo, for independence; and the greater strength in economic and military resources of the Serbs, who form the majority in the region as a whole.

As more immediate causes, analysts refer to the movements for independence and wars in Slovenia, Croatia, and Bosnia, which encouraged the Albanians in Kosovo to seek their own independence, while helping to inflame Serbian nationalism. As in the case of Rwanda, analysts note the willingness of politicians to exploit ethnic nationalism to gain and hold power.

Appendix 7

EUROPE NEWS MAY 27, 2011 Serbia Arrests Fugitive Gen. Mladic
Bosnian Serb, Accused of Leading
http://webcache.googleusercontent.com/search?q=cache:LcvrSKg6rKMJ:online.wsj.com/article/SB10001424052702304520804576346960916648594.html+serbian+general+war+crimes&cd=7&hl=en&ct=clnk&gl=ca&source=www.google.ca

Ratko Mladic, the fugitive Bosnian Serb general considered Europe's most wanted war criminal, was captured in Serbia on Thursday after a decade and a half on the run from an indictment for genocide.

Gen. Mladic, who is accused of directing the 1995 Srebrenica massacre of some 8,000 Muslim men, was the last of the major figures accused of war crimes in the 1992-95 Yugoslav wars to evade capture.

The arrest's timing—amid heightened European Union pressure on Serbia to bring the 69-year-old former general to face international trial—triggered speculation about whether Serbian authorities already knew where Gen. Mladic was. But the arrest was nevertheless widely welcomed as a turning point for Serbia's reintegration with its neighbors and Europe as a whole.

Serbia's President Boris Tadic announced the arrest at a news conference, where he described Gen. Mladic's capture as "good for Serbia," and said it would open the doors for his country to start talks to join the EU.

"I think today we finished a difficult period in our recent history. We clear our name and the name of all Serbs, wherever they are," Mr. Tadic said. Gen. Mladic's extradition to the International Criminal Tribunal for Former Yugoslavia in The Hague was under way, he said.

The EU is currently discussing whether to let Serbia have candidate status later this year, a move that has been blocked pending Belgrade's full cooperation with The Hague tribunal. Many Serbs saw the arrest as a tactical move designed to open the gates to the EU, at a time when Serbia's economy has been badly hit and popular resistance to handing over Gen. Mladic would be low.

In a report that began circulating last week, the tribunal's special prosecutor criticized Serbia's cooperation, largely due to the failure to arrest Gen. Mladic.

"We need results before summer," European Commission President José Manuel Barroso said, also last week, adding that Serbia's cooperation with the tribunal was "of critical importance" if it was to gain EU candidate status by year's end.

Ratko Mladic: Apprehended May 26, 2011. Former Bosnian Serb general. Indicted on charges of genocide, persecution, extermination and murder, deportation and inhumane acts and unlawfully inflicting terror upon civilians.

Ante Gotovina: Sentenced in 2011 to 24 years in prison. Former Croatian general. Convicted of persecutions, deportation, murders and cruel treatment.
Slobodan Milosevic: Died in 2006 before trial ended. Former president of Yugoslavia. Accused of ordering the deportation of 800,000 Kosovo Albanian civilians and the murders of hundreds of Kosovo Albanian civilians.

Ramush Haradinaj: Acquitted of all Tribunal war-crimes charges in 2008, ordered retried on some. Former Commander of the Kosovo Liberation Army and former Kosovo prime minister. Accused of involvement in persecution and murder.
Gen. Mladic was arrested in Lazarevo, a village north of Belgrade, close to the border with Romania, early Thursday morning. Mr. Tadic declined to give details of how he was found. The wartime general was carrying two pistols but put up no resistance, a Serbian war-crimes official told national television.

Unlike wartime Bosnian Serb President Radovan Karadzic, who was captured in the Serb capital of Belgrade in 2008, Gen. Mladic wasn't disguised, according to Serbian media reports. He was living under an alias, Milorad Komadic, these reports said.

"There are many questions to be asked," Tomislav Nikolic, leader of the opposition Serbian Progressive Party, told Serbia's B92 television. "Who saw this man yesterday and recognized him? Did Serbia perhaps know all along where Mladic was? What made them decide to arrest him today?"

In response to reporters' questions, President Tadic repeatedly denied the government had "calculated" the arrest to help its EU membership bid. He said his government had always cooperated to the fullest with the tribunal. He also said an investigation would be launched into how and why it had taken so many years to find Gen. Mladic, who was indicted in 1995.

In a statement Thursday, the tribunal's special prosecutor said "we recognize" Serbia's effort in detaining Gen. Mladic.

Leaders from the EU, the North Atlantic Treaty Organization and from around the world welcomed Thursday's arrest as a moment of closure for the Balkans and for the more than 100,000 victims of Europe's bloodiest conflict since World War II. Mr. Barroso called the arrest "great news" that showed Serbia's determination to get closer to the EU.

Many—especially younger—Serbs quietly welcomed the capture of Gen. Mladic as allowing the country to move beyond the war and toward EU membership. The Belgrade stock market rose 3% on news of the arrest, before selling off half of those gains.

Of the 161 people that the Yugoslav tribunal in The Hague indicted for war crimes, only one—Goran Hadzic, the wartime leader of Serbs in Croatia—remains at large.

To many Bosnian Muslims, Gen. Mladic was the greatest monster of the war, the man they believe personally directed the separation and execution of thousands of men and boys in Srebrenica, a United Nations protected enclave in Bosnia, over a few days in July 1995.

The Mladic indictment describes him as responsible for the siege of Sarajevo, the Bosnian capital; for taking United Nations peacekeepers hostages; and for helping to plan and carrying out the deliberate ethnic cleansing of Muslims from Bosnian territory, including at Srebrenica. He is charged with genocide and crimes against humanity and violations of the laws or customs of war.

But Gen. Mladic remains a war hero to large numbers of Serbs, among whom The Hague tribunal is widely considered biased. Serbia's B92 television reported that about 150 villagers in Lazarevo confronted media crews camped outside the house where Gen. Mladic was arrested Thursday, pulled the plug on B92's satellite truck and sang patriotic songs. About 50 people also demonstrated in Belgrade.

Gen. Mladic was revered by men under his command and liked to refer to himself as God. He was filmed on Serbian TV entering Srebrenica with his troops.

"The time has come to take revenge on the Turks in this region," he said on camera, in footage that is likely to play an important role in his trial, according to Mark V. Vlasic, a U.S. lawyer, who served as a prosecuting attorney in the trials of former Serbian President Slobodan Milosevic and Gen. Mladic's deputy commander in Srebrenica, Radislav Krstic.

In the ensuing days, some 8,000 males were separated and executed en masse, many with a bullet to the back of the head, and buried in mass graves. Milosevic died of a heart attack in 2006, five years into his trial. Mr. Krstic was found guilty of abetting genocide at Srebrenica.

As the tribunal awaited Gen. Mladic's arrival Thursday, Mr. Vlasic said the sheer volume of "insider witness" evidence already established in previous cases should speed the trial process.

When first indicted, Gen. Mladic reportedly sought refuge in a bunker designed to resist nuclear attack, in Bosnia. Later he moved to Belgrade and in the late 1990s was photographed attending a wedding, and was reported to have attended football matches and other events. Those appearances sowed widespread doubt as to Belgrade's commitment to arresting him.

There had been no reliable sightings of Gen. Mladic for years, however. Last year his wife filed an official request to have him declared dead.

Appendix 8

Serbian war criminals: Slobodan Milosevic profile
Ratko Mladic was the last of three Serbian leaders wanted for war crimes following the capture of Slobodan Milosevic and Radovan Karadzic.
Wednesday 17 August 2011
By Victoria Ward
2:58PM BST 26 May 2011
http://www.telegraph.co.uk/news/worldnews/europe/serbia/8538575/Serbian-war-criminals-Slobodan-Milosevic-profile.html

Milosevic, the former Yugoslav President, died of a heart attack in 2006 before his own trial was concluded.

He was born and raised in Yugoslavia, where he studied law before becoming an economic adviser the Mayor of Belgrade.

In 1987, as number two in the Serbian Communist Party, he was sent to Serbia's troubled province of Kosovo by his leader Ivan Stambolic.

Amid deepening animosity between Serbs and Albanians, he addressed a crowd of rioting of Serbs, declaring: "No one should dare to beat you again."

Stambolic would later say that he had seen that day as "the end of Yugoslavia".

Within two years, Milosevic was president of Serbia. Stambolic was abducted and murdered in 2000, allegedly by Milosevic's secret police.

Milosevic embraced and promoted nationalism, manipulating the grievances of Serbs.

In 1991, when Slovenia and Croatia seceded from Yugoslavia, Serbia went to war. Croatia, Slovenia and later Bosnia were pounded and besieged under his rule.

Ethnic cleansing became a reality as whole populations were forced from their homes and hundreds of thousands were killed. All three wars were fought and lost.

Milosevic reinvented himself, signing the Dayton Peace Treaty on behalf of Bosnian Serbs in 1995. In abandoning claims for a Greater Serbia he was rewarded with a partial lifting of international sanctions. In 1997, Milosevic became Yugoslav president.

But the following year, Kosovo's ethnic Albanians rose up against Serbian rule, demanding independence.

During the Kosovo war, Milosevic was indicted for war crimes.

In 2000, the struggling leader called an election and lost. The new Serbian government handed him to the War Crimes Tribunal in The Hague the following year and six months later he was tried for crimes against humanity.

In his last interview before his arrest, Milosevic denied any responsibility for the carnage and chaos wreaked during his 13 years in power.

"I did my best to defend my people and I did not make any move detrimental to the interests of the country, people and citizens," he said.

He claimed that his indictment by The Hague tribunal for war crimes was the result of score-settling by foreign enemies collaborating with his political opponents and former colleagues within Yugoslavia.

He died mid-trial in his cell in 2006.

Appendix 9

UN war crimes tribunal convicts two former Croatian generals over atrocities
ICTY courtroom
15 April 2011 –
http://webcache.googleusercontent.com/search?q=cache:8YiyrQk4T8gJ:www.un.org/apps/news/story.asp%3FNewsID%3D38125%26Cr%3Dicty%26Cr1%3D+Croatian+Operation+Storm+in+Krajina&cd=10&hl=en&ct=clnk&gl=ca&source=www.google.ca

Two former top Croatian generals were today convicted and sentenced to lengthy jail terms by a United Nations war crimes tribunal over atrocities carried out against ethnic Serb civilians during a military offensive in the Balkan conflicts of the 1990s.
But a third ex-general was acquitted by judges at the International Criminal Tribunal for the former Yugoslavia (ICTY) on charges relating to his role in the same offensive, known as Operation Storm, in the Krajina region of Croatia in mid-1995.

Judges serving on the ICTY trial chamber found Ante Gotovina and Mladen Markac guilty of various crimes against humanity, including murder, persecutions, deportation and plunder. Both were acquitted of charges of inhumane acts (forcible transfer).

Mr. Gotovina, 55, who commanded the Split military district of the Croatian army from 1992 to 1996, was sentenced to 24 years in prison. Mr. Markac, 55, who served as the Assistant Interior Minister in charge of Special Police matters after 1994, was jailed for 18 years.

Ivan Cermak, 61, who commanded the Knin Garrison from August 1995, was acquitted of all charges, including murder, persecutions, deportation and the wanton destruction of cities, towns or villages.

The judges noted that Operation Storm took place within a wider armed conflict in the former Yugoslavia and followed years of Serb-Croat ethnic tensions in the Krajina region and crimes committed against Croats.

But Judge Alphons Orie, who presided over the trial, said that the case was not about the legality of resorting to and conducting war.

"This case was about whether Serb civilians in the Krajina were the targets of crimes and whether the accused should be held criminally liable for these crimes," he stressed.

The judges found that "a high number of crimes" were carried out during Operation Storm, which had the objective of permanently removing ethnic Serbs from the Krajina region by either force or threat of force.

At the end of July 1995 the then Croatian president Franjo Tudman met with high-ranking military officials – including Mr. Gotovina and Mr. Markac – to discuss Operation Storm, which began on 4 August.

Military forces and special police under the control or influence of Mr. Gotovina and Mr. Markac shelled a series of towns and villages, murdered several elderly residents of another village and burned or looted property belonging to ethnic Serb civilians.

The men created a climate of impunity and were aware of the involvement of subordinates in the commission of these crimes, but did nothing to stop them.

The judges found, however, that Mr. Cermak did not have effective control over army units outside of his own subordinates at the Knin garrison, and there was no reliable evidence that those subordinates committed crimes.

The joint trial of the three former generals was one of the ICTY's longest, beginning in March 2008 and concluding in September last year. The tribunal, which is based in The Hague, has concluded proceedings against 125 people and is still conducting proceedings against 34 others.

Appendix 10

Croatian general convicted of war crimes
The Associated Press
Posted: Apr 15, 2011
http://www.cbc.ca/news/world/story/2011/04/15/croatia-serbia-war-crimes-un.html

A commander hailed by Croats as a hero of the Balkan conflict was convicted of war crimes by a UN court Friday and sentenced to 24 years in prison for a campaign of shelling, shootings and expulsions aimed at driving Serbs out of a Croatian border region in 1995.

The conviction of Gen. Ante Gotovina was a blow to the Croatian view of its wartime generals as national heroes who reclaimed Croatian land from a more powerful Serb force.

Thousands of Croatian war veterans watched the verdict live on a large video screen at Zagreb's main square, and jeered and booed the ruling.

"We have heard the shameful verdicts of the so-called Hague court, but in fact a Serbian court," Zvonimir Trusic, one of their leaders, told the angry crowd. "We don't recognize that tribunal."

"The war is not over, it continues," he said, as some 5,000 people stood frozen in disbelief, some crying.

Former Croatian Army General Mladen Markac sits in the courtroom of the International Criminal Tribunal for the former Yugoslavia in The Hague on Friday. Markac was sentenced to 18 years.Jerry Lampen/Reuters
Gotovina was convicted of committing war crimes and crimes against humanity, including murder, deportation, persecution and inhuman acts, during and immediately after a lightning campaign called Operation Storm that seized back land along Croatia's eastern border taken over by rebel Serbs early in the Balkan wars. Dozens of Serbs were killed and tens of thousands forced to flee their homes.

Presiding Judge Alphons Orie cited one witness who recalled finding his elderly mother and mentally ill brother shot dead after hearing a Croatian soldier say, "I killed another one."

The first prosecution witness in the case recalled artillery shells raining down on the city of Knin, hitting apartment blocks and a medical clinic.

"As I ran, shells were falling around me," the witness said. Her identity was not released by the court.

The offensive is still a source of friction between Balkan neighbours Croatia and Serbia. Zagreb celebrates it with a national holiday, while Belgrade regards it as one of the worst crimes against Serbs committed during the Balkan wars.

In Zagreb, former Foreign Minister Mate Granic, who testified at the trial, criticized the verdicts as "shameful and not based on evidence." He added that the verdicts attempted to "change history and the historic truth."

General will appeal

Defence lawyer Greg Kehoe said Gotovina would appeal.

"We all are disappointed," he said. "We all believed…that we would be taking the general home today."

The Yugoslav war crimes tribunal judgment said Croatia's then-president, Franjo Tudjman, led a "joint criminal enterprise" to repopulate the Krajina region with Croats after driving out Serbs. Tudjman died in 1999 while under investigation by the tribunal.

Gotovina's "orders to unlawfully attack civilians…amounted in and of itself to a significant contribution to the joint criminal enterprise," Orie said. He said the terror spread by Croat shelling "created an environment in which those present there had no choice but to leave."

The court also convicted a second general, Mladen Markac, and sentenced him to 18 years, but cleared a third, Ivan Cermak, of all charges and ordered him released.

Gotovina and Markac both stood upright and showed no emotion as they were convicted and sentenced. Cermak looked down at the desk in front of him as Orie pronounced his acquittal of all charges.

The judgment was one of the most significant ever handed down by the UN court dealing with crimes against Serbs. Belgrade often accuses the tribunal of anti-Serb bias since the vast majority of suspects convicted are Serbs.

Defence lawyers for Gotovina and Markac unsuccessfully argued during the three-year trial that crimes in the Krajina were committed not by Croatian armed forces and special police, but by Croats exacting revenge on Serbs who forced them from their homes years earlier.

Appendix 11

Caucasus
http://www.forgottendiaries.org/en/diaries/caucasus/

The name of the region has its origin in the high mountains that cover the region from the Black Sea to the Caspian Sea. The Caucasus Mountains divides the region in two: South Caucasus (also called Trans Caucasus) and North Caucasus. North Caucasus consists of: Karatchaevo-Tcherkessia, Kabardino – Balkaria, North Ossetia, Inguschetia, Chechnya, and Dagestan. South Caucasus consists of Georgia, Armenia, Azerbaijan.

Nagorno-Karabakh

Nagorno-Karabakh is a region in the South Caucasus. It encompasses the Nagorno-KarabakhRepublic, a de facto independent republic, and is officially part of the Republic of Azerbaijan.

The issue of Nagorno-Karabakh first came to surface in 1918. After the collapse of the Russian empire Armenia and Azerbaijan faced the problem of border delimitation. In July 1918 the congress of the Karabakh Armenians declared Nagorno-Karabakh as an administrative andpolitical unit. Reacting to Azerbaijan's territorial claims the League of Nations recognized Nagorno-Karabakh as a disputed territory.

After the establishment of the Soviet rule in the South Caucasus, Soviet Azerbaijan declared its refusal of any claims over Nagorno-Karabakh. In July 1921 the Nagorno-Karabakh issue was discussed at the Caucasus Plenum and Nagorno-Karabakh had then to be included in the territory of the Soviet Socialist Republic of Armenia (ArmSSR). The following day the decision was revised, resulting in the annexion of Nagorno-Karabakh to the Azerbaijani Soviet Socialistic Republic (AzSSR).

In August 1991 Azerbaijan declared the restoration of the state independence of the Azerbaijani Democratic Republic of 1918-1920. In September of the same year the 'Declaration of the proclamation of Nagorno-Karabakh Republic' based on the right of the nations to self-determination was adopted. The declaration was followed by a referendum in December, where 99.89% of the population voted for the independence of the Nagorno-Karabakh Republic. The referendum was boycotted by local Azerbaijanis, and a full-scale war erupted. By the end of 1993 the conflict had caused thousands of casualties and hundreds of thousands on refugees on both sides. At that stage and for the first time, Nagorno-Karabakh was recognised as a third party in the conflict. A cease-fire was subsequently reached in May 1994.

Over the years the OSCE Minsk Group – created to encourage a peaceful resolution to the conflict – has suggested different solution packages to the parties, but all of them have been rejected. At the moment the proposed solution consists of the combination of the international principle of self-determination, the preservation of territorial integratity and avoidance of the use of force.

Chechnya

The conflict in Chechnya originated from a dispute between the former Chechnyan Autonomous Republic and Russia when the latter refused to acknowledge the self-proclaimed Chechnyan independence in 1993. In the first war against Russia (1994-1996), almost every Chechnyan group was involved. In the second war (1999 – onwards), it is the groups from Southern Chechnya who fought Russia. Whereas the first war was a war of independence, the second has the characteristics of a religious war.

For more than 250 years, Chechnya's relations to Russia have been characterised by resistance and revolt. The Caucasian wars in the 18th century and Stalin's deportations of Chechnyans in 1994 caused strong anti-Russian sentiments among most Chechnyans. In the early 1980s, Moscow's Glasnost and Perestroika policies reinforced already existing nationalist feelings in Chechnya, and popular nationalist movements were created here as well as in the other Caucasian republics.

The conflict in Chechnya is the most important of the conflicts in the Caucasus, with nationalist as well as religious aspects, and it is also the deadliest. Since 1994, at least 150,000 people have died as a result of the conflict and another 300,000 has left the republic. Before the war, Chechnya had 1.1 million inhabitants, but today it is estimated that only 715,000 remain in the republic. Although Russia's President Putin has claimed for years that the war is over and supports a pro-Russian government in Chechnya, there are clashes occurring daily and the conflict is far from over. It remains one of the major destabilizing factors in the Caucasus

Dagestan

Dagestan is a republic with many potentially destabilizing factors. In the early 1990s, Dagestan witnessed an "Islamic Renaissance" in which hundreds of mosques were constructed with support from abroad.

Although there are more than 20 ethnic groups in the country and no single group form a majority, the turmoil in Dagestan has been of a religious nature. Since 1992, the Saudi Wahhabist ideology has become very popular in many parts of the country. Tensions between groups adhering to the traditional Muslim Sufi tradition and the fundamentalist Islamic movement "Wahhabi" escalated in 1998 and turned into an armed conflict between local and Russian forces against the Wahhabis. As we have seen above, this conflict created the background for the Second Chechnyan war in 1999. Since 2002, the number of terrorist guerrilla actions has risen in Dagestan. The situation is very tense, and many fear that Dagestan could become a new Chechnya.

Ingushetia

The Republic of Ingushetia, the western neighbour of Chechnya, has also witnessed an increase in terror and guerrilla attacks. When Ingushetia lost control of Prigorodnyj to North Ossetia, many Ingush felt betrayed by Moscow and some joined the rebellion against Russian forces in Chechnya. The presence of the Ingush refugees from Prigorodnyj and Chechnyan refugees fleeing the conflict in their country has affected the economy of Ingushetia and the rates of unemployment are high. As in Dagestan, the situation remains tense.

Georgia

Observers have often labelled Georgia a failed state because of the central government's difficulties with its provinces. The Georgian economy has struggled with high rates of unemployment and poverty ever since the country gained independence. The mass demonstrations of 2003 developed into a revolution that forced President Shevardnadze to step down. The young and charismatic Sakashvili was elected President in 2004.

The expectations for the new President were high, and many Georgians hoped that their situation would improve. The long awaited finalization of the strategically and economically important oil pipeline, Baku-Tbilisi-Ceyhan, in September 2005 has further increased the optimism. But Georgia is still facing serious challenges. The main areas of problems are: South Ossetia/Tsjikanvili, Abkhazia, Ajara, Javakheti, The Kvemo Kartli Region, The Pankisi Valley.

Appendix 12

Analysis: roots of the conflict between Georgia, South Ossetia and Russia
Anatol Lieven
From The Times, August 11, 2008
http://www.timesonline.co.uk/tol/news/world/europe/article4498709.ece

Many factors are involved in the present conflict but the central one is straightforward: the majority of the Ossetes living south of the main Caucasus range in Georgia wish to unite with the Ossetes living to the north, in an autonomous republic of the Russian Federation; and the Georgians, regarding South Ossetia as both a legal and an historic part of their national territory, refuse to accept this.

Twice in the past century, when the empire to the north weakened and Georgia declared its independence, the southern Ossetes revolted against Georgian rule. It happened in 1918-20, between the collapse of the Russian empire and the Soviet Union's conquest of Georgia in 1921; and it happened again in our own time with the fall of the Soviet Union.

In 1918-20, between 5,000 and 15,000 people died, depending on whose figures you believe. For the conflicts since 1990, the figure is about 4,000 and rising.

As the Soviet Union began to crumble in 1989, and Georgian nationalist moves for independence gathered pace, so too did Ossete nationalism and demands for separation from Georgia.

The Ossete national movement was encouraged by the Soviet Government in an effort to exert pressure against Georgian independence.

In November 1989 the Soviet assembly of the South Ossetian autonomous region passed a motion calling for union with North Ossetia. Thousands of Georgian nationalists marched on Tskhinvali, the South Ossetian capital, in protest but were blocked by Soviet forces.

A year later, after the election in Georgia of a pro-independence government led by the extreme nationalist Zviad Gamsakhurdia, the same assembly declared South Ossetia a Soviet republic separate from Georgia. The Gamsakhurdia Government then sent thousands of Georgian armed police and nationalist militia into the region. These were fought to a standstill by local Ossete militia backed by Soviet Interior Ministry troops.

I was in Georgia at the time, reporting for The Times, and could hardly have imagined that this obscure conflict would one day create a major international crisis. Tskhinvali was a typical grey Soviet Caucasian Nowheresville, of bleak, crumbling concrete offices, potholed roads and faceless compounds. The only colour I remember was on the uniforms of the Georgian fighters: one was wearing a blue and white bobble hat, another had made for himself the uniform of an officer in the Georgian forces of 1918-21.

The Russian conscripts by contrast were not colourful at all: drab, demoralised and loathing the whole situation. They were, however, much better armed than the Georgians – and still are today.

The conflict rumbled on for several years, with peaks of fighting interspersed with truces. When in 1991 the Soviet Union collapsed and Georgian independence (within the borders of the Georgian Soviet Republic, and therefore including South Ossetia and Abkhazia) was recognised by the international community, South Ossetia rejected this and continued to assert its independence. Georgia declared the South Ossete autonomous republic abolished.

Russia has not recognised this, but Russian forces have remained as the de facto defenders of the South Ossetian separatist region.

In 1996 the Organisation for Security and Cooperation in Europe (OSCE) brokered an agreement whereby Russian and Georgian peacekeepers would patrol different sectors of the region.

The OSCE remained until the Georgian Government of Eduard Shevardnadze, the former Communist leader, was overthrown in the Rose Revolution and replaced by the radical nationalist administration of Mikhail Saakashvili.

Russia's policy is driven by a mixture of emotion and calculation. The Russian security establishment likes the Ossetes, who have been Russian allies for more than 250 years. They loathe the Georgians for their antiRussian nationalism and alliance with the US. For a long time they hoped to use South Ossetia initially to keep Georgia within the Soviet Union and later in a Russian sphere of influence.

That Russian ambition has been abandoned largely in the face of the Georgians' determination to escape from this influence.

What remains is an absolute determination not to be defeated by Georgia and not to suffer the humiliation of having to abandon Russia's South Ossete client state, with everything that this would mean for Russian prestige in other areas. Vladimir Putin's Kremlin made it clear again and again that if Georgia attacked South Ossetia, Russia would fight. Georgian advocates in the West claimed that Moscow was only bluffing. It wasn't.

Anatol Lieven is a professor at King's College London and a senior Fellow of the New America Foundation in Washington DC. In 1990-96 he was a correspondent for The Times in the former Soviet Union, including Georgia

Appendix 13

Press release - US support for OSCE policing drive will help fight terrorism and organized crime
http://webcache.googleusercontent.com/search?q=cache:eASxra2UYhcJ:www.osce.org/spmu/54763+OSCE+more+effective+than+united+nations&cd=2&hl=en&ct=clnk&gl=ca

WASHINGTON D.C., 23 October 2002 - More effective policing in the volatile Central Asia region adjoining Afghanistan is among measures that will help the United States and its allies in the region to combat terrorism and crime, the Organization for Security and Co-operation in Europe (OSCE) said today.

International terrorism and organized crime both thrive in an environment of lax security, where trust in the police is low and legitimate expressions of differing political opinion are often suppressed. The results can be felt far from the original source of the problems.

The OSCE, a 55-nation security organization with a strong human rights record, is urging the United States and its international partners to back a new drive to build up the quality of policing in OSCE participating States.

"With its broad membership and comprehensive approach to security, the OSCE is uniquely placed to prevent conflicts and deal with post-conflict situations," OSCE Secretary General Jan Kubis said. "The OSCE has a proven expertise in policing, gained in the Balkans, where many U.S. police officers have served with distinction."

He was speaking in Washington after meeting with senior officials from the U.S. State Department and National Security Council.

The Secretary General said the OSCE, comprising the United States, Canada, all the countries of Europe and the former Soviet Union, including the former Soviet republics of Central Asia and the Caucasus, had refocused its activities in the wake of the terrorist atrocities in the USA on September 11.

"The OSCE's current focus in the fight against terrorism is in four key areas - policing, border security, anti-trafficking and cutting off terrorist financing," he said. "These are areas in which the OSCE has, or is rapidly developing, a real comparative advantage."

Improved policing would not only reduce crime and improve the lives of ordinary people in the countries concerned. It would also help to curb the international spread of transnational organized crime which could threaten the fabric of society in the United States, Western Europe and elsewhere.

"Criminals are already co-operating internationally," Secretary General Kubis said. "It is vital that the international community should unite to tackle this modern scourge. The OSCE is keen to play its part."

The OSCE's comprehensive approach to security includes the promotion of human rights, democratization and economic well-being, alongside political and politico-military measures. The Organization is heavily operational, with nearly 4,000 international and local staff working in 19 field missions in south-eastern Europe, the Caucasus and Central Asia.

The Organization's newly-appointed Senior Police Adviser, Richard Monk, is spearheading a drive to build up police capacity in countries such as Kyrgyzstan, Uzbekistan, Tajikistan and Kazakhstan.

Monk, a former New Scotland Yard Commander who has 35 years of police experience in Britain and abroad, is asking the United States and other OSCE countries to provide experienced, top-quality police officers with proven expertise in areas such as forensics, crime intelligence systems, hostage rescue and public order.

The officers would be deployed on short-term assignments in the countries concerned, where they would provide training and share their expertise with their local counterparts.

"There is an inclination in some quarters to regard terrorism as being beyond the sphere of conventional criminal activity," said Monk, a former Commissioner of the United Nations International Police Task Force (IPTF) in Bosnia-Herzegovina.

"Well, it isn't. Its darkly sinister aims are nothing other than a criminal conspiracy and it sustains itself and executes its purpose by means which are entirely criminal."

The OSCE countries neighbouring Afghanistan face major problems including poverty, rampant organized crime, religious fanaticism, and trafficking in weapons, drugs and human beings: "In many cases, the police forces are ill-equipped and lack proper training to tackle serious crime," Monk said.

"There is ample evidence to show that policing plays a vital role in preventing conflict, preserving social stability during a political crisis and in post-conflict rehabilitation. It is equally apparent that without effective law enforcement and respect for the institutions of the rule of law, there can be no social, political or economic stability."

"The OSCE alone has experiences from its strong field presence and operations, institutional influence and broad membership to provide the long-term engagement required."

The OSCE's Strategic Police Matters Unit will offer OSCE participating States long-term assistance programmes, run by experienced professionals with the experience and authority to win the respect of their local police partners. It aims to build up a database of police experts who can be deployed as required.

"Respect for the human rights of detainees will be a constant thread running through our programmes," Richard Monk said. "Honesty, integrity and the respect of the community are vital for effective policing."

For example, proper training in interviewing victims and witnesses or interrogating suspects enables police to make maximum use of information essential to successful enquiries. "If you get this right, there is no need for the aggressive or abusive treatment of detainees which is all too common in some countries," Monk said.

Likewise, effective crime intelligence systems, enabling analysts to link crimes and criminals, are a cornerstone of modern police investigation techniques: "Sophisticated systems help to open up additional lines of enquiry for investigating officers and provide proof for courts, removing the need to rely on interrogation and confessions," Monk added.

The OSCE has gained invaluable experience of law enforcement in Croatia, the Federal Republic of Yugoslavia (including Kosovo and southern Serbia) and the former Yugoslav Republic of Macedonia.

Richard Monk wants to build on that expertise and create new practical police programmes that will make a measurable difference in new areas.

"The United States has some of the finest police officers in the world and it has been generous in supporting policing activities in the Balkans," he said. "U.S. backing for this new police programme, with a particular focus on Central Asia, will help us to tackle international terrorism and organized crime effectively and at source."

Steve Bennett, Director of the Kosovo Police Service Training School, said the OSCE's experience in Kosovo, Serbia, Bosnia-Herzegovina and the former Yugoslav Republic of Macedonia had proven that long-term programmes to improve policing do bear fruit.

"In all the countries where the OSCE has been involved in policing, things have improved as a result of our presence," said Bennett, a former U.S. Marine Corps trainer and member of the state of Oregon's board of public safety.

That experience has also demonstrated that even officers trained in a more authoritarian tradition can make the switch to a democratic style of policing: "We have had a lot of success in changing the culture of those organisations," Bennett said. "A lot of the old-line police leadership have, to different degrees, come on board with the new ideas."

Since it was established in 1999, Kosovo's police school has put more than 5,500 Kosovo Police Service officers - from all ethnic groups in the province - through basic training. Despite the region's recent history of bitter ethnic conflict, officers from both the ethnic Albanian and Serbian communities now patrol the streets side by side.

Alongside fundamental police skills - everything from defensive tactics to traffic control and criminal investigation - recruits also learn basic principles of human rights, police ethics and community relations.

A dramatic improvement in the province's crime statistics testifies to improved security in Kosovo, helped by the success of the training programme. The number of murders fell 52 per cent in 2001 from a year earlier while robberies were down 73 per cent, arson fell 58 per cent and the number of burglaries dropped more than 10 per cent.

"Kosovo's crime rate now stands comparison with that of almost any western country," Bennett said.

He has no doubt that a sustained improvement in policing can help to stem cross-border crime and terrorism: "Borders are becoming increasingly insignificant," Bennett said.

"Because of the mobility of crime, countries have to work together. If there is a major crime problem and a lack of internal controls in any state which is left unchecked, then it can grow into something that becomes a threat to everybody in the world.

"Look at Afghanistan and the Taliban. It was the neglect of what they were doing in that country that allowed them to have a terrorist base of operation. A different type of policing apparatus could have checked that earlier and maybe saved us from September 11."

Appendix 14

Security committee to debate larger OSCE role in N. Africa
COPENHAGEN, 27 June 2011
http://webcache.googleusercontent.com/search?q=cache:f7Kx6Ap7AhAJ:oscepa.org/index.php%3Fview%3Darticle%26id%3D1084%253Asecurity-committee-to-debate-larger-osce-role-in-n-africa%26option%3Dcom_content%26Itemid%3D70+OSCE+more+effective+than+united+nations&cd=7&hl=en&ct=clnk&gl=ca

The Organization for Security and Co-operation in Europe should provide assistance when asked in the fields of democracy and human rights in North Africa, according to a proposed resolution released today by the OSCE Parliamentary Assembly.

"With the rapid change we are seeing in our partner countries of Tunisia and Egypt and elsewhere, the time is now for the OSCE to step up and lend its considerable experience to countries who seek help to build democratic institutions," said Tonino Picula (Croatia), rapporteur of the politico-security committee and author of the resolution.

The Parliamentary Assembly's Committee on Political Affairs and Security will consider the resolution at the Belgrade Annual Session beginning 6 July under the theme "Strengthening the OSCE'S Effectiveness and Efficiency – A New Start After the Astana Summit."

The resolution is being considered for inclusion in the Assembly's Belgrade Declaration, which helps shape OSCE and national policy. Parliamentarians from more than 50 countries will vote on the resolution and declaration in Belgrade.

A More Effective OSCE through international co-operation

The committee's draft resolution calls for strengthening co-operation with the United Nations, European Union and others. Specifically, the resolution identified food security as a "new and major challenge" deserving of priority treatment within the OSCE.

"This resolution should be the impetus for action in all our parliaments," said Karl-Georg Wellmann (Germany), committee chairman. "With high food prices forcing millions of people into poverty, our countries must act to keep agricultural prices in check and fund rural development that balances food and energy demands."

A More Efficient OSCE though transparency and accountability

To ensure greater transparency and accountability, the OSCE's decision making body, the Permanent Council should allow public and the press to attend its meetings, the resolution says.

"We live in world that demands more visible examples of multilateral diplomacy in action," Mr. Picula said. "OSCE meetings need to be open to the public to raise the profile of this important work."

The resolution also recommends modifying the consensus rule for OSCE decision-making, at least for decisions related to personnel, budget and administration. The resolution would encourage the OSCE to employ outside, independent, professional auditors and to make the audits available to the OSCE PA.

The Belgrade Annual Session, including committee debates and votes, is open to the press and public. The session runs 6-10 July 2011. For more information on the Annual Session, click here.

The OSCE Parliamentary Assembly is comprised of 320 parliamentarians from 55 countries spanning, Europe, Central Asia and North America. The Assembly provides a forum for parliamentary diplomacy, monitors elections, and strengthens international cooperation to uphold commitments on political, security, economic, environmental and human rights issues.

Media Contact:

Neil Simon
Director of Communications, OSCE PA

Appendix 15

UNODC and organized crime
http://webcache.googleusercontent.com/search?q=cache:dEb-wZEw_sMJ:www.unodc.org/unodc/en/organized-crime/index.html+drug+trafficking+into+an+international+perspective&cd=1&hl=en&ct=clnk&gl=ca

Transnational organized crime is considered as one of the major threats to human security, impeding the social, economic, political and cultural development of societies worldwide. It is a multi-faceted phenomenon and has manifested itself in different activities, among others, drug trafficking, trafficking in human beings; trafficking in firearms; smuggling of migrants; money laundering; etc. In particular drug trafficking is one of the main activities of organized crime groups, generating enormous profits. UNODC works closely with Governments, international organizations and civil society to strengthen cooperation to counter the pervasive influence of organized crime and drug trafficking.

The United Nations Convention against Transnational Organized Crime is the main international instrument to counter organized crime.

UNODC helps countries use the provisions of the Convention to create domestic criminal offences to counter the problem; to adopt new frameworks for mutual legal assistance; to facilitate extradition; law enforcement cooperation; technical assistance and training.

As globalization has expanded international trade, so the range of organized crime activities has broadened and diversified. The traditional hierarchical forms of organized crime groups have diminished; replaced with loose networks who work together in order to exploit new market opportunities. For example organized crime groups involved in drug trafficking are commonly engaged in smuggling of other illegal goods. The links between drug trafficking and other forms of transnational organized crime calls for a more integrated approach to address this nexus. The signing of the United Nations Convention against Transnational Organized Crime in 2000 was a historic step forward in countering this threat.

The United Nations Convention against Transnational Organized Crime, which entered into force in September 2003, is the main international instrument to counter organized crime. The Convention commits states to introduce a range of measures, including the creation of domestic criminal offences to counter the problem; the adoption of new frameworks for mutual legal assistance; extradition; law enforcement cooperation; technical assistance and training.

UNODC works closely with national governments, organizations and civil society to enhance international cooperation to counter the pervading influence of organized crime and drug trafficking. The Unit has initiated and oversees numerous counter-narcotics and anti-organized crime projects.

Assisting Member States in the ratification and implementation of the TOC Convention;
- Monitoring the implementation of the Convention;
- Developing and promoting best practice in countering organized crime across the globe;
- Improving the exchange of information; judicial cooperation and mutual legal assistance between law enforcement officials and;
- Determining the most effective method for collecting information on organized crime from a regional and global perspective and ensuring that such information is available to policymaking and technical assistance projects.

Appendix 16

Links between Terrorism and Drug Trafficking: A Case of "Narco-terrorism"?
by Alex Schmid
January 27, 2005
http://english.safe-democracy.org/causes/links-between-terrorism-and-drug-trafficking-a-case-of-narcoterrorism.html

This article explores the nature of links between terrorism and trafficking in illicit narcotic drugs. It discusses some of the empirical evidence on the simultaneous presence of armed conflict, including the terrorist variety, and the cultivation, processing and trafficking of narcotic drugs. While some authors postulate close links - and even convergence - between terrorist groups and organized crime groups, the author of this article is more skeptical about the nature and extent of this connection. He points out both similarities and differences between these two types of organizations and also explores the possible reasons which might tempt - and restrain - groups of one type to establishing connections with groups of a significantly different mindset. He finds that the "in-house" development of organized crime activities by terrorist organizations is a more imminent problem than a close alliance or convergence of organized crime and terrorist organizations. Consequently, he recommends that the Palermo Convention against Transnational Organized Crime be used to prevent terrorist organizations from acquiring the financial resources needed to launch and maintain terrorist campaigns. At the same time he is skeptical about the use of the concept of "narco-terrorism". Its implication, the fusing of the "war on drugs "and the "war on terror," might do a disservice to both.

Introduction

On December 9th 1994, the General Assembly of the United Nations issued a Declaration on Measures to Eliminate International Terrorism wherein it expressed, inter alia, its concern "at the growing and dangerous links between terrorist groups and drug traffickers and their paramilitary gangs, which have resorted to all types of violence, thus endangering the constitutional order of states and violating basic human rights".

Since then, much stronger and broader statements have been made, especially in Security Council resolution 1373 (2001) wherein the Council "Notes with concern the close connection between international terrorism and transnational organized crime, illicit drugs, money-laundering, illegal arms-trafficking, and illegal movement of nuclear, chemical, biological and other potentially deadly materials...."

Of all the alleged and real links between terrorism and other forms of crime, the one between illicit drug trafficking and terrorist and guerrilla organizations seems to be the strongest. It certainly appears to be the best documented. Yet, while there are hundreds of terrorist organizations and at least as many drug trafficking organizations, the evidence, which is said to exist, is derived from relatively few cases.

For some thirty countries, a link between armed conflicts and illicit drug production and trafficking can be established with reasonable certainty. Yet according to UN estimates, there are more than 100 countries involved in some way in the illicit drug trade, either in terms of cultivation, processing, trafficking, distribution, or the laundering of illicit profits. While in most countries where drugs are produced, trafficked or consumed there is a causal link to crime, including violent crime, these are not necessarily terrorist crimes. There is often only sparse empirical evidence for some of the frequently cited cases of alleged connections between illicit drugs and terrorism. Even where these links have been established with reasonable certainty, estimates about the profits from drug trade going to terrorists vary widely. Lack of conclusive proof is often compensated by deductive reasoning such as this: with the end of the Cold War state-supported terrorism declined and terrorists had to look for alternative sources of financing and found it, inter alia, in the production, taxing and trafficking of illicit drugs like cannabis, heroine and cocaine.

The crucial question is: are these known and probable linkage cases, as it were, the tip of an iceberg, or are they, on the contrary, the exceptions to the rule that terrorist organizations and drug traffickers do in general, not work together?

Narco-terrorism

In 1983, the term "narcoterrorism" was introduced by Peruvian President Belaunde Terry. It became very popular in a very short time . Grant Wardlaw, a senior Australian criminologist, wrote a few years later:

"Narcoterrorism has emerged as a potent weapon in the propaganda war waged by governments against terrorists, insurgents, organised crime, drug traffickers, and even other sovereign states (…). Where "narcoterrorism" is used as an analytical concept intended to convey information about the dimensions of an activity and methods of countering it, it must have well defined boundaries and not subsume under the one rubric a variety of activities of different types, involving different sorts of actors and having a range of (sometimes) contradictory law enforcement and national security implications. In fact, these contradictions are violated by most uses of the term "narcoterrorism".
A look at a dozen existing definitions (see Appendix II) supports the statement above.

Grant Wardlaw even suggested that we should scrap the term "narcoterrorism" in an effort to encourage a more critical and specific study of drug links to terrorist and insurgent groups. This advice is still worth pondering. If one looks at the activities of organized crime groups and terrorist groups in terms of their respective motivations and group goals rather than demonizing them in terms of a drug mafia-cum-terrorist conspiracy, one is in a better position to understand the extent - and the limits - of cooperation between organized crime groups and secular and non-secular terrorist groups.

One author who has utilized such an approach is Chris Dishman. He has argued that transnational organized crime groups (TOCs) and terrorist groups will, in general, not cooperate with each other to advance aims and interests, preferring to utilize their "in-house" capabilities to undertake criminal and political acts. He postulates the adaptation by these groups of each other's "core competencies" (for example, a transnational organized crime group's experience in smuggling drugs or a guerrilla group's expertise in detonating bombs from a distance). He holds that: "The disinterest of TOCs and guerrillas to forge lasting alliances is a pattern supported by the limited number of examples where collaboration between the two groups has actually occurred."

However, sometimes the development of "in-house" capabilities takes more time than is available and in such cases each other's services are sought. In the case of Colombia, there were reports indicating that cocaine kingpin Pablo Escobar hired ELN (National Liberation Army) guerrilleros to plant car bombs in 1993. In another instance, there were reports that the explosion of 1,100 pounds of dynamite in front of the Department of Administrative Security in Bogota was executed by a Spanish terrorist with ties to the Basque ETA.

The cross-over between terrorist and criminal organizations has caused some analysts - and even more politicians - to lump these two types of underworld organizations together. When it comes to the question of whether one should keep terrorism and organized crime conceptually (and operationally) apart or place them together under some label like "narco-terrorism", a number of considerations arise. A case has been made for both positions. The argument for keeping them apart has been argued forcefully by Alison Jamieson:

"Organised crime and terrorism are correctly viewed as quite distinct phenomena. Essentially, the terrorist is a revolutionary, with clear political objectives involving the overthrow of a government or the status quo, and a set of articulated strategies to achieve them. Organised crime actors are inherently conservative: they tend to resist political upheaval and seek conditions of order and stability, those more conductive to their business activities. Unlike terrorists, who project an 'ideal state' for which they are prepared to sacrifice their lives, organised crime sees no virtue in sacrifice, has no comparable sense of 'victory' or 'defeat', but operates according to a set of short and medium-term goals to be realised with maximum profit and minimum risk.
In general, the organised criminal power system is not "anti-state", but a parallel organisational model with its own legal and ethical rules, hierarchy of authority and military force. (…) Thus, unlike terrorist actors whose raison d'etre is direct

confrontation with the state against which they practice violence, the survival of an organised crime group depends upon operating within the state, on the penetration by criminal actors of the legitimate political, economic and social spheres".

On the other side, there are those who tend to label all armed groups "terrorist groups" and equate all insurgents with criminals. With regard to the second they are right in the sense that under domestic law, an internal uprising against the state is considered a crime by those holding state power and by the law of the land. Only international law gives some insurgent groups the status of privileged combatants. This finds its expression in the additional protocols to the Geneva Conventions formulated in 1977. These should not, however, apply to terrorists since their deliberate attacks on non-combatants should deprive them of combatant status. Were it war, such acts would be war crimes and the fact that these are committed in peacetime makes them even more objectionable. Terrorists and war criminals have much in common. Yet, what are the commonalities between terrorist and organized crime groups?

Appendix 17

America gripped by fear of 'dirty bomb' attack
By Rupert Cornwell in Washington
Thursday, 13 February 2003
http://webcache.googleusercontent.com/search?q=cache:G80C7yPnmSYJ:www.independent.co.uk/news/world/americas/america-gripped-by-fear-of-dirty-bomb-attack-745846.html+fear+of+dirty+bomb+in+schools&cd=2&hl=en&ct=clnk&gl=ca

From the anti-aircraft missiles around Washington to government recommendations that families prepare bunkers in their homes against biological, chemical, radiological weapons, America is suffering its most acute bout of terror jitters since the attacks of 11 September.

From the anti-aircraft missiles around Washington to government recommendations that families prepare bunkers in their homes against biological, chemical, radiological weapons, America is suffering its most acute bout of terror jitters since the attacks of 11 September.

Nerves began to jangle last week when the new Department of Homeland Security raised its colour-coded threat alert to orange, denoting a "high" risk of an attack. Then came the latest purported Osama bin Laden tape, urging more suicide attacks against American citizens.

And yesterday, George Tenet, the CIA director, issued his grimmest warning yet, telling a Senate panel that a strike could come as early as this week, either in America or in the Arabian peninsula, perhaps involving a dirty bomb. The threat was "the most specific we have ever seen", he warned.

Hours earlier, the Pentagon confirmed that anti-aircraft Stinger missiles had been deployed around key sites in Washington, considered with New York the likeliest targets for the terrorists. But all along the eastern seaboard tensions are running high, and ordinary people are taking precautions.

"Duct tape, plastic sheeting, can openers; you name it, we're selling it," the manager of Candey's hardware store, just half-a-dozen blocks from the White House, said yesterday.

The run was sparked when Homeland Security officials issued a list of instructions on how to prepare for an emergency. Families are being urged to designate a "safe room" in their house, which could be sealed with plastic sheeting and tape.

They should stockpile three days of food and water, at the rate of a gallon per person per day, as well as blankets, torches, radios and spare batteries. Families should also have pre-arranged plans on how to keep in contact if separated.

The government insists the precautions are "prudent planning", just as people should prepare for natural disasters such as hurricanes, tornados or floods. But officials freely compare the measures to steps taken by Israel, whose citizens face the risk of attack every day.

The threat of a terrorist outrage in America in the next three weeks was "perhaps the equivalent of eight on a scale of one to 10", Tom Ridge, the Homeland Security Secretary, has said.

Most at risk now are not traditional targets such as airports and government buildings, but so-called soft targets, such as schools, banks, shopping centres and sports arenas. The attacks could be more insidious too, with bombs replaced by poison in the water supply.

Appendix 18

NIDA InfoFacts: High School and Youth Trends
http://webcache.googleusercontent.com/search?q=cache:YZqa5kWtUxAJ:www.drugabuse.gov/infofacts/hsyouthtrends.html+drugs+in+schools+facts&cd=1&hl=en&ct=clnk&gl=ca

Since 1975 the Monitoring the Future (MTF) survey has measured drug, alcohol, and cigarette use and related attitudes among adolescent students nationwide. Survey participants report their drug use behaviors across three time periods: lifetime, past year, and past month; for some drugs, daily use is also reported.

Initially, the survey included 12th-graders only, but in 1991 it was expanded to include 8th- and 10th-graders. The MTF survey is funded by NIDA and is conducted by the University of Michigan's Institute for Social Research. The 36th annual study was conducted during 2010.2

This year's Monitoring the Future Survey raises concerns about increases in drug use among the Nation's teens, particularly the youngest.

Daily Marijuana use increased among 8th, 10th, and 12th graders from 2009 to 2010. Among 12th graders it was at its highest point since the early 1980s at 6.1%. This year, perceived risk of regular marijuana use also declined among 10th and 12th graders suggesting future trends in use may continue upward.

In addition, most measures of marijuana use increased among 8th graders between 2009 and 2010 (past year, past month, and daily), paralleling softening attitudes for the last 2 years about the risk of using marijuana.

Marijuana use is now ahead of cigarette smoking on some measures (due to decreases in smoking and recent increases in marijuana use). In 2010, 21.4 percent of high school seniors used marijuana in the past 30 days, while 19.2 percent smoked cigarettes.

Steady declines in cigarette smoking appear to have stalled in all three grades after several years of improvement on most measures.

Appendix 19

Bomb Threat Showed Absence of Safety Plan
January 31, 2005
Daniel B. Prieto and Robert Knake
Boston Herald
http://webcache.googleusercontent.com/search?q=cache:kFnf7pvQ3b0J:www.hks.harvard.edu/news-events/news/commentary/bomb-threat-showed-absence-of-safety-plan+dirty+bomb+threat+in+schools&cd=3&hl=en&ct=clnk&gl=ca

During the Cold War, Americans in large cities went about their daily lives accepting the very real possibility of nuclear attack. Faced with that reality, they did not flee in large numbers, stop going to work or divest from the stock market. Instead, Americans, in their finest tradition, developed a culture of preparedness.

School children learned to duck and cover. Store owners turned their basements into fallout shelters and fathers dug them in the yard.

In short, given a far greater threat, Americans went about their daily lives but did so knowing what to do should the sum of all fears be realized.

Recently, Bostonians of this generation faced a threat of both higher probability than nuclear war and of lesser impact. A radiological or dirty bomb, though devastating, is altogether a much lower order of magnitude threat. Moreover, education and preparation about this threat can dramatically reduce the loss of life in a way that preparations for nuclear war with the Soviet Union could not.

At his press conference, Boston Mayor Tom Menino urged calm, but failed to take the opportunity to discuss preparedness. In so doing, a critical opportunity was lost.

Regardless of whether four Chinese and two Iraqis ever posed a threat to Boston is largely irrelevant. If and when an attack on this or any other city occurs, it is likely that the public and possibly law enforcement will not know about it until there is a boom followed by a column of smoke. Such was the case on 9/11 for New Yorkers.

Calm should only be the product of proper preparation. Business as usual should mean that individuals, communities and businesses, confident in their preparations, will be ready should disaster strike.

A dirty bomb disperses radioactive material in the dust created by the explosion. The overarching goal of anyone exposed is therefore simple: Avoid inhaling dust that could be radioactive.

If you are outdoors in the vicinity of an explosion, cover your nose and mouth with your clothing and get indoors.

If you are indoors, and the explosion has not affected your building, stay there. Close windows, turn off ventilation systems and wait for authorities to tell you it is safe to exit. If you have been exposed, shower thoroughly. More information can be obtained from the RAND Corp. at www.rand.org/publications/mr1731 . Alarmingly, the federal government's online resource for terrorism planning does not provide as much useful information.

Every family should have a disaster kit with enough water and food to avoid going outside for three days as well as any medications you might need. Families should discuss disaster planning with their children, emphasizing that the most important thing, while counter to instinct, may not be to return home. Cell phones may not work and transit will likely be clogged.

Boston's dirty bomb scare was a time for officials to ask with a sense of urgency whether the citizenry and municipal agencies are prepared for such a crisis. Public health officials should ask how hospitals would handle not only large numbers of casualties but also thousands of the worried well. In short, civic leaders should use crises even if they turn out to be false alarms as invaluable opportunities to transform fear into preparedness.

HBO recently premiered "Dirty War," a film that realistically depicts a dirty bomb attack on London. The film shows an ill- informed public running rampant. Every Bostonian should watch it (PBS will run it starting Feb. 23). The tagline of the film is, "How do you prepare for the unthinkable?"

The answer is that such an attack is not unthinkable.

Appendix 20

Foreign Terrorist Organizations
Office of the Coordinator for Counterterrorism
September 15, 2011
http://www.state.gov/s/ct/rls/other/des/123085.htm

Foreign Terrorist Organizations (FTOs) are foreign organizations that are designated by the Secretary of State in accordance with section 219 of the Immigration and Nationality Act (INA), as amended. FTO designations play a critical role in our fight against terrorism and are an effective means of curtailing support for terrorist activities and pressuring groups to get out of the terrorism business.

Current List of Designated Foreign Terrorist Organizations:

- Abu Nidal Organization (ANO)
- Abu Sayyaf Group (ASG)
- Al-Aqsa Martyrs Brigade (AAMS)
- Al-Shabaab
- Ansar al-Islam (AAI)
- Asbat al-Ansar
- Aum Shinrikyo (AUM)
- Basque Fatherland and Liberty (ETA)
- Communist Party of the Philippines/New People's Army (CPP/NPA)
- Continuity Irish Republican Army (CIRA)
- Gama'a al-Islamiyya (Islamic Group)
- HAMAS (Islamic Resistance Movement)
- Harakat ul-Jihad-i-Islami/Bangladesh (HUJI-B)
- Harakat ul-Mujahidin (HUM)
- Hizballah (Party of God)
- Islamic Jihad Union (IJU)
- Islamic Movement of Uzbekistan (IMU)
- Jaish-e-Mohammed (JEM) (Army of Mohammed)
- Jemaah Islamiya organization (JI)
- Kahane Chai (Kach)
- Kata'ib Hizballah (KH)
- Kongra-Gel (KGK, formerly Kurdistan Workers' Party, PKK, KADEK)
- Lashkar-e Tayyiba (LT) (Army of the Righteous)
- Lashkar i Jhangvi (LJ)
- Liberation Tigers of Tamil Eelam (LTTE)
- Libyan Islamic Fighting Group (LIFG)
- Moroccan Islamic Combatant Group (GICM)

- Mujahedin-e Khalq Organization (MEK)
- National Liberation Army (ELN)
- Palestine Liberation Front (PLF)
- Palestinian Islamic Jihad (PIJ)
- Popular Front for the Liberation of Palestine (PFLP)
- PFLP-General Command (PFLP-GC)
- al-Qaida in Iraq (AQI)
- al-Qa'ida (AQ)
- al-Qa'ida in the Arabian Peninsula (AQAP)
- al-Qaida in the Islamic Maghreb (formerly GSPC)
- Real IRA (RIRA)
- Revolutionary Armed Forces of Colombia (FARC)
- Revolutionary Organization 17 November (17N)
- Revolutionary People's Liberation Party/Front (DHKP/C)
- Revolutionary Struggle (RS)
- Shining Path (Sendero Luminoso, SL)
- United Self-Defense Forces of Colombia (AUC)
- Harakat-ul Jihad Islami (HUJI)
- Tehrik-e Taliban Pakistan (TTP)
- Jundallah
- Army of Islam (AOI)
- Indian Mujahideen (IM)

Identification

The Office of the Coordinator for Counterterrorism in the State Department (S/CT) continually monitors the activities of terrorist groups active around the world to identify potential targets for designation. When reviewing potential targets, S/CT looks not only at the actual terrorist attacks that a group has carried out, but also at whether the group has engaged in planning and preparations for possible future acts of terrorism or retains the capability and intent to carry out such acts.

Designation

Once a target is identified, S/CT prepares a detailed "administrative record," which is a compilation of information, typically including both classified and open sources information, demonstrating that the statutory criteria for designation have been satisfied. If the Secretary of State, in consultation with the Attorney General and the Secretary of the Treasury, decides to make the designation, Congress is notified of the Secretary's intent to designate the organization and given seven days to review the designation, as the INA requires. Upon the expiration of the seven-day waiting period and in the absence of Congressional action to block the designation, notice of the designation is published in the Federal Register, at which point the designation takes effect. By law an organization designated as an FTO may seek judicial review of the designation in the United States Court of Appeals for the District of Columbia Circuit not later than 30 days after the designation is published in the Federal Register.

Until recently the INA provided that FTOs must be redesignated every 2 years or the designation would lapse. Under the Intelligence Reform and Terrorism Prevention Act of 2004 (IRTPA), however, the redesignation requirement was replaced by certain review and revocation procedures. IRTPA provides that an FTO may file a petition for revocation 2 years after its designation date (or in the case of redesignated FTOs, its most recent redesignation date) or 2 years after the determination date on its most recent petition for revocation. In order to provide a basis for revocation, the petitioning FTO must provide evidence that the circumstances forming the basis for the designation are sufficiently different as to warrant revocation. If no such review has been conducted during a 5 year period with respect to a designation, then the Secretary of State is required to review the designation to determine whether revocation would be appropriate. In addition, the Secretary of State may at any time revoke a designation upon a finding that the circumstances forming the basis for the designation have changed in such a manner as to warrant revocation, or that the national security of the United States warrants a revocation. The same procedural requirements apply to revocations made by the Secretary of State as apply to designations. A designation may be revoked by an Act of Congress, or set aside by a Court order.

Legal Criteria for Designation under Section 219 of the INA as amended

It must be a foreign organization.

The organization must engage in terrorist activity, as defined in section 212 (a)(3)(B) of the INA (8 U.S.C. § 1182(a)(3)(B)),* or terrorism, as defined in section 140(d)(2) of the Foreign Relations Authorization Act, Fiscal Years 1988 and 1989 (22 U.S.C. § 2656f(d)(2)),** or retain the capability and intent to engage in terrorist activity or terrorism.

The organization's terrorist activity or terrorism must threaten the security of U.S. nationals or the national security (national defense, foreign relations, or the economic interests) of the United States.

Legal Ramifications of Designation

It is unlawful for a person in the United States or subject to the jurisdiction of the United States to knowingly provide "material support or resources" to a designated FTO. (The term "material support or resources" is defined in 18 U.S.C. § 2339A(b)(1) as " any property, tangible or intangible, or service, including currency or monetary instruments or financial securities, financial services, lodging, training, expert advice or assistance, safehouses, false documentation or identification, communications equipment, facilities, weapons, lethal substances, explosives, personnel (1 or more individuals who maybe or include oneself), and transportation, except medicine or religious materials." 18 U.S.C. § 2339A(b)(2) provides that for these purposes "the term 'training' means instruction or teaching designed to impart a specific skill, as opposed to general knowledge." 18 U.S.C. § 2339A(b)(3) further provides that for these purposes the term 'expert advice or assistance' means advice or assistance derived from scientific, technical or other specialized knowledge."

Representatives and members of a designated FTO, if they are aliens, are inadmissible to and, in certain circumstances, removable from the United States (see 8 U.S.C. §§ 1182 (a)(3)(B)(i)(IV)-(V), 1227 (a)(1)(A)).

Any U.S. financial institution that becomes aware that it has possession of or control over funds in which a designated FTO or its agent has an interest must retain possession of or control over the funds and report the funds to the Office of Foreign Assets Control of the U.S. Department of the Treasury.

Other Effects of Designation

- Supports our efforts to curb terrorism financing and to encourage other nations to do the same.
- Stigmatizes and isolates designated terrorist organizations internationally.
- Deters donations or contributions to and economic transactions with named organizations.
- Heightens public awareness and knowledge of terrorist organizations.
- Signals to other governments our concern about named organizations

Appendix 21

Poll: Muslim-Americans feel targeted by terror policies
By HOPE YEN
updated 8/30/2011
http://webcache.googleusercontent.com/search?q=cache:4nDmp5WcoCUJ:www.msnbc.msn.com/id/44327070/ns/us_news-life/t/poll-muslim-americans-feel-targeted-terror-policies/+islamic+names+and+law+enforcement&cd=9&hl=en&ct=clnk&gl=ca

WASHINGTON — More than half of Muslim Americans in a new poll say government anti-terrorism policies single them out for increased surveillance and monitoring, and many report increased cases of name-calling, threats and harassment by airport security, law enforcement officers and others.

Still, most Muslim Americans say they are satisfied with the way things are going in the U.S. and rate their communities highly as places to live.

The survey by the Pew Research Center, one of the most exhaustive ever of the country's Muslims, finds no signs of rising alienation or anger among Muslim-Americans despite recent U.S. government concerns about homegrown Islamic terrorism and controversy over the building of mosques.

"This confirms what we've said all along: American Muslims are well integrated and happy, but with a kind of lingering sense of being besieged by growing anti-Muslim sentiment in our society," said Ibrahim Hooper, spokesman for the Council on American-Islamic Relations, a Washington, D.C.-based Muslim civil rights group.

"People contact us every day about concerns they've had, particularly with law enforcement authorities in this post-9/11 era," he said.

Appendix 22

Arab & Islamic Names Analysis
http://webcache.googleusercontent.com/search?q=cache:9b7yIQxCrZQJ:www.redcellig.com/pages/training/seminars/arab-islamic-names-analysis.php+islamic+names+and+law+enforcement&cd=10&hl=en&ct=clnk&gl=ca

Red Cell IG teaches this course in conjunction with our partners at Harbinger Technologies Group. The Arab and Islamic Names Analysis course provides soft skills to compliment the training offered by your organization or unit.

The course gives those personnel deploying to and working with the Arab and Islamic World the edge they need to more effectively and intelligently deal with the various naming conventions and other names related issues.

This two to four hour course, designed by Global War on Terror veterans and Islamic/Arab culture experts, provides the basic information needed to understand the cultural naming patterns of the Islamic World.

Individuals will learn how a deeper understanding of these names aids in properly screening individuals and finding out who is a friend or foe.

It is a must-have for anyone involved in the questioning of individuals from the region and for those trying to understand how the names interrelate to other biographical information.

Appendix 23

Selected Strategic, Intelligence & Military Courses
http://webcache.googleusercontent.com/search?q=cache:V0dpefhFDbQJ:www.htgcorp.com/Selected_Courses_I.html+islamic+names+and+law+enforcement&cd=17&hl=en&ct=clnk&gl=ca

Islamic World Familiarization Course™ (IWFC)
These courses combine historical and cultural background with practical application skills. Personnel will learn how a deeper understanding of Arab and Islamic culture provides the edge they need to more effectively and intelligently combat Islamic terrorism and build relationships of trust with the community and other partners.

In Depth Study of al-Qaeda
This course offers students a look at the religion, culture, and personalities that led to the creation of one of America's greatest threats, providing a study of the history, formation, and activities of al-Qaeda.

Arab & Islamic Names Analysis
This course goes step-by-step to reveal the complexities of Arab and Islamic naming convention. Personnel will learn how to improve intelligence-gathering by simply unlocking complex naming patterns. The course also reveals the security breaches inherent to bringing Arab and Islamic names into the Western world.

Police Source Operations Course®
These courses enable law enforcement personnel to identify and defeat specific threats on the home front, providing in-depth studies of terrorist, drug, and gang methodology and incidents, including Arab and Islamic culture in America and "myth busting". These intense courses move quickly through the essentials in order to provide a core competency in identifying and handling relevant sources in the local community.

Focused Security Approach (FSA®)
This course enhances and refines the ability of law enforcement and security personnel to identify individuals that pose higher potential threats. Security professionals learn to focus their attention based on potential threat levels resulting in a better allocation of security resources, improved efficiency and increased effectiveness of the overall security system. The course delineates industry-pertinent disciplines and methodologies that have proven successful in high-risk areas around the world. It can be tailored to suit your organization's specific needs, interest, and desired level of intensity.

Appendix 24

Irish surnames explained - the meaning behind the top ten clan names
By ANTOINETTE KELLY, IrishCentral Staff Writer
Published Thursday
http://webcache.googleusercontent.com/search?q=cache:wyLA-CJlo6sJ:www.irishcentral.com/roots/Irish-surnames-explained---the-meaning-behind-the-top-ten-clan-names-128338993.html+law+enforcement+%26+irish+names&cd=6&hl=en&ct=clnk&gl=ca

Irish and Irish-Americans alike tend to be immensely proud of their surnames.

Many a Irish family proudly declare their Irish roots by displaying the crest of their clan in their homes.

Appendix 25

Top 100 Irish last names explained: Find out more about your Irish roots and where your family name hails from
By BRYAN FITZGERALD,
IrishCentral.com Staff Writer
Published Friday, September 17, 2010
http://www.irishcentral.com/roots/Top-100-Irish-last-names-explained-103125099.html#ixzz1YgevJKrX

IrishCentral.com has put together a list of the top 100 common Irish surnames with a little explanation of where these names come from.

Whether you're looking to trace your family crest or trying to trace your family roots this list will point you in the right direction.

Aherne - (Ó hEachtighearna/Ó hEachthairn) (each, steed tightearna, lord). Originally Dalcassian, this sept migrated from east Clare to Co. Cork. In County Waterford the English name Hearn is a synonym of Hearn.

Allen - This is usually of Scottish or English origin but sometimes Ó hAillín in Offaly and Tipperary has been anglicized Allen as well as Hallion. Occasionally also in Co. Tipperary. Allen is found as a synonym of Hallinan. As Alleyn it occurs frequently in mediaeval Anglo Irish records. The English name Allen is derived from that of a Welsh saint.

MacAleese - MacGiolla (son of the devotee of Jesus). The name of a prominent Derry sept. There are many variants of the name such as MacIliese, MacLeese, MacLice, MacLise, etc. The best known of this spelling, the painter Daniel MacLise, was a family of the Scottish highlands, know as MacLeish, which settled in Cork.

MacAteer - Mac an tSaoir (saor, craftsman) An Ulster name for which the Scottish MacIntyre, of similar derivation, is widely substituted. Ballymacateer is a place-name in Co. Armagh, which is its homeland. Mac an tSaoir is sometimes anglicized Wright in Fermanagh.

MacAuley - Awley. There are two distinct septs of this name, viz. MacAmhalghaidh of Offaly and West Meath, and the more numerous MacAmhlaoibh, a branch of the MacGuires which as MacAmhlaoibh gives the form Gawley in Connacht. Both are derived from personal names. The latter must not be confused with MacAuliffe.

MacAuliffe - Mac Amhlaoibh. An important branch of the McCarthys whose chief was seated at Castle MacAuliffe. The name is almost peculiar to south-west Munster

Appendix 26

Baby-Naming Trends
by Cleveland Kent Evans
http://webcache.googleusercontent.com/search?q=cache:bcDShBaXaIAJ:tlc.howstuffworks.com/family/baby-name-trends-ga2.htm+cultural+naming+of+children&cd=1&hl=en&ct=clnk&gl=ca

Cultural and Ethnic Influences on Baby Names

As long as there has been language, there have been names. Naming is the first task of speech through which we differentiate one person or thing from all others. Every society has a naming system, and all these systems have certain common elements.

Throughout the world, each child is assigned a sound or series of sounds that will be his or her name. Because that name is a part of the language of the child's parents, it immediately identifies the child as belonging to a particular society. So our names identify us both as individuals and as members of a group.

In many parts of Africa, a child's naming day is a festive occasion that usually occurs a week or so after the birth. Girls are named sooner than boys, but only by a day or two. An older person bestows the name, first by whispering it to the baby, because a newborn should know his or her name before anyone else does, then by announcing the name to everyone attending the ceremony.

Many Native Americans developed naming systems in which a person's individual name included the name of his or her clan. For example, all the members of a clan that has the bear as its totem animal have names relating to bears, such as Black-Bear Tracks and Black-Bear Flashing Eyes.

In some groups, children are given secret names that are not revealed until the child reaches puberty or another important stage of life. In other Native American nations, an event that occurs at a child's birth may become the child's name. Today, a person living on a reservation may have one name at home but a different name when he or she is off the reservation.

In China, all given names are created out of words in the Chinese language that have an obvious, immediate meaning. Names are believed to reflect the character of the person, and great care is taken in selecting a child's name. Usually about a month after the child is born, the parents attempt to create an original name. Many girls are given names that signify beauty, such as Sweet Willow or Morning Star. Boys are given names that reflect strength and good health. In rural areas, many Chinese names still include a "generation name," a word or syllable that is the same for all children born in a family in the same generation. Three sisters, for example, might be named Yuan-Chun, Ying-Chun, and Xi-Chun, which mean "First Spring," "Welcome Spring," and "Cherish Spring."

With China's one-child policy, this custom is fading in urban areas, but some Americans of Chinese descent continue this tradition by giving all their children names containing the same syllable (such as Mar- as seen in Marco, Marisa, Marla, Marlene, Marshall, Martha, and Marvin). Most Chinese-Americans give their children American-style first names, though they often give a Chinese-language name as the middle name, as in Brittany Ngon Lee.

Jewish names are some of the oldest names in use today. A Jewish boy is named officially when he is circumcised on the eighth day after his birth. A girl is named as soon as possible after her birth. Traditionally, an Ashkenazic Jewish child is not named for a living person for fear that the Angel of Death will mistake the child for the older person if their names are the same.

African-American Names

In the 1960s, some African-Americans began to give their children names from African cultures. Some adults also changed their names to African or Muslim names. Because slaves were often assigned the surnames of their owners and given common first names, choosing African names is a way for African-Americans to acknowledge their heritage before slavery. However, only a few genuine African names, such as Ayana, Kwame, and Jabari, have become widely popular in the African-American community. Muslim names from the Arabic language, such as Iesha, Jamal, Malik, and Aaliyah, have been more popular recently, even with African-Americans who have not adopted the Islamic religion.

Since the 1970s it has become more common for African-Americans to create new names for their children by combining their own set of fashionable sounds and syllables. Names for girls formed in this way are called "Lakeisha names" after one of the prime examples. Lakeisha names are created by linking a fashionable prefix, such as Sha-, La-, Ka-, Shan-, or Ty-, with a fashionable suffix, such as -isha, -ika, -onda, -ae, -ique, or -ice. The resulting names are almost always accented on the second syllable.

In the 1970s and 1980s, names beginning with La- such as Lashonda and Lashay were most popular. In the 1990s, Sha- names such as Shameka, Shanae, and Shaniqua were fashionable. In 2004, names starting with Ja- or ending in -iyah such as Jakayla, Jamya, Janiyah, and Taniyah were in vogue. But the point of this custom for most parents is to create a unique name for their child, and many are successful. Even in states as large as Pennsylvania, each year the average

African-American girl receives a name that no other African-American girl born in that state is given. It was not possible to include many of these unique names, such as Azanae, Kyaire, and Zaterria, but they are now the most typical kind of names for African-American girls. Names for boys that have been created similarly include DeJuan, Deonte, Jamarion, Ladarius, and Quantavious.

Hispanic-American Names

Traditionally, Hispanic-American babies were often given saints' names, and both male and female saints were considered appropriate. Hispanic-American boys are often given religious names such as Jesus, Angel, and Salvador. Girls are often named in honor of the Virgin Mary, using words from her devotional titles such as Araceli, Rocio, Consuelo, Dolores, and Mercedes.

Other traditional Spanish names popular in the Hispanic-American community include Carlos, Enrique, Fernando, Francisco, Jaime, Javier, Jorge, Jose, Juan, Julio, Luis, Marcos, and Miguel for boys and Adriana, Beatriz, Carolina, Daniela, Gabriela, Isabel, and Maria for girls.

Traditional boys' names remain especially common in the Hispanic-American community, because there is still the expectation that most boys will be named after their fathers or grandfathers, a custom that is now rare in other ethnic groups.

However, not all the names popular with Hispanic-Americans are traditionally Spanish names. Hector, Oscar, and Rene have long been popular names for boys in Latin America, and non-Spanish immigrants to Central and South America, as well as the modern media, have introduced many new names. In particular, Spanish-language television programs called telenovelas, most of which are produced in Mexico, have popularized the names of their stars and characters wherever they are shown, including in the United States. For example, Vanessa, a very British name, is popular in the Hispanic-American community because it was the name of the title character in a television program starring Lucia Mendez, one of Mexico's most popular actresses.

Other non-Spanish names more popular with Latinos than Anglos in the United States include Astrid, Daisy, Evelyn, Leslie, Lizbeth, and Yasmin for girls and Axel, Edgar, Edwin, Elmer, George, Giovanni, Omar, and Yahir for boys. Ariel and Alexis are very common names for Hispanic-American boys, while other ethnic groups now give them mostly to girls. Some Latino parents also create brand-new names for their children, especially daughters. At the moment, invented names beginning with the letter Y are in vogue, and many Hispanic girls are being given names like Yaritza, Yanelis, Yosayra, and Yuritzi.

Other Ethnic Influences

Historically, first-generation immigrants to the United States from Europe and East Asia have tried to adopt American naming customs, though since they are not completely assimilated into the culture they often give their children names that seem out of style. For example, recent immigrants from China and Korea are much more likely to name daughters Linda or Eunice than other Americans.

The second generation of an immigrant group usually gives their children names that are no different from those of the majority. The third and fourth generations, however, often begin to revive names from their ancestry. Many Irish-Americans began this process in the 1940s, re-introducing traditional Irish names such as Sean, Kevin, Sheila, and Caitlin that have gone on to become generally popular. This process has now begun with Italian-Americans, who, since 1990, have strongly increased their use of traditional Italian names such as Isabella, Gianna, Lorenzo, and Leonardo.

Because of the strong influence of Islam and Hinduism, immigrants from the Middle East and South Asia don't adopt "Western" names as readily, though they do often try to choose names from their religious traditions that they think will be easier for other Americans to pronounce. Muslim-Americans give their children names such as Ali, Fatima, Zaynab, and Ziad; Hindu-Americans use names such as Aryan, Diya, Mira, and Rohan. Many names popular with East Indian-Americans, such as Arjun and Shreya, have been influenced by the stars of India's huge Bollywood film industry

Appendix 27

Are Privacy Rights of Citizens Being Eroded Wholesale?
By Angela Jarvis
http://webcache.googleusercontent.com/search?q=cache:uY9hIxTyyBoJ:www.forensic-evidence.com/site/ID/facialrecog.html+problems+in+Identifying+criminal+Subjects&cd=41&hl=en&ct=clnk&gl=ca

Facial identification is the fastest growing biometric technology today. According to many industry experts, it is also the most controversial of all biometrics. Despite their lingering questions regarding the practical usefulness of facial identification technology, law enforcement and military facial identification systems have been in place for several years without arousing too much controversy. According to industry insiders, this is because these applications have proven quite successful in carrying out specific objectives and the public is often unaware of these uses. Although facial recognition technology has not been proven to be an accurate and effective way of identifying terrorists or wanted suspects, some of the proposed post-September 11 uses of the technology – such as in immigration and airport security – have been welcomed by the general public. Are we too eager to buy into a new technology without clearly evaluating its effectiveness and without weighing the potential harms involved with its use?

Before September 11, the public viewed the technology with much more skepticism than it does today. Many people remain skeptical when it comes to widespread use of the technology in areas other than public safety and security. The possibility of identity theft and privacy infringement are the most common concerns voiced by people.

Much of the skepticism may be attributed to the very visible and troubling past uses of the technology. Tampa, Florida is one such questionable application.

Viisage Technology's software matched 19 faces in the Tampa Super Bowl crowd to persons whose purported likenesses were contained in a law enforcement database, all of whom had criminal records but were not wanted by police, nor were there outstanding warrants for the individuals' arrests.

Ybor City, a nearby coastal village, installed 36 of the surveillance systems. Many visitors to the city and civil libertarians expressed their utter disgust with the system, calling it a "virtual lineup." The program was likened to Big Brother and people feared that the technology would worsen racial profiling practices and would accidentally identify innocent people as criminals. These criticisms persist even though the law is pretty clear, at least so far, that visual privacy rights don't apply in public places.

In spite of the harsh criticism of the Florida systems, Virginia Beach became the second city in the U.S. to use the technology when it installed a similar facial-recognition system in November 2001 at the Oceanfront. Although Mayor Meyera E. Oberndorf initially disapproved of Virginia Beach's plan to incorporate the technology for security purposes, she changed her opinion about the technology in light of the September 11 terrorist attacks. The public is more at ease with the idea of giving up a little privacy if it means the possibility of preventing even greater tragedies. "Possibility" is the keyword here, indeed. In actuality, the systems have yet to identify one "bad guy."

Some facial identification advocates say that the cameras have not caught any suspects because the systems have been successful in deterring terrorists and other criminals from entering the protected area. Others, like the single dissenter of the Virginia Beach decision, are more skeptical. Her research of the software led her to conclude that it was not worth giving up a sense of liberty for the marginal security benefits that these products provide.

For many, privacy is the most obvious and overriding concern. One aspect that bothers many people is both the incompleteness or the over-inclusive content of the database against which individuals' likeness is being compared. Virginia Beach police have minimized this concern with an agreement stating that they will only enter pictures of runaways, wanted felons and people suffering from dementia into the database. The Visionics' CEO announced that its system, FaceIt facial recognition, captures the images of faces taken from security cameras in airports and creates a unique mathematical identifier called a "faceprint" for each face. The faceprint is compared to those already stored in the database and if it doesn't match one of a terrorist, then the subject is not stopped and there is no record of that particular faceprint going through the system. The system simply doesn't recognize or identify the face.

Tampa police, who have a different system, have said that it is their practice to discard information on seemingly innocent faces in the crowd, but there is no requirement to do so. Nor is there any rule against the police scanning drivers license photos of passersby. The president of Visionics Corp. seems to be committed to minimizing privacy concerns involved with using his technology. He agrees that the federal government needs to regulate the use of facial identification systems.

Limiting the class of persons whose images are stored in a database is an important issue to be addressed by Congress. Although this may be a start, for many this doesn't safeguard the public from routine violations of privacy. Even facial recognition corporations admit the possibility of people getting unauthorized access to the data collected with the technology. The more widespread the technology becomes, the higher the privacy risks associated with its use.

Those concerned with privacy also point out the fact that the software only helps in situations where security services are aware of certain individuals. Some insist that these databases are not effective in catching unknown, foreign visitors to the United States and that those are the types of people we are trying to stop at the terminal.

The accuracy of the systems has also been a real concern. Even if a subject's face is stored in the database, a disguise or even a minor change in appearance, like wearing sunglasses or wearing or growing a mustache can often fool the system. Even an unusual facial expression can confuse the software. Facial identifiers often cannot distinguish twins. Other factors affecting the reliability of the images are changes in the lighting and the angle at which the photos are taken.

The industry is working hard to make the systems "smarter." After September 11, Visionics redoubled its efforts to create reliable facial recognition equipment. According to one National Institute of Justice Standards and Technology study, the industry still has a lot of work to do. The systems often have difficulty recognizing the effects of aging. NIJ's study found that digitally-compared photographs of people taken 18 months apart produced false rejections by the face identification program approximately 43 percent of the time. Manually controlled face identifiers, which are used by casinos, driver's license bureaus, welfare offices, for instance, are more successful than public surveillance systems because they allow the user to obtain high-quality photos of subjects. The pictures are taken in the same lighting, with the same camera, and the user typically requires the subject to look straight into the camera for the photo. These uses are not as troubling to those concerned with privacy infringement because in many of these circumstances, you give up a little privacy when you choose to participate in certain activities or services. The thought of being watched every time we step outside our homes, however, makes almost anyone squeamish, doesn't it?

Visionics' FaceIt technology measures 80 facial structures and calculates a "face print," which contains the physical measurements of your skull and your face. The company maintains that this face print is identity specific and is not affected by aging, viewing conditions, and superficial disguises. Other experts warn that the company, and other companies like it, may be misrepresenting the actual accuracy of their systems. While the actual technology is quite accurate, the systems that use the software are not always the best quality, nor are the databases' stored images. This is where the true problems with accuracy occur, according to industry leaders. Taking into account these factors, one company has estimated that the probability of capturing a terrorist, using facial recognition technology, is between 60 to 90 percent. Considering the deterrent effect this likely has on terrorist travelers, the use of these systems in airports may well be seen as a positive security measure.

Industry insiders rave about how exciting it is that this software is often compatible with the computers and cameras already in use by airports, banks, and other corporations. Because the technology is getting less expensive, it is becoming more and more attractive to private institutions as a way of preventing fraud. Many access-control uses of the technology are more acceptable when our safety and identity is in need of protection. However, public video surveillance uses of the technology raise unique privacy concerns that will need to be addressed in the courts.

The Senate is expected to address some very important issues regarding the use of these systems in airports, including whether or not the database information will be available on the Internet. Assuming that the law will require that database information be kept secure on discrete systems, the laws will also have to address how entities can ensure and maintain that level of privacy for the protection of their customers' or the public's rights.

The public understandably fears the worst with this modern and mysterious capability. There is no doubt that facial recognition systems can have a very positive impact on modern commerce as well as on crime-fighting, but there must be guidelines and limitations to the use of the technology to make it more privacy-friendly.

Some current and projected uses of the technology:

• The city of Santa Ana, California uses "MugMatch," a current generation automated mug shot system, which uses face pattern recognition algorithms, of which can be accessed and searched from a PC.

• In 1988, the Lakewood Division of the Los Angeles County Sheriff's Department started using composite drawings of a suspect or video images to conduct a search on its database of digitized mugshots. The same department also plans to search for suspects on a photo database of registered sex offenders

• . National Institute of Justice is funding projects involving the development and integration of software with facial identification modules. It has successfully integrated face recognition with still photographs. Still in the developmental stages is the integration of face recognition for video, newsgroup search agents, text categorization, and age progressio

• n. Gang Reporting Evaluation Tracking (GREAT) system can be queried using photographs of suspects so that law enforcement can circumvent any false identification cards and information presented by gang membe

• rs. In 1998, West Virginia became the first state to integrate facial identification technology into the drivers license application system. The system keeps a digital record of an applicant's image to prevent people from getting a driver's license under a false identity. Fingerprints can also be stored on the licenses to safeguard proper identification at stores and other locati

- ons. The Illinois State police and Secretary of State will have digitized the photographs of everyone licensed to drive in the state.
More than 100 American casinos use Biometrica Systems, a type of facial recognition system, to scan for cheaters and dishonest money counters

- . Integrated Law Enforcement Face-Identification System (ILEFIS) has been called the "next generation" face-identification technology. It incorporates a novel 3D-composite technology that can more easily identify angled-view face shots. This system will be helpful in correctly identifying non-cooperative suspects or subjects caught from a distance on a video surveillance camera.
The U.S. Army and West Virginia University have highly respected biometrics programs

- . West Virginia's Missing Children Clearinghouse uses the technology to look for missing children. Scanned pictures found on the internet are digitally compared to the images of children stored in its databas

- e. There is still talk about a national ID card even though such proposals have been rejected by the President's administration and the idea was not favored by most security industry experts. Other uses of biometrically encoded ID cards: passports, institutional and commercial uses for limiting access to secure areas or accounts, for verifying government benefit recipients, driver's licenses, and government ID car

- ds. The London borough Newham, numerous U.S. embassies, and the Los Angeles area have all used face recognition syst

- ems. Britain uses more than 200,000 video cameras for surveillance. Many of these are now being set up with facial recognition software. These systems generally use a computer that monitors the cameras, which are looking for known criminals. When the system identifies someone, the police are called to res

- pond. One new biometric system is the actual infrared heat pattern of the face. This allows the system to work in the dark.
Fresno International Airport uses facial recognition technology

- . The Israeli-Palestinian border uses both face recognition and hand geometry and will be incorporating INSPASS, a hand geometry system that is used for immigration in the U.S. and Canad

- a. The Department of Defense has a facial recognition system in place.

Appendix 28

Biometrics FAQ
http://www.inttelix.com/face-recognition-faq.php

1. What is biometrics?

Biometrics is the science of measuring and studying biological data. In I.T., biometrics refers to technologies that measure and analyze human body characteristics, such as fingerprints, eye retinas and irises, voice patterns, facial patterns and hand measurements, for authentication purposes.

2. What is the most common biometrics?

Fingerprints have been using successfully in a law enforcement environment for over 100 years. New biometrics systems have emerged in recent years including Hand Geometry, Iris Recognition, Retina Recognition, Signature Verification, Vein Patterns, Facial Recognition and DNA.

3. What is a Facial Recognition System?

Facial Recognition system is a computer program that is used for identifying a person automatically. Research on this technology started in the mid 1960s. The technology works by using several facial features in a person's image and comparing these with existing images in the database. Facial recognition systems are used as an additional and mass security measure and are comparable to the other biometric security systems available today such as retina scanners, fingerprint scanners, etc.

4. How well do biometrics work?

Used in the right environment, biometrics can make a major contribution to improving security. It has to be understood that no single biometric that can be used in real-time is 100% accurate. However when used in conjunction with a personal identifier such as an ID card or PIN, it can be a very effective means for verifying one's individuality. Its importance generally comes as an aid to recognition rather than guaranteeing someone's identity.

5. How are biometrics selected?

While the emphasis will differ in different applications, the following criteria are used to determine which biometric should be used in a specific application:
accuracy
speed
intrusiveness

6. How does biometrics work?

Almost all biometrics work essentially in the same way. The finger/face/iris is scanned and the locations of key features of the pattern relative to each other are determined. This information is transformed into a digital string and then it is added to the individual's record. When a match is undertaken, the process is repeated and a second string is generated. By matching this string with the one on the individual's record and comparing the result to a user-specified acceptance threshold, the system can establish the facts on the individual's claim on his identity.

7. What is the Technology behind Facial Recognition Systems?

The most important factor in Facial Recognition systems is its ability to differentiate between the background and the face. This is very important when the system has to identify a face within a crowd. The system then makes use of a person's facial features - its peaks, valleys and landmarks - and treats these as nodes that can be measured and compared against those that are stored in the system database. There are approximately 80 nodes comprising the face print that the system makes use of and this includes the jaw line length, eye socket depth and distance between the eyes, cheekbone shape, and the width of the nose.

8. What is FAR, FRR ?

The accuracy of face recognition system is often defined in terms of two parameters, False Rejection Rate (FRR) and False Acceptance Rate (FAR).

FRR measures how often an authorized user, who should be granted access, is not recognized, while FAR measures how often non-authorized user, who should not be granted access, is falsely recognized.

The control of FRR and FAR through recognition threshold adjustment defines the accuracy of face recognition system. When the recognition threshold is increased, it will adversely cause FAR to decrease. At the same time however, the increase of recognition threshold will result in the increase of FRR. For example, when recognition threshold is set at 100%, FRR rate will increase to its highest level.

9. What is Live Detection?

Live Detection Technology detects and memorizes the background where the camera is facing as part of parameters for identification and verification process. It can effectively detect the difference between a photo and a person in order to prevent imposters to gain access using photos

10. What is Moving Detection?

Face Recognition System is equipped with moving detection function that analyzes the captured image periodically to identify the presence of a moving object and its position. The face detection function then analyzes images to detect a human face and its position.

These two functions can be integrated to provide automated surveillance for detecting moving faces, positioning and data recording. The records can be used in Face Recognition System for enrollment purpose.

11. Three-Dimensional facial Recognition Systems

The new facial recognition systems make use of three-dimensional images and are thus more accurate than their predecessors. Just like two-dimensional facial recognition systems, these systems make use of distinct features in a human face and use them as nodes to create a face print of a person. Unlike two-dimensional face recognition systems, however, they have the ability to recognize a face even when it is turned 90 degrees away from the camera. Moreover, they are not affected by the differences in lighting and facial expressions of the subject.

Appendix 29

20 Years Later, the Lockerbie Terror Attack Is Not as Solved as We Think
By Nathan Thrall
January 2, 2009
http://webcache.googleusercontent.com/search?q=cache:vhl86yRlg2kJ:www.us
news.com/opinion/articles/2009/01/02/20-years-later-the-lockerbie-terror-
attack-is-not-as-solved-as-we-
think+terror+Lockerbie+Scotland&cd=3&hl=en&ct=clnk&gl=ca

Twenty years after Pan Am 103 exploded over Lockerbie, Scotland, killing all 259 passengers and crew, as well as 11 residents of the town below, it appears that resolution has finally come to the decades-long mystery surrounding the worst terrorist attack in British history and the deadliest attack on American civilians before 9/11.

A Libyan intelligence officer has been convicted of murdering Lockerbie's 270 victims; the Libyan government, in a letter to the United Nations, has "accepted responsibility for the actions of its officials"; and less than two months ago, Libya completed payments of $1.5 billion to victims of terrorism, including Lockerbie's 189 American victims (35 of them Syracuse University students returning home from study abroad). Sanctions against Libya have been lifted, the United States has granted Libya immunity from further terrorism-related lawsuits, and the Senate confirmed the first U.S. ambassador to Libya in 36 years.

"We're proud to announce we won, and Libya has been held accountable," Sen. Frank Lautenberg, a New Jersey Democrat, said at a November news conference with the families of victims. One of the victims' relatives added, "We are free now to close this chapter in our nightmare."

But though a chapter may have closed, the Lockerbie case is today further from resolution than it has been since the investigation began 20 years ago.

An official Scottish review body has declared that a "miscarriage of justice may have occurred" in the conviction of the Libyan intelligence officer, Abdelbaset al-Megrahi. The reviewers examined a secret document, provided to the United Kingdom by a foreign government and seen during Megrahi's trial by only the prosecution, that they said cast serious doubts on Megrahi's guilt. A new appeal of Megrahi's conviction is scheduled for this coming spring. The U.N. special observer appointed by Kofi Annan to Megrahi's trial, Hans Koechler, has declared that Megrahi was wrongfully convicted, as have the legal architect of his special trial, Prof. Robert Black, and a spokesperson for the families of the British victims, Jim Swire.

Piece by piece, the major elements of the prosecution's case are falling apart. A high-ranking Scottish police officer has said vital evidence was fabricated. One of the FBI's principal forensic experts has been discredited. The lord advocate—Scotland's chief legal officer—who initiated the Lockerbie prosecution has called the credibility of the government's primary witness into question, stating that the man was "not quite the full shilling...an apple short of a picnic." Another prosecution witness now claims, in a July 2007 sworn affidavit, to have lied about the key piece of evidence linking Libya to the bombing. So if the case against Megrahi and his government is so thin, why would Libya pay compensation to the families of Lockerbie's victims?

One answer came from Libya's prime minister. He told the BBC that his government took no responsibility for Lockerbie and had merely "bought peace," agreeing to pay compensation to the families of victims because it was the only means of ending the far more costly sanctions against his country. Saif al-Qadhafi, the Libyan leader's son and one of the regime's most prominent spokespersons, recently told CNN that Megrahi "had nothing to do with Lockerbie." When asked why his government would pay the victims of a terrorist act in which they played no role, Qadhafi responded, "There was no other way around. Because there was a resolution from the Security Council, and you have to do it. Otherwise, you will not get rid of the sanctions. It was very political. Very political."

Megrahi has been diagnosed with prostate cancer and may not live to see his second appeal. If he does live and his appeal succeeds, a new and independent international investigation—as has been called for by the U.N. observer to the Lockerbie trial—may commence. If it does, the investigators will return to the primary suspect of the first year and a half of the original investigation: a cell of the Popular Front for the Liberation of Palestine-General Command, whose bank account, according to a CIA officer involved in the investigation, received a transfer of $11 million two days after Lockerbie and whose leaders the investigators believed had been contracted by Iran to avenge America's inadvertent shooting down of an Iranian civilian airliner carrying 290 passengers and crew.

Appendix 30

7 July 2005 London bombings
http://webcache.googleusercontent.com/search?q=cache:5o2EQX_0f2cJ:en.wikipedia.org/wiki/7_July_2005_London_bombings+tube+bombing+in+london&cd=1&hl=en&ct=clnk&gl=ca

Bombers - Profiles

The four suicide bombers were later identified and named as:

The four bombers captured on CCTV at Luton station at 7:21 am on 7 July 2005. From left to right: Hasib Hussain, Germaine Lindsay, Mohammad Sidique Khan, and Shehzad Tanweer.

Mohammad Sidique Khan: aged 30 and of Pakistani descent. Khan detonated his bomb just after leaving Edgware Road on a train travelling toward Paddington, at 8:50 a.m. He lived in Beeston, Leeds, with his wife and young child, where he worked as a learning mentor at a primary school. The blast killed seven people, including Khan himself.

Shehzad Tanweer: aged 22 and also of Pakistani descent. He detonated a bomb aboard a train travelling between Liverpool Street and Aldgate, at 8:50 a.m. He lived in Leeds with his mother and father, working in a fish and chip shop. He was killed by the explosion along with seven members of the public.

Germaine Lindsay: 19-year-old Jamaican-born Lindsay detonated his device on a train travelling between King's Cross-St. Pancras and Russell Square, at 8:50 a.m. He lived in Aylesbury, Buckinghamshire, with his pregnant wife and young son. His blast killed 27 people, including Lindsay himself.

Hasib Hussain: the youngest of the quartet at 18 years of age, Hussain, who was of Pakistani descent, detonated his bomb on the top deck of a double-decker bus at 9:47 a.m. He lived in Leeds with his brother and sister-in-law. Fourteen people, including Hussain, perished in the explosion in Tavistock Square.

Charles Clarke, Home Secretary when the attacks occurred, described the bombers as "cleanskins," a term describing them as previously unknown to authorities until they carried out their attacks.

Appendix 31

Deadliest terrorist strikes, worldwide
http://webcache.googleusercontent.com/search?q=cache:47vN6aEW89AJ:www.johnstonsarchive.net/terrorism/wrjp255i.html+worst+terrorist+acts&cd=1&hl=en&ct=clnk&gl=ca

Date of attack, location and fatalities injuries:

- 11 Sep 2001 crashing of hijacked planes into World Trade Center, New York City, New York, Pentagon in Alexandria, Virginia, and site in Pennsylvania, USA 2,993 8,900
- 14 Aug 2007 multiple car bombings in Al-Qataniyah and Al-Adnaniyah, Iraq 520 1,500
- 20 Aug 1978 arson of theater in Abadan, Iran 477 ?
- 1-3 Sep 2004 hostage taking at school in Beslan, Russia (includes 30 terrorists killed) 366 747
- 23 Jun 1985 mid-air bombing of Air India flight off Ireland, and attempted bombing of second flight in Canada 331 4
- 12 Mar 1993 15 bombings in Bombay, India 317 1,400
- 8 Aug 1998 truck bombings of U.S. embassies in Nairobi, Kenya, and Dar es Saalam, Tanzania 303 4,954
- 23 Oct 1983 truck bombings of U.S. Marine and French barracks, Beirut, Lebanon 301 161
- 22 Sep 1997 attack at Ben Talha, Algeria 277 ?
- 30 Dec 1997 attack at Ami Moussa, Algeria 272 ?
- 21 Dec 1988 mid-air bombing of Pan Am flight over Lockerbie, Scotland 270 12
- 20 Nov-5 Dec 1979 hostage taking at Grand Mosque in Mecca, Saudi Arabia (includes 87 terrorists killed) 240 600
- 21 Feb 2004 armed attack and arson at refugee camp, Uganda 239 60
- 29 Aug 1997 attacks at Sidi Moussa and Hais Rais, Algeria 238 ?
- 31 Oct 1999 intentional crash of Egypt Air flight off Massachusetts, USA, by pilot 217 0
- 12 Oct 2002 car bombing outside nightclub in Kuta, Indonesia 202 350
- 23 Nov 2006 multiple car bombings in Baghdad, Iraq 202 250
- 11 Jul 2006 multiple bombings on commuter trains in Mumbai, India 200 714
- 18 Apr 2007 multiple bombings in Baghdad, Iraq 193 197
- 11 Mar 2004 bombings of four trains in Madrid, Spain 191 1,876
- 2 Mar 2004 multiple suicide bombings at shrines in Kadhimiya and Karbala, Iraq 188 430

- 14 Sep 2005 multiple suicide bombings and shooting attacks in Baghdad, Iraq 182 679
- 7 Jul 2007 multiple suicide truck bombings in Armili and area, Iraq 182 270
- 26-29 Nov 2008 multiple shooting and grenade attacks and hostage takings in Mumbai, India (includes 9 terrorists killed) 174 370
- 4 Jan 1998 attacks at Had Chekala, Remka, and Ain Tarik, Algeria 172 ?
- 19 Sep 1989 mid-air bombing of French UTA flight near Bilma, Niger 171 0
- 26 Oct 2002 hostage taking and attempted rescue in theater in Moscow, Russia (includes 41 terrorists killed) 170 656
- 19 Apr 1995 truck bombing of federal building, Oklahoma City, Oklahoma, USA 169 675
- 16 Apr 1925 bombing of cathedral in Sophia, Bulgaria 160 ?
- 25 Oct 2009 two vehicle bombings at government buildings in Baghdad, Iraq 155 540
- 27 Mar 2007 two truck bombings in Tal Afar, Iraq 152 347
- 10 Aug 2001 attack on train south of Luanda, Angola 152 146
- 14 May 1985 armed attack on crowds in Anuradhapura, Sri Lanka 150 ?
- 14-19 June 1996 hostage taking in Budennovsk, Russia, and two failed rescue attempts 143 435
- 18 Oct 2007 bombing of motorcade in Karachi, Pakistan 140 540
- 3 Aug 1990 armed attack at two mosques in Kathankudy, Sri Lanka 140 70
- 3 Feb 2007 truck bombing in marketplace in Baghdad, Iraq 137 334
- 6 Mar 2007 two suicide bombings and additional attacks in Hilla, Iraq 137 310
- 28 Feb 2005 car bombing outside medical clinic in Hilla, Iraq 135 130
- 2 Oct 1990 crash of hijacked PRC airliner in Guangzhou, PRC 132 49
- 13 Sep 1999 bombing of apartment building in Moscow, Russia 130 150
- 8 Dec 2009 five car bombings in Baghdad, Iraq 127 448
- 18 Apr 1987 roadway ambush near Alut Oya, Sri Lanka 127 64
- 23 Nov 1996 crash of hijacked Ethiopian Air flight off Comoros 127 48
- 29 Aug 2003 car bombing outside mosque in Najaf, Iraq 125 500
- 5 Jan 2006 bombings in Karbala, Ramadi, and Baghdad, Iraq 124 203
- 13 Aug 1990 armed attack at mosque in Eravur, Sri Lanka 122 79
- 28 Oct 2009 bombing at marketplace in Peshawar, Pakistan 118 213
- 27 Feb 2004 bombing and fire on ferry near Manila, Philippines 118 9
- 29 Nov 1987 mid-air bombing of Korean Air flight near Burma 115 0
- 23 Sep 1983 crash of Gulf Air flight following mid-air bombing over the UAE 112 0
- 27 Nov 1989 mid-air bombing of Avianca flight in Bogota, Columbia 110 ?

- 1 Feb 2004 two suicide bombings of political party offices in Irbil, Iraq 109 240
- 21 Apr 1987 bombing of bus depot in Columbo, Sri Lanka 106 295
- 22 Sep 1993 crash of airliner struck by missile in Sukhumi, Georgia 106 26
- 17 Feb 2008 suicide bombing at dogfighting festival, Kandahar, Afghanistan 105 65
- 24 Jun 2004 multiple bombings and armed attacks in several cities in Iraq 103 324
- 16 Oct 2006 suicide bombing of military convoy near Habarana, Sri Lanka 103 150
- 11 Jan 1998 attack on movie theater and mosque at Sidi Hamed, Algeria 103 70
- 19 Aug 2009 multiple bombings at government sites in Baghdad, Iraq 102 500
- 10 May 2010 multiple bombings in Hilla, Basra, al-Suwayra, and other cities, Iraq 102 350
- 4-10 Jul 2007 hostage taking and army storming of mosque in Islamabad, Pakistan 102 ?
- 22 Jan 2007 multiple bombings and mortar attack on marketplaces in Baghdad and Baquba, Iraq 101 186
- 13 Dec 1921 bombing of Bolgard palace in Bessarabia (modern Moldova) 100 ?
- 18 May 1973 mid-air bombing of Aeroflot airliner, Siberia 100 0
- 4 Dec 1977 crash of hijacked Malaysian airliner near Malaysia 100 0

Appendix 32

Significant terrorist acts using unconventional weapons
http://webcache.googleusercontent.com/search?q=cache:47vN6aEW89AJ:www.johnstonsarchive.net/terrorism/wrjp255i.html+worst+terrorist+acts&cd=1&hl=en&ct=clnk&gl=ca

Date of attack, location and fatalities injuries:

- Apr 2007 suicide bombing with truck carrying chlorine tanks in Ramadi, Iraq 35 50
- 6 Sep 1987 water poisoning with pesticide at constabulary in Zamboanga City, Philippines 19 140
- 21 Jan 1994 attack with chemical grenades on village of Ormancik, Turkey 16 ?
- 28 Jan 2007 explosion of truck bomb carrying chlorine tank 16 ?
- 20 Mar 1995 sarin nerve gas attack in subway in Toyko, Japan 12 5,511
- 20 Feb 2007 bombing of chlorine tanker truck in Taji, Iraq 9 150
- 16 Mar 2007 two suicide bombings using trucks carrying chlorine tanks in Falluja, Iraq 8 350
- 27 Jun 1994 nerve gas attack in Matsumoto, Japan 7 270
- 21 Feb 2007 explosion of car bomb carrying chlorine tanks in Baghdad, Iraq 6 73
- 9 Oct 2001 anthrax-laced letters mailed to Washington, DC, USA 4 7
- 18 Sep 2001 anthrax-laced letters mailed to West Palm Beach, Florida, USA, and New York City, New York, USA 1 10
- 19 Apr 1946 cyanide poisoning in prison near Nuremberg, Germany 0 2,283
- 9-19 Sep 1984 salmonella poisoning in restaurants in The Dalles, Oregon, USA 0 751
- 19 Apr 1995 tear gas attack in Yokohama, Japan 0 272

Appendix 33

Terrorist attacks producing high numbers of non-fatal injuries*
http://webcache.googleusercontent.com/search?q=cache:47vN6aEW89AJ:www.
johnstonsarchive.net/terrorism/wrjp255i.html+worst+terrorist+acts&cd=1&hl=e
n&ct=clnk&gl=ca

* Includes attacks resulting in 300 or more injuries apart from fatalities. Note than these figures are not as consistently defined by reporting authorities. This listing is incomplete.

Date of attack, location and fatalities injuries:

- 11 Sep 2001 crashing of hijacked planes into World Trade Center, New York City, New York, Pentagon in Alexandria, Virginia, and site in Pennsylvania, USA 2,993 8,900
- 20 Mar 1995 sarin nerve gas attack in subway in Toyko, Japan 12 5,511
- 8 Aug 1998 truck bombings of U.S. embassies in Nairobi, Kenya, and Dar es Saalam, Tanzania 303 4,954
- 19 Apr 1946 cyanide poisoning in prison near Nuremberg, Germany 0 2,283
- 11 Mar 2004 bombings of four trains in Madrid, Spain 191 1,876
- 14 Aug 2007 multiple car bombings in Al-Qataniyah and Al-Adnaniyah, Iraq 520 1,500
- 12 Mar 1993 15 bombings in Bombay, India 317 1,400
- 31 Jan 1996 suicide truck bombing of bank in Colombo, Sri Lanka 91 1,400
- 26 Feb 1993 truck bombing in garage of World Trade Center, New York City, USA 6 1,040
- 6 Dec 1989 truck bombing at federal police building in Bogota, Columbia 52 1,000
- 9-19 Sep 1984 salmonella poisoning in restaurants in The Dalles, Oregon, USA 0 751
- 1-3 Sep 2004 hostage taking at school in Beslan, Russia (includes 35 terrorists killed) 372 747
- 11 Jul 2006 multiple bombings on commuter trains in Mumbai, India 200 714
- 1 Oct 1982 truck bombing in public square in Tehran, Iran 60 700
- 7 Jul 2005 bombings of three subway trains and one bus in London, UK 54 700
- 8 Oct 2006 possible poisoning of food in Numaniyah, Iraq 7? 700?
- 14 Sep 2005 multiple suicide bombings and shooting attacks in Baghdad, Iraq 182 679

- 19 Apr 1995 truck bombing of federal building, Oklahoma City, Oklahoma, USA 169 675
- 26 Oct 2002 hostage taking and attempted rescue in theater in Moscow, Russia (includes 41 terrorists killed) 170 656
- 27 Dec 2002 two car bombings outside government house, Chechnya, Russia 71 640
- 20 Nov-5 Dec 1979 hostage taking at Grand Mosque in Mecca, Saudi Arabia (includes 87 terrorists killed) 240 600
- 17 Jul 1996 bombing of train in Sri Lanka 70 600
- 25 Oct 2009 two vehicle bombings at government buildings in Baghdad, Iraq 155 540
- 18 Oct 2007 bombing of motorcade in Karachi, Pakistan 140 540
- 15 Aug 1998 two car bombings in Omagh, Northern Ireland, UK 29 530
- 26 Jun 1996 truck bombing at U.S. military housing complex in Dhahran, Saudi Arabia 19 515
- 29 Aug 2003 car bombing outside mosque in Najaf, Iraq 125 500
- 19 Aug 2009 multiple bombings at government sites in Baghdad, Iraq 102 500
- 16 Sep 1999 car bombing in Volgodonsk, Russia 17 480
- 8 Dec 2009 five car bombings in Baghdad, Iraq 127 448
- 14-19 June 1996 hostage taking in Budennovsk, Russia, and two failed rescue attempts 143 435
- 2 Mar 2004 multiple suicide bombings at shrines in Kadhimiya and Karbala, Iraq 188 430
- 30 Oct 2008 12 bombings in Guwahati, Kokrajhar, Barpeta Road, and Bongaigaon, India 84 400
- 20 Nov 2003 suicide bombings of British consulate and bank in Istanbul, Turkey 30 400
- 26-29 Nov 2008 multiple shooting and grenade attacks and hostage takings in Mumbai, India 174 370
- 12 Oct 2002 car bombing outside nightclub in Kuta, Indonesia 202 350
- 10 May 2010 multiple bombings in Hilla, Basra, al-Suwayra, and other cities, Iraq 102 350
- 16 Mar 2007 two suicide bombings using trucks carrying chlorine tanks in Falluja, Iraq 8 350
- 27 Mar 2007 two truck bombings in Tal Afar, Iraq 152 347
- 3 Feb 2007 truck bombing in marketplace in Baghdad, Iraq 137 334
- 24 Jun 2004 multiple bombings and armed attacks in several cities in Iraq 103 324
- 26 Sep 1980 suicide bombing in Munich, West Germany 13 312
- 6 Mar 2007 two suicide bombings and additional attacks in Hilla, Iraq 137 310
- 1 Aug 1980 bombing at railway station in Bologna, Italy 85 300
- 1 Oct 1981 car bombing in Beirut, Lebanon 83 300

- 14 Jul 1987 twin car bombs and two other bombs in shopping area in Karachi, Pakistan 72 300
- 15 Dec 1976 bombing at airport in Baghdad, Iraq 40 300
- 16 Sep 1920 bombing near bank in New York City, New York, USA 34 300
- 5 Mar 1998 bombing of bus in Colombo, Sri Lanka 32 300

Appendix 34

March 20, 1995: Poison Gas Wreaks Tokyo Subway Terror
By Randy Alfred 03.20.09
http://webcache.googleusercontent.com/search?q=cache:kcYThoVV0NEJ:www.wired.com/science/discoveries/news/2009/03/dayintech_0320+20+Mar+1995+sarin+nerve+gas+attack+in+subway+in+Toyko,+Japan&cd=3&hl=en&ct=clnk&gl=ca

1995: Religious cultists release the toxic nerve gas sarin at multiple locations in the Tokyo subway. A dozen people will die, and thousands suffer injuries ranging from mild to severe.

Aum Shinrikyo was a Japanese cult combining bits of Buddhism, Hinduism, shamanism and end-of-days Christianity. The name combined the Buddhist mantra om with the Japanese for "supreme truth."

With a worldwide membership of 20,000 to 40,000, Aum had a net worth in 1995 of about $1.5 billion. It made money through standard religious techniques like donations, tithing and paraphernalia sales. It also employed the New Age technique of high-priced indoctrination seminars. In addition, it ran some businesses, including a restaurant chain and a computer factory that assembled Taiwanese electronic components into computers it sold at its own downtown Tokyo store.

The cult also built a facility to manufacture biological and chemical weapons by the ton. Aum experimented with botulin toxin, anthrax, cholera, Q fever and the Ebola virus. Operatives tried to release botulin near the Diet in 1990, and near the imperial palace in 1993. An anthrax release from its Tokyo office building in 1993 caused foul smells, brown steam, pet deaths and stains on cars and sidewalks. None of these attacks is known to have caused death or injury.

Things changed on June 27, 1994. Cult members drove a truck to a residential neighborhood in Matsumoto, about 200 miles northwest of Tokyo, then used a computer system to remotely release a cloud of sarin. Their primary targets were three judges who lived there and were about to rule against the cult in a big real estate case.

Sarin was first created in Nazi Germany. The volatile nerve agent is 500 times more toxic than cyanide: A single pinhead-size drop can kill an adult. The Matsumoto sarin attack killed seven people and injured 500, of whom 200 were admitted to hospitals at least overnight.

Despite all that, Aum Shinrikyo managed to pull off its most audacious — and deadly — attack just nine months later. In the Monday morning rush hour of

March 20, five cult members boarded different subway trains converging on central Tokyo.

Four of them each carried two plastic bags loaded with sarin, and the fifth had three bags. At nearly the same moment, they each dropped the bags to the floor of the jam-packed train and punctured them with a specially sharpened umbrella tip. The cultists then quickly stepped off the trains as they pulled into the next station. Getaway drivers were waiting outside the station for each of them.

The liquid began vaporizing, and people began getting sick. Some of them got off the trains at subsequent stations, stumbling onto the platforms. At each stop, more gas spread, and more liquid was tracked off the trains and into the stations. The deadly sarin vapor also clung to the clothes and bodies of its victims, sickening those who rushed to their aid.

Some of the trains continued traveling — one for an hour and 40 minutes — before finally stopping to deal with the emergency ... and stop spreading it. Emergency and hospital services later got heavily criticized for the uncoordinated response.

Symptoms included bleeding from the nose and mouth, coma, convulsions, difficulty breathing, extreme sensitivity to light, flulike symptoms, foaming at the mouth, fevers, loss of consciousness, loss of memory, loss of vision, nausea, vomiting, paralysis, respiratory problems, seizures and uncontrollable trembling. Some survivors suffered these problems permanently, along with disturbed sleep, nightmares and post-traumatic stress disorder.

Many victims with initially mild symptoms went to work before sickening later and going to the hospital. Others probably never sought medical care. Estimates of the injured range from 3,800 up to 6,000. The sarin killed 12 people.

Police began raiding cult buildings and property all over Japan within 48 hours, wearing hazmat equipment that had been issued to them for this purpose ... the week before the Tokyo attack. The cult had in fact gotten wind of an impending crackdown and unleashed its subway attack to kill police officers.

The Japanese government revoked Aum Shinrikyo's status a religion and seized as many of the cult's assets as it could find. Some members later reorganized on a much smaller scale as Aleph (the first letter of the Hebrew alphabet and a key symbol in mathematical set theory).

About 200 people were arrested. About 20 are either still in Japan's lengthy trial process standing trial or have already been convicted. At least eight Aum members, including the founder, have received death sentences for their roles in the attack.

Appendix 35

A Prescription for Safeguarding Against Terrorist Attacks
July 2006
http://www.homelandsecurity.org/journal/Default.aspx?oid=146&ocat=1

Since the 11 September attacks, much of the literature on terror has focused on the psychology of terrorism rather than on identifying attacks that may occur. While the psychology of terrorists is important, it doesn't do much to help those responsible for defending against terrorist acts. One thing should be remembered: terrorists, whoever they may be (Middle Eastern, Asian, European, or domestic), will use whatever tools are most suitable that they're trained to use and are available.

In "A Terrorist Target Selection and Prioritization Model" (2003),[1] the senior authors described a mathematical model they believed to be of the type used by al-Qaeda planners in selecting targets. By using this model, those responsible for safeguarding against acts of terrorism would have a heads-up as to which targets terrorists are likely to attack. To demonstrate the model, a terrorist assessment team of eight specialists played the role of terrorists in an action where the target was a Florida county with no obvious strategic sites. Using the model in a process of several steps, they identified 99 terrorist events, then determined the impact and likelihood for each event. The product of a given event's impact and likelihood constitutes that event's "expected value." By ordering the 99 events according to their expected value, those responsible for providing safeguards reduce to a relatively small number the events for which to prepare.

Next, the assessment team developed three scenarios (involving six terrorist events). Using one scenario (involving two events), they easily carried out a simulated terrorist attack.

In 2003, Joshua Sinai[2] concluded that the failure to anticipate 9/11 was not an intelligence failure but that 9/11 was simply beyond the imagination of those responsible for intelligence and law enforcement. He also emphasized the necessity to "adopt proactive measures to anticipate, defend against, and preempt new types of terrorist threats" and that "terrorists, especially al-Qaeda planners, always seek to exploit new vulnerabilities and new and innovative modes of warfare in order to evade detection and inflict maximum damage." Firmly agreeing with Sinai's conclusions, we believe that we must think like terrorists, determine what they are likely to undertake, and develop appropriate countermeasures.

Since 11 September, much has been done to bolster defenses in the United States. These steps have focused on such sites as airports, tunnels, and bridges. Consequently, these types of sites have become hard targets, a fact of which terrorists are well aware. Even so, the question is whether those focusing on these hard targets are focusing on the areas in which we truly are vulnerable.

In dealing with terrorists, particularly al-Qaeda, we cannot rely on historical trends with regard to sites and attack modes. Instead, we must anticipate unconventional methods, techniques, and targets—which means that we simply must think like terrorists. Furthermore, it would be a another failure in imagination if we as a nation focused exclusively, or nearly exclusively, on geographic areas with many potential hard targets. We should also consider areas where hard targets are scarce, where little thought has been given to the possibility of terrorist attacks.

Methodology

We came to the conclusion that to meaningfully identify potential domestic terrorist attacks, we would need to look at relatively small geographic areas (for example, county by county) rather than at the nation. For this reason we selected Charlotte County, FL, for testing the effectiveness of our Terrorist Target Selection and Prioritization Model. The county is devoid of strategic targets. People who live there, like those in many other areas of the United States, go about their business every day without being particularly concerned about terrorist attacks. Charlotte County3 has approximately 150,000 residents; 35% are age 65 or older. County government and medical and health providers are the leading employment segments, along with the varied retail industry. The county has another interesting and distinguishing feature: it accommodated several of the 11 September terrorists. Mohammed Atta visited restaurants, facilitated overseas cash transfers, and sought aid in a local hospital there. It is reasonable to assume that the county is well known to al-Qaeda planners.

To identify potential terrorist attacks in Charlotte County, we created a team of eight "terror planners" (the authors of this article) with backgrounds in physics-math, psychology, infectious disease, radiation oncology, emergency room medicine, emergency management, environmental health planning, and senior levels of the U.S. military.

Using the equations described in Stungis and Schori's 2003 article on the Terrorist Target Selection and Prioritization Model, our team, thinking like terrorists, identified 99 possible terrorist events (target sites and modes of attack) that might take place in Charlotte County. The planning team judged the likelihood of success (from a terrorist perspective) for each event. Then the team made judgments, using the Stevens Power Function,4 of the impact that each event would have on three terrorist objectives (publicity, with a weight of 0.2; casualty count, with a weight of 0.3; and economic impact, with a weight of 0.5). Cross-impact matrices were also constructed. The product of the likelihood rating and the overall weighted impact associated with each terrorist event constitutes the expected value to the terrorists. Since the likelihood scores are probabilities and the impact scores can range from 0 (no impact on the terrorist objectives) to 8 (maximum on each terrorist objective), the resulting terrorist alert scores can range from 0 to 8.

Results

We believed that it would not be necessary to further consider potential terrorist events that had terrorist alert scores less than 3.0. The terrorist alert scores themselves can be thought of as a type of desirability index (from a terrorist perspective) and as a terrorist alert index (from the perspective of those responsible for safeguarding against terrorist attacks). Thus, we have been able to logically reduce the number of events so that countermeasures can be implemented (see Table 1).

The most attractive event (from a terrorist vantage point) would be a biological attack at a shopping mall in Charlotte County, followed by a suicide bomber attack at a major festival in the county.

For any given terrorist event (such as a biological attack at a shopping mall), terrorists could choose to carry it out in dozens of ways. To provide a look into the thinking of terrorists, we developed three scenarios for carrying out some of the 14 events.

Scenario 1: Vehicle bomb attack, then chemical attack, at a major festival.

Objective: To stage a terrorist attack in Charlotte County, FL, that will kill many and maim many more and thus instill hysteria.

Strategy: A truck bomb attack followed immediately by a chemical attack.

Plan: At a very popular Charlotte County festival, while the maximum number of people is present, three terrorists drive small pickup trucks, through separate festival entrances, directly into the crowds of people. Simultaneously, each terrorist will detonate a 500-lb. charge. Each explosion is expected to kill more than 50 persons and injure many more. Then, coinciding with the explosions, just as soon as survivors are huddling at a point equally distant from the three explosions, a fourth terrorist will use a fire hose to spray the survivors with anhydrous ammonia. At least 10% of those sprayed with the ammonia are likely to die. Many of those who survive will be blinded or horribly burned. So many burns will occur that the county's health services will be unable to handle the volume and severity of the injuries.

These attacks will be completely unexpected and will result in mass panic, not only in the county but across the state and country as well. The immediate economic impact of these attacks will not be great. Only a few hundred people will be killed, and perhaps a thousand or so will be severely injured. The fear that will be created will far exceed the impact of any economic cost.

Scenario 2: Vehicle bomb attack, then a chemical attack at a major shopping mall.

Objective: To stage an attack that will convince the American public that government is powerless to protect them.

Strategy: A vehicle bomb attack will be used to cover an even more deadly chemical attack.

Plan: While crowds are at a maximum, three terrorists will simultaneously, at high speed, drive automobiles into separate entry points of a major shopping mall, directly into the crowds, where each terrorist will detonate 500 pounds of explosives. Each explosion is expected to kill 15 persons and injure another 125. Coinciding with the vehicle detonations, aerosolized sarin (which is more deadly than sarin applied to skin) will be dispensed throughout the mall through the ventilation system. At least 30% of those in the mall remaining alive after the vehicle detonations are likely to die from breathing the gas. There will be many deaths and so many injured that the county's healthcare system will be sorely taxed.

That the attack will have occurred in a quiet, unassuming Florida county will frighten the American public far more than did the deaths and destruction that occurred in New York City on 9/11.

According to the 1997 Economic Census,5 49% of Charlotte County's revenue is attributable to retail sales—a much higher proportion than for the country as a whole. County revenue, then, will be devastated by the economic impact of these attacks. But it will go far beyond Charlotte County. Throughout the country, people will stay away from shopping malls because if such an attack can happen in a county in Florida, it can happen anywhere. The recession from which the country is emerging will return with a vengeance.

Scenario 3: Biological attacks in hospitals followed by suicide bomber attacks in a popular shopping mall.

Objective: To paralyze the state of Florida and have an impact on the entire United States.

Strategy: To surreptitiously attack a key industry—health care—and overtly attack the retail industry.

Plan: Three individuals armed with two-ounce hairspray containers filled with a critical solution of smallpox virus in water would enter Charlotte County's three hospitals approximately 15 minutes before the peak lunch hour. They would proceed to the hospital cafeteria and approach the salad bar, fruit bar, or suitable equivalent. They would carefully spray the solution over the bar, obtain a salad, and go to a nearby table and observe. Afterward they would leave the hospital at a leisurely pace. The process would be repeated before dinner—again in the cafeteria. The same steps would be taken the next day.

After 12 days, the infection rate for healthcare workers would be about 80%, while that for hospital patients would probably be around 90%; families of workers and patients would also have a very high rate of exposure that would, in all likelihood, lead to infection.

On the 12th day, at dinnertime, all three terrorists would independently proceed to the food court in Charlotte County's main shopping mall. Sitting separately at key locations, they each would detonate explosive packs of 25 pounds of a nitrate compound. This would kill about 50 people and injure another 100 or so. The casualties would be rushed to hospitals that are severely biologically contaminated. At this point, hospital personnel and others would be at the threshold of showing the pox symptoms. County deaths could easily be in the thousands, and an ultimate financial loss of millions of dollars could be expected.

The terrorists would have released a videotape describing their mission and telling Americans to expect more. Across Florida and the United States, the healthcare system would be in panic and the retail industry would crumble. Two-thirds of the U.S. gross national product6 is accounted for by consumer spending. In all probability, the United States would rapidly go into a depression.

With all the discussion in the news media about terrorists and the potential for terrorist attacks, rational people might be led to believe that many safeguards have been put into place. Shortly after deaths started occurring from anthrax contamination of the U.S. mail, there was much discussion, for example, about the possibility of terrorists staging smallpox attacks. One might assume that hospitals, at least, would have implemented safeguards.

The three scenarios we described are just that—scenarios, not forecasts of doom. All in all, Charlotte County is no doubt a low-probability target for terrorist events. In fact, while a cutoff terrorist alert score of 3.0 may make sense for a given county in identifying what deserves to be safeguarded against, the government of the state in which that county is located should probably not become involved for county terrorist alert scores lower than 5. Likewise, the federal government should probably not become involved for county terrorist alert scores lower than 6.

Our intent was to demonstrate how an attack process unfolds and what the targets and modes of attack might be. Most of the counties in Florida (or any other state) could be handled, using the Terrorist Target Selection and Prioritization Model, in a similar way. Larger areas in Florida (such as Miami-Dade County or Tampa–St. Petersburg–Clearwater) would be evaluated somewhat differently.

The process shows the overall steps involved in planning an attack. Obviously, defenders cannot plan for all possible contingencies. The procedure is not a replacement for good intelligence data (which are not always available). Using the model allows a structure for attacks, a reduction of possible attack targets and modes, and the ability to view alternatives—facilitating defense planning and allocation of resources.

Conclusions

Starting with no a priori beliefs as to what terrorists might undertake, we were able to use the mode to cost-effectively identify and prioritize what terrorists might undertake within the county. By knowing what constitutes high-priority potential targets, those responsible for the at-risk entities (hospitals, festivals, etc.) have the opportunity to implement countermeasures designed to avoid (or reduce the severity of) terrorist attacks.

Not only political or military entities may become targets of terrorist attacks. Consider Illinois State University, with 22-story twin dormitories in which over 2,000 students reside, and State Farm Insurance Company's national headquarters a mile or so away. It would make sense for planners in such entities to assess their vulnerabilities to terrorist acts but, unfortunately, they probably aren't doing so. As Joshua Sinai indicated, as a nation, we don't suffer from intelligence failures so much as from failures in imagination.

Recommendations

Because it is both effective and cost-efficient, the Stungis-Schori Terrorist Target Selection and Prioritization Model should be widely used by federal, state, county, and city governments and other entities to assess vulnerabilities to terrorist attacks.

If the methodology we used in Charlotte County is faithfully followed in assessing other entities, the resulting terrorist alert scores will be useful in comparing the vulnerabilities in one entity with those in another. In Charlotte County, a terrorist alert score of 3.0 is the point at which one should start developing countermeasures, as opposed to ignoring the threats.

Author Contact Information
George E. Stungis, Ph.D.

Thomas R. Schori, Ph.D.
Mark O. Asperilla, M.D.
Larry G. Beebe
Raymond A. James, D.O.
Rufus C. Lazzell
David J. Rice, M.D.
Wayne P. Salladé

References

1. George E. Stungis and Thomas R. Schori, "A Terrorist Target Selection and Prioritization Model," Journal of Homeland Security, March 2003.

2. Joshua Sinai, "How to Forecast and Preempt al-Qaeda's Catastrophic Terrorist Warfare," Journal of Homeland Security, August 2003.

3. Robert Carpenter, Charlotte County, Florida, Statistical Prospectus, 2002-2003 edition, Charlotte County Chamber of Commerce, Punta Gorda, FL.

4. G.A.V. Borg and L. E. Marks, "Twelve Meanings of the Measure Constant in Psychological Power Functions," Bulletin of the Psychonomic Society, vol. 21, pp. 73-75, 1983.

5. 1997 Economic Census, U.S. Census Bureau, Washington, DC.

6. 2002 Statistical Abstract of the United States, U.S. Census Bureau, Washington, DC.

Appendix 36

Terrorist Targets
http://www.historyofwar.org/articles/concepts_terrortargets.html

The choice of target for a terrorist organisations is far from random. What often defines a terrorist group as opposed to those who claim to be freedom fighters or a liberation movement is that a terrorist organisations will strike against non-military targets. There has been a radical change in the targeting policy of terrorist groups, traditional politically motivated terrorist groups often seen in the west such as the IRA or the Italian Red Brigades chose to strike at high profile political targets or against targets that would guarantee media attention like the bombing of commercial centres. The targeting was determined mainly by two factors, maximum media attention and little loss of life, the so called Propaganda of the deed, and the by the survival / escape of the terrorists carrying out the attack. The aim of minimising loss of life might seem strange until you consider that such terrorist groups rely on public support and a large number of deaths quickly destroys any ground swell of support from the local population and makes it easier for the authorities to label the groups as criminals. Western style terrorists are not normally motivated by religion and rarely have a desire to become a martyr so escape is a priority, hence the use of snipers, remote bombs or IED's , methods which allow the terrorist to be a far away from the scene of the crime as possible.

With the growth of religious fundamentalist terrorism the nature of terrorist targets has changed. Attacks which now result in a large number of deaths or civilian causalities are now firmly on the agenda for many terrorist groups, as the attacks of 9/11 horrifically demonstrated. This type of attack has been present in the Middle East for some time with a long tradition of suicide bombings of crowded civilian areas such as bars and night clubs. Secondly for this type of terrorist survival is not a major concern and for some definitely not a desirable outcome as they actively seek death as a planned part of the attack. This means that targets that were previously thought to be safe from attack are now at risk and the chances of a terrorist successfully reaching their target if their own survival is not a consideration is much, much greater. In fact actually stopping a suicide bomber from causing deaths, apart from their own is virtually impossible.

So what do terrorists look for in a potential target? Firstly there is a risk analysis, by this I mean the terrorist organization will consider the potential benefits of attacking a particular target as opposed to the cost in resources and the likelihood of success. Here definitions of 'Hard' and 'Soft' targets become useful. A 'Hard' target is one which is guarded or has considerable security; this means that a terrorist attack runs the risk of being intercepted often with potentially lethal force. Examples of 'Hard' targets would include military bases, and political organisations and high ranking politicians and heads of state such as Presidents. A 'Soft' target is one which has little or no military protection or security and hence is an easy option for a terrorist attack. This includes commercial shopping centres, power stations, and leisure facilities such as football grounds and sports stadiums. Of course a soft target may become a harder one if a particular event or situation raises the risk, for example the Olympics or a major sporting or diplomatic event , but due to the large amounts of civilian visitors, and the shear number of access points to control they are still generally very vulnerable. Airports since 9/11 fall into this category as although they are more secure since the attacks they still have vast numbers of visitors and many access points, all of which are potential points of entry for a terrorist. It is also worth considering the potential press coverage an attack on a particular target would generate. All types of terrorist seek the maximum media coverage for an attack so a target which has lots of international visitors is a preferred target. For example why target a small local airport in the UK when you could target an international airport like Heathrow which has visitors from many nations. Any attack on such a target would cause causalities among many nationalities and therefore generate maximum international media coverage. What is clear that despite increased security measures the vast majority of potential terrorist targets are impossible to protect, any measures to secure them are often more to calm public fears that in any real hope of preventing an attack. The true hope of preventing terrorist attacks lies in good intelligence and intercepting the terrorist cells before an attack takes place.

How to cite this article: Dugdale-Pointon, TDP. (26 May 2005), Terrorist Targets, http://www.historyofwar.org/articles/concepts_terrortargets.html

Appendix 37

Robert S. Mueller, III
Director
Federal Bureau of Investigation
InfraGard 2005 National Conference
Washington, D.C.
August 09, 2005
http://www.fbi.gov/news/speeches/working-together-to-protect-national-infrastructure-from-crime-and-terrorism

Good afternoon. Nearly 10 years ago, we joined forces with you to defend our critical national infrastructure. Since then, we have worked side-by-side to protect our businesses, our communities, and our families from crime and terrorism.

We have diverse backgrounds and different specialties--from emergency responders to entrepreneurs, from computer programmers to chemical engineers, from FBI Agents to farmers. But we face the same threats to our way of life.

Through InfraGard, you have become vital members of a long-standing partnership between the FBI and the private sector. Today, our partnership is more important than ever, because the threats we face are more diverse than ever. And the only way to defeat these threats is by standing strong together.

Today I want to talk about what we in the FBI are doing to protect our national infrastructure from crime and terrorism. I want to talk about the value of working together and sharing information through programs like InfraGard. And I want to talk about what each of us can and must do to prevent crime and to prevent the next terrorist attack.

I. The FBI: Protecting Our Infrastructure

Our national infrastructure is a soft target, ranging from bridges and buildings to public utilities and power grids across the country. More than 90 percent of our infrastructure is owned and operated by private industry or state and local governments. And it is increasingly managed by computer networks and the Internet.

The Internet has opened the doors to a new world of communication and commerce. But technology is a double-edged sword. Entrepreneurs and engineers are not the only ones who recognize the vast potential of the Internet. Criminals and terrorists do, too.

For example, in Australia, a computer hacker used a laptop and a two-way radio to hack into a sewage control computer system, releasing more than 250 million tons of raw sewage on to the grounds of a luxury resort hotel.

In Russia, hackers took control of a gas pipeline for 24 hours by penetrating electronic control systems.

In Ohio, the Slammer worm computer virus attacked a nuclear power plant, preventing the plant's computers from communicating with each other and disrupting safety systems for more than five hours.

And we have all heard story after story about one of today's most pervasive threats: identity theft. Every day, cyber criminals steal our most personal information--from our financial data to our social security numbers to our security passwords.

Terrorists who shun our way of life are more than willing to use our technology to carry out and publicize their attacks--from airplanes used as missiles, to coordinated attacks on mass transportation, to videotaped beheadings posted on the Internet.

These examples show that as technology evolves, so does crime. International jet travel, cell phones, and the Internet have erased geographical boundaries.

In his new book, "The World is Flat," New York Times columnist and author Tom Friedman asserts that advances in technology, travel, and communication have broken down walls between continents, countries, and individuals. Now, anyone can hop online, on board, or on the phone and connect with the world.

The advantage to this is that we are collaborating and connecting in ways never before imagined. The disadvantage is that Al Qaeda and other criminal organizations are using that same technology to wreak havoc around the world. Criminals and terrorists no longer need to be in the same room, or even the same country, to plan, finance, and execute attacks. Increasingly, technology and the global community of the Internet are used not only to break down walls, but to sustain and nurture hatred and violence.

Fortunately, we, too, are breaking down walls. We are using technology to win the war against crime and terror. We are creating a "flat world" within the Bureau, and within the intelligence and law enforcement communities. And we are working together in new ways and with new partners.

For example, agents and analysts in our Cyber Division protect against theft of intellectual property, child pornography, online fraud, and computer intrusions. Our Cyber Action Teams travel around the world on a moment's notice to assist in computer intrusion and counterterrorism cases.

Our Joint Terrorism Task Forces combine the resources of special agents and analysts, police officers, the CIA, the Department of Homeland Security, and the IRS, just to name a few. Together, these task forces investigate cases and share information.

We are also working with our partners around the world to defeat crime and terrorism. We have joined forces with the Hungarian National Police to tackle organized crime syndicates in Eastern Europe. We are gathering intelligence in Iraq and Afghanistan and hunting down terrorists with our partners in Pakistan, Morocco, and Indonesia.

II. The InfraGard Program

We are not limiting our collaborative efforts to our international partners, or to law enforcement and intelligence agencies. We are also working with members of the private sector and sharing information through programs like InfraGard.

To date, there are more than 11,000 members of InfraGard. From our perspective, that amounts to 11,000 contacts…and 11,000 partners in our mission to protect America.

InfraGard is one of our most important links to the private sector. We recognize that in certain areas we lack the expertise that you possess. We lack the specific knowledge of threats that affect individual businesses every day. That is why we need your help, and why we continue to ask for your cooperation.

The threat to our infrastructure is broad, from computer intrusions to breaches of physical security to terrorist threats. Today, a command sent over a network to a power station's control computer could be just as deadly as a backpack full of explosives, and the perpetrators might be more difficult to identify and apprehend. But we stand a much greater chance of preventing an attack on our infrastructure by working together.

Someone who understood the value of working together, Henry Ford, once said: "Coming together is a beginning. Keeping together is progress. Working together is success."

Working together, we have already had successes.

For example, an InfraGard member in Colorado was the first to alert the FBI to the theft of computer software templates used by energy providers in the United States. We might not have been aware of this theft without the information provided by our InfraGard member.

InfraGard members serve as resources to agents and analysts in pending investigations. While working on a highly sensitive counterterrorism case last year, agents in Phoenix turned to several InfraGard members for information on a complicated high-tech issue.

And in San Francisco, InfraGard members briefed agents and analysts on risks associated with different infrastructures, including power grids, air traffic control, and chemical and nuclear facilities.

The InfraGard program has been so successful that we are taking it in new directions.

In 2003, through our Albuquerque Field Office, we started a program called AgriGard. Members of the agricultural community share information with scientists, academic institutions, state and local law enforcement, and the FBI through a secure web portal. Members can pose questions about farm and food security, and alert the FBI to any suspicious or unusual activity.

We are implementing a similar program for those in the chemical industry.

III. Our Collective Roles in Preventing Crime and Terror

Partnerships enhance our collective knowledge and improve our ability to confront criminal and terrorist threats. But information sharing is a two-way street. We cannot investigate if we are not aware of the problem. Those of you in the private sector are the first line of defense.

Let me give you an example. In late 2004, a computer hacker infiltrated CardSystems, Inc., a credit card processing company in Tucson, Arizona. Thousands of credit card numbers were stolen.

When the company discovered the breach earlier this year, representatives quickly contacted the FBI to initiate an investigation, based on the recommendation of an employee who is an InfraGard member. Because of CardSystem's quick response, we were able to start the investigation immediately, before the trail went cold. Unfortunately, timely reporting like this is only too rare.

According to a survey by the Computer Security Institute and the FBI, only 20 percent of companies that experienced computer intrusions in 2004 reported those incidents to law enforcement. Respondents said they did not alert authorities because they feared negative publicity and loss of competitive advantage.

We know that you have practical concerns about reporting breaches of security. You may believe that calling us will adversely impact your organization's image and competitive position in the marketplace. You may need to protect confidential information to maintain the trust of your customers and clients.

We know that putting on raid jackets and rushing in may not be the best way to get the job done. We need to minimize the disruption to your business and protect your interests. But we must find a way to stop these attacks. Maintaining a code of silence will not benefit you or your company in the long run.

President Reagan once said, "To sit back, hoping that someday, some way, someone will make things right is to go on feeding the crocodile, hoping he will eat you last--but eat you he will."

Our safety lies in protecting not just our own interests, but our critical infrastructure as a whole. There are cyber criminals who will hit company after company. Disgruntled employees who will use knowledge gained on the job against their employers. Terrorists who may attempt to harm our infrastructure in a multitude of ways. We cannot continue to feed the crocodile.

If you note suspicious activity or an unusual event--from a computer intrusion, to a disgruntled employee, to a breach of physical security--notify your InfraGard coordinator, the Department of Homeland Security, the FBI, or your local police. We must be constantly alert to the possibility of crime and terrorism.

There is an example that drives the point home. Roughly one year ago, police arrested a man for possession of homemade ricin--a deadly poison. He had placed a large order for castor seeds-- the material used to make ricin--with a seed company in New York.

Employees of the seed company became suspicious and called the FBI. When FBI agents searched the man's home, they found jars clearly labeled "Caution--ricin poison." They also found large amounts of castor seeds and both the chemicals and the equipment used to manufacture ricin.

We found this man before he could harm anyone, based on the tip from the seed company employees. This is an example of the private sector and the FBI working together to fight crime and terrorism.

And this partnership extends "outside of the office." While shopping in a home improvement store, an InfraGard member noticed several teenagers buying items that could be used to build a pipe bomb. He took down the license plate number of their car, and called the authorities.

As it turns out, these teenagers were planning to build a pipe bomb. This individual's vigilance and quick response to a potential threat may have thwarted a deadly attack.

Success stories like these reinforce the need for vigilance and cooperation.

No person, no police officer, no agency, no company, and no country can prevent crime and terrorism on its own. There are too many potential weapons, too many avenues of attack, too many unlocked doors.

Baseball great Babe Ruth once said that "the way a team plays as a whole determines its success. You may have the greatest bunch of individual stars in the world, but if they don't play together, the club won't be worth a dime." The way our team plays as a whole will determine our success.

In this era of globalization, in this flat world, working side-by-side is not just the best option, it is the only option. It is vital that we use our collective resources to protect our national infrastructure. It is by working together through programs like InfraGard that we will win this war. Partnerships strengthen our response against the many forces who seek to do us harm. From Portland to Phoenix to Philadelphia, we must stand together to protect our communities, our businesses, and our families. Together, we will keep our nation safe.

Thank you and God Bless.

Appendix 38

Three killed in Gaza convoy blast
Agencies
guardian.co.uk, Wednesday 15 October 2003 16.31 BST
http://www.guardian.co.uk/world/2003/oct/15/israel.usa

A Palestinian miltant group was today reported to have claimed responsibility for a bombing of a US diplomatic convoy in Gaza that left three Americans dead and one wounded.

A three-vehicle convoy carrying US officials to interview Palestinian students for scholarships at American universities was hit in the blast. The three dead were all security guards travelling in the second car, which took the brunt of the explosion.

Agence France Presse said that the Popular Resistance Committee, a umbrella group of Gaza militants, had claimed responsibility for the attack.

It was the first time that a convoy of US diplomats, who travel in Gaza almost daily, had been targeted since the current violence began three years ago.

The main Palestinian militant groups were quick to deny involvement in the attack.

Hamas and Islamic Jihad, responsible for the bulk of the attacks on Israelis, reiterated that they have no interest in taking aim at non-Israeli targets.

An Islamic Jihad spokesman, Nafez Azzam, said the group's battle was "with the occupiers only" and did not want to engage anyone else. "In the land of Palestine, it's not proper to target Americans nor any other nations," he said.

But resentment against the US has been growing steadily, with many Palestinians complaining that Washington sides with Israel.

A US state department spokeswoman said it would pursue the people behind the attack until they were brought to justice and an FBI team has been dispatched to Gaza to investigate.

"Our sympathies go out to these brave men and their families. ... The United States will pursue the perpetrators until they are caught and brought to justice," she said.

The Palestinian prime minister, Ahmed Qureia, immediately condemned the bombing, expressing "deep regret" at the deaths and injuries. Colin Powell, the US secretary of state, later asked him to act against militant group.

The US said it would continue to work for an end to Palestinian-Israeli violence despite the attack but advised all its citizens to leave Gaza for their own safety.

Around 200 to 400 Americans, some of them of Palestinian descent, work in the Gaza Strip, many for NGOs.

Mohammed Radwan, a Palestinian taxi driver, said that he had been at a nearby petrol station when the blast happened.

"I was about to fill up my car with gas when I saw the American convoy passing," Mr Radwan said. "There was a Palestinian police car in front and then three big [US] cars. When the third one passed, an explosion went off."

"The first two cars drove quickly and stopped far form the explosion. Palestinian security people jumped out of the car and rushed to the car that had blown up.

"When I tried to approach them, they shouted at me to leave. I saw two people covered with blood lying next to the car." The body of one of the US victims was taken to Shifa Hospital in Gaza City.

The device exploded on Gaza's main north-south road, about one mile south of the Erez crossing between Israel and Gaza. The explosion tore the jeep in half, leaving twisted wreckage and the tyres pointing up into the air.

An Associated Press reporter saw a grey wire with an on-off switch leading from the scene of the attack to a small concrete room at the side of the road.

Contrary to initial reports, John Wolf, the head of the US team monitoring progress on a Middle East peace plan, was not in the convoy, the US embassy told Israeli daily newspaper Ha'aretz.

Appendix 39

State Department updates warning to Americans overseas
July 26, 2011, By Jill Dougherty, CNN Foreign Affairs Correspondent
http://articles.cnn.com/2011-07-26/us/state.department.caution_1_islamic-maghreb-target-both-official-qaeda?_s=PM:US

The State Department is warning Americans that al Qaeda and affiliated organizations continue to plan terrorist attacks against U.S. interests around the world, including Europe, Asia, Africa, and the Middle East.

"These attacks may employ a wide variety of tactics including suicide operations, assassinations, kidnappings, hijackings, and bombings," the department said in its latest Worldwide Caution report, issued Tuesday.

There is an "enhanced potential" for more anti-American violence around the world, it says, in the wake of Osama bin Laden's killing by U.S. special forces in May.

Extremists, the warning says, may use "conventional or non-conventional weapons" and target both official and private interests. It points to targets like "high-profile sporting events, residential areas, business offices, hotels, clubs, restaurants, places of worship, schools, public areas, and other tourist destinations both in the United States and abroad where U.S. citizens gather in large numbers, including during holidays."

The so-called "Arab Spring" movements in the Middle East and North Africa, meanwhile, have resulted in civil unrest and large-scale protests and the State Department warns that even "peaceful" demonstrations can turn violent, that riots can occur "with little or no warning."

A number of al Qaeda-affiliated groups and other extremists continue to operate in and around Africa, the State Department says, and it notes increased threats across East Africa.

Groups like al-Shabaab, al Qaeda in the Lands of the Islamic Maghreb (AQIM) and Taliban elements like Lashkar-e-Tayyiba pose a threat to U.S. citizens as well, the department said in its report, the latest update since a similar warning was posted in January.

U.S. citizens considering travel by sea near the Horn of Africa or in the Southern Red Sea "should exercise extreme caution," it says, as there has been a notable increase in armed attacks, robberies and kidnappings for ransom by pirates.

In Pakistan, extremist groups continue to target U.S. and other Western citizens and interests as well as Pakistani government and military and law enforcement personnel.

The State Department urges U.S. citizens living overseas or planning to travel abroad to enroll in its Smart Traveler Enrollment Program (STEP), which provides updates on safety and security and makes it easier for the U.S. Embassy to contact them in emergencies.

Appendix 40

World Wide Caution: U.S. Citizens Overseas
January 17, 2008
http://windhoek.usembassy.gov/u2.s._citizens_overseas

This Worldwide Caution updates information on the continuing threat of terrorist actions and violence against Americans and interests throughout the world. American citizens are reminded to maintain a high level of vigilance and to take appropriate steps to increase their security awareness. This supersedes the Worldwide Caution dated October 9, 2007.

The Department of State remains concerned about the continued threat of terrorist attacks, demonstrations and other violent actions against U.S. citizens and interests overseas. Current information suggests that al-Qaida and affiliated organizations continue to plan terrorist attacks against U.S. interests in multiple regions, including Europe, Asia, Africa and the Middle East. These attacks may employ a wide variety of tactics including suicide operations, assassinations, kidnappings, hijackings and bombings.

Extremists may elect to use conventional or non-conventional weapons, and target both official and private interests. Examples of such targets include high-profile sporting events, residential areas, business offices, hotels, clubs, restaurants, places of worship, schools, public areas and locales where Americans gather in large numbers, including during holidays. In August 2007, two bombs exploded almost simultaneously at an amusement park and a restaurant in India, killing at least 42 people. In June 2007, two unexploded car bombs were discovered in London.

Americans are reminded of the potential for terrorists to attack public transportation systems. Recent examples include multiple terrorist attacks on trains in India in 2006, the July 2005 London Underground bombings, and the March 2004 train attacks in Madrid. In addition, extremists may also select aviation and maritime services as possible targets, such as the August 2006 plot against aircraft in London, or the December 2006 bomb at Madrid's Barajas International Airport. In June 2007, a vehicle was driven into the main terminal at Glasgow International Airport and burst into flames, but the bomb failed to detonate.

The Middle East and North Africa
Credible information indicates terrorist groups seek to continue attacks against U.S. interests in the Middle East and North Africa. Terrorist actions may include bombings, hijackings, hostage taking, kidnappings, and assassinations. While conventional weapons such as explosive devices are a more immediate threat in many areas, use of non-conventional weapons, including chemical or

biological agents, must be considered a possible threat. Terrorists do not distinguish between official and civilian targets. Increased security at official U.S. facilities has led terrorists and their sympathizers to seek softer targets such as public transportation, residential areas, and public areas where people congregate, including restaurants, hotels, clubs, and shopping areas.

On December 11, 2007, two vehicle-borne explosive devices were detonated at the UN headquarters in Algiers and the Algerian Constitutional Council. Three other suicide bomb attacks in July and September of 2007 in Algeria killed more than 80 people. In July 2007, suspected al-Qaida operatives carried out a vehicle-borne explosive device attack on tourists at the Bilquis Temple in Yemen, which resulted in the deaths of eight Spanish tourists and their two Yemeni drivers. There was a series of bombings in Morocco in March and April 2007, two of which occurred simultaneously outside the U.S. Consulate General and the private American Language Center in Casablanca. Additionally, an attack took place on the American International School in Gaza in April 2007. These events underscore the intent of terrorist entities to target facilities perceived to cater to Westerners. The September 2006 attack on the U.S. embassy in Syria and the March 2006 bombing near the U.S. consulate in Karachi, Pakistan illustrate the continuing desire of extremists to strike American targets.

Potential targets are not limited to those companies or establishments with overt U.S. ties. For instance, terrorists may target movie theaters, liquor stores, bars, casinos, or any similar type of establishment, regardless of whether they are owned and operated by host country nationals. Due to varying degrees of security at all such locations, Americans should be particularly vigilant when visiting these establishments.

The violence in Iraq, clashes between Palestinians and Israelis, clashes between terrorist extremists and the Lebanese Armed Forces, and the violence in Pakistan following the assassination of former Prime Minister Benazir Bhutto on December 27, 2007 have the potential to produce demonstrations and unrest throughout the region. Americans are reminded that demonstrations and rioting can occur with little or no warning. In addition, the Department of State continues to warn of the possibility for violent actions against U.S. citizens and interests in the region. Anti-American violence could include possible terrorist actions against aviation, ground transportation, and maritime interests, specifically in the Middle East, including the Red Sea, Persian Gulf, the Arabian Peninsula, and North Africa.

The Department is concerned that extremists may be planning to carry out attacks against Westerners and oil workers on the Arabian Peninsula. Armed attacks targeting foreign nationals in Saudi Arabia that resulted in many deaths and injuries, including U.S. citizens, appear to have been preceded by extensive surveillance. Tourist destinations in Egypt that are frequented by Westerners were attacked in April 2006 resulting in many deaths and injuries, including Americans. Extremists may be surveilling Westerners, particularly at hotels, housing areas, and rental car facilities. Potential targets may include U.S. contractors, particularly those related to military interests. Financial or economic venues of value also could be considered as possible targets; the failed attack on the Abqaiq oil processing facility in Saudi Arabia in late February 2006 and the September 2006 attack on oil facilities in Yemen are examples.

East Africa

A number of al-Qaida operatives and other extremists are believed to be operating in and around East Africa. As a result of the conflict in Somalia, some of these individuals may seek to relocate elsewhere in the region. Americans considering travel to the region and those already there should review their plans carefully, remain vigilant with regard to their personal security, and exercise caution. Terrorist actions may include suicide operations, bombings, kidnappings or targeting maritime vessels. Terrorists do not distinguish between official and civilian targets. Increased security at official U.S. facilities has led terrorists to seek softer targets such as hotels, beach resorts, prominent public places, and landmarks. In particular, terrorists may target civil aviation and seaports. Americans in remote areas or border regions where military or police authority is limited or non-existent could also become targets.

Americans considering seaborne travel near the Horn of Africa or in the southern Red Sea should exercise extreme caution, as there have been several incidents of armed attacks, robberies, and kidnappings for ransom at sea by pirates during the past several years. Merchant vessels continue to be hijacked in Somali territorial waters, while others have been hijacked as far as 200 nautical miles off the coast of Somalia in international waters.

The U.S. Government maritime authorities advise mariners to avoid the port of Mogadishu, and to remain at least 200 nautical miles off the coast of Somalia. In addition, when transiting around the Horn of Africa or in the Red Sea, it is strongly recommended that vessels travel in convoys, and maintain good communications contact at all times.

Central Asia

The U.S. Government continues to receive information that terrorist groups in Central Asia may be planning attacks in the region, possibly against U.S. Government facilities, American citizens, or American interests. Elements and supporters of extremist groups present in Central Asia, including the Islamic Jihad Union (IJU), al-Qaida, the Islamic Movement of Uzbekistan (IMU), and the Eastern Turkistan Islamic Movement, have expressed anti-U.S. sentiments in the past and have demonstrated the capability to conduct terrorist operations in the region. Previous terrorist attacks conducted in Central Asia have involved improvised explosive devices and suicide bombers and have targeted public areas, such as markets, local government facilities, and, in 2004, the U.S. and

Israeli Embassies in Uzbekistan. In addition, hostage-takings and skirmishes have occurred near the Uzbek-Tajik-Kyrgyz border areas.

Before You Go
U.S. citizens living or traveling abroad are encouraged to register with the nearest U.S. Embassy or Consulate through the State Department's travel registration web site at https://travelregistration.state.gov/ibrs/ui/ so that they can obtain updated information on travel and security. Americans without Internet access may register directly with the nearest U.S. Embassy or Consulate. By registering, American citizens make it easier for the Embassy or Consulate to contact them in case of emergency.

U.S. citizens are strongly encouraged to maintain a high level of vigilance, be aware of local events, and take the appropriate steps to bolster their personal security. For additional information, please refer to "A Safe Trip Abroad" found at http://travel.state.gov/.

U.S. Government facilities worldwide remain at a heightened state of alert. These facilities may temporarily close or periodically suspend public services to assess their security posture. In those instances, U.S. embassies and consulates will make every effort to provide emergency services to U.S. citizens. Americans abroad are urged to monitor the local news and maintain contact with the nearest U.S. embassy or consulate.

Appendix 41

Oil tanker terror hijacks easy, attacks complex
By Katharine Houreld
Associated Press Sunday, May 22nd, 2011
http://globalnation.inquirer.net/2173/oil-tanker-terror-hijacks-easy-attacks-complex

NAIROBI, Kenya—Supertankers — the hulking, slow-moving ships that transport half the world's oil — have few defenses against terrorist hijackers like those envisioned by Osama bin Laden, security experts said Saturday.

Al-Qaeda operatives with enough training could easily manage to capture ships carrying millions of gallons of oil or liquefied natural gas. All they would have to do is imitate the tactics of Somali pirates who already use small boats to overpower tanker crews in mostly remote locations, the experts said. Few supertankers have armed guards, due to gun import laws and the risk of accidental gunfire igniting explosive cargos.

But once terrorists captured a supertanker, it wouldn't be so easy to sow the economic chaos and costly environmental destruction bin Laden desired and outlined in secret files captured from his Pakistan hideout. It's actually extremely complex to blow up a supertanker or even sink it near heavily guarded oil shipping lanes like the Suez Canal, the Panama Canal or the Strait of Hormuz at the end of the Persian Gulf.

"It would only be a risk if they could sail it undetected and had worked out how to blow it up, which is pretty complicated," said Graeme Gibbon-Brooks, the head of Dryad Maritime Intelligence.

The FBI and the US Department of Homeland Security issued a confidential warning to authorities and the energy industry Friday that al-Qaeda was seeking information on the size and construction of tankers.

The newly revealed plot showed that while bin Laden was scheming about the next strike to kill thousands of Americans, he also believed an attack on the oil industry in "non-Muslim waters" could create a worldwide economic panic that would send oil prices soaring and hurt Westerners at the gas pump.

Other bin Laden documents revealed that the terror group identified New York, Washington, Los Angeles and Chicago as important cities that should be attacked. Al-Qaeda also identified key dates for those attacks, including the 10th anniversary of the September 11, 2001 attacks, Christmas, July 4th and during Obama's State of the Union address in January.

Oil already is a known target. On Saturday, a truck tanker carrying oil for NATO forces in Afghanistan exploded in northwestern Pakistan as people tried to siphon off fuel, killing 15. Fourteen other NATO oil trucks were damaged in a bombing at a nearby border town, but no one was hurt.

The hundreds of seafaring oil tankers that travel across the planet daily are theoretically capable of igniting massive fires with the capability for extensive destruction.

Intelligence gathered from bin Laden's hideout revealed that al-Qaeda realized the tankers would have to be boarded so explosives could be planted inside them. Security experts say, however, blowing them up would be difficult because the tankers have double hulls and compartmentalized holds that prevent oil spills in groundings and can withstand direct hits from rocket propelled grenades.

Plus, getting enough explosives aboard the tankers would mean using more speedboats than Somali hijackers normally do to take over the ships and hold crews hostage, Gibbon-Brooks said.

Somali pirates have already captured five supertankers, proving that men with little training and basic weapons can easily seize the giant ships. Supertankers move slowly when fully loaded, can be longer than three football fields and generally only have around 20 unarmed crew onboard.

Although the size of the ships makes them vulnerable, their slow speed also makes it harder for terrorists to sneak one into a port or a narrow shipping passage. Ships are closely tracked via satellite and any unexplained deviations from their travel plans would immediately raise alarms.

While al-Qaeda's most brazen sea attack was on the USS Cole in Yemen, the explosives that knocked a hole in the destroyer and killed 17 sailors in 2000 would not sink a double-hulled oil tanker.

Other marine attacks have been botched. An attempt to blow up the USS The Sullivans warship failed in 2000 when the plotters overloaded their speedboat with explosives and it sank en route to the mission.

The 2002 suicide bombing of a tanker off the coast of Yemen damaged the ship but didn't sink it. And last year a suicide bomber only slightly damaged the Japanese tanker M. Star in the Straits of Hormuz, which handles 40 percent of the world's tanker traffic. An obscure al-Qaeda-linked group claimed responsibility.

After those attempts, al-Qaeda decided attackers have to board a ship and blow it up from the inside, according to documents seized by US special forces from the compound where bin Laden was killed nearly three weeks ago.

Despite the difficulties, warnings abound that several groups have the capability to pull off a terror attack on a supertanker, especially in Asian waters.

The al-Qaeda-affiliated Abu Sayyaf extremists remotely detonated a bomb on a ferry in Manila Bay in the Philippines in 2004, igniting an inferno that killed 116 people.

Small cargo barges and fishing boats have been attacked by militants, some of whom have taken diving lessons that Filipino authorities suspect were preludes to maritime attacks. In March 2010, Singapore's navy raised its security alert, warning that an unspecified terrorist group was planning attacks on oil tankers and other vessels in the Malacca Strait, which separates Malaysia from the Indonesian island of Sumatra.

While authorities fear that al-Qaeda may link up with the Somali pirates who have become so adept at hijacking cargo ships, experts say the chance of any such alliance is remote because the pirates are in the hijacking business for the multimillion-dollar ransoms they get from holding ship crews hostage.

If the pirates started working with terrorists, that could seriously hurt their business, said Roger Middleton, a piracy expert with London's Chatham House think tank.

"They're multimillionaires running a very important business and don't want to see that jeopardized by too much politics," he said.

To counter attacks, tanker owners have begun putting barbed wire around ship guardrails and installing firehoses that can launch high pressure jets of water at attackers. They are also installing bulletproof glass around ship bridges and accommodation quarters, a vessel's two most vulnerable areas, said Chris Austen, the head of Maritime and Underwater Security Consultants.

Some shipping companies also insist their tankers travel through pirate-infested waters only in convoys, added Crispian Cuss, program director at Olive Group, one of the biggest security companies working in the Middle East.

If hijackers decide they can't get onboard and steer a ship toward a target without detection, they might try to seize a vessel in port — but that would be much riskier given the global port security measures in effect in the last decade.

The al-Qaeda plot found in bin Laden's hideout also mentioned attacking oil facilities, but most oil terminals are considered strategic installations —

meaning they are protected by roving coast guard boats, radar, divers who conduct inspections and heavy security. Brazil, for example, is justifying the cost of developing a nuclear submarine to protect its vast offshore oil fields.

Security levels vary, but the ports that terrorists value the most generally have the heaviest protection, Cuss said.

"A port in Sudan is not going to have the same level of security as Houston," he said.

The latest plots show that bin Laden was clearly thinking about the economic consequences of his attacks and might even have been planning a devastating oil spill, said Tim Hart, a maritime security analyst at Maritime and Underwater Security Consultants.

That means Western security forces might have to take strong action sometime at sea.

In 2007, a Japanese tanker was hijacked carrying 40,000 tons of benzene, a highly explosive chemical. Intelligence officials feared at first that terrorists might try to crash the tanker into an offshore oil platform or use it as a gigantic bomb. In the end, it proved to be just another attack by pirates seeking ransom.

Naval forces were, however, ready to attack the ship and blow it up at sea if it approached populated areas, a Western diplomat confirmed, speaking on condition of anonymity because he was not authorized to talk to the media.

With reports from Cassandra Vinograd, Raphael Satter and Meera Selva in London; Adam Schreck in Dubai; and Jim Gomez in Manila, Philippines

Appendix 42

Terror's next target
By Gal Luft and Anne Korin
The Journal of International Security Affairs, December 2003.
http://www.iags.org/n0111041.htm

Terrorist organizations have always been interested in targeting oil and gas facilities. Striking pipelines, tankers, refineries and oil fields accomplishes two desired goals: undermining the internal stability of the regimes they are fighting, and economically weakening foreign powers with vested interests in their region. In the past decade alone, there have been scores of attacks against oil targets primarily in the Middle East, Africa and Latin America. These attacks have never received much attention and have been treated as part of the 'industry's risk.'

However, after the attacks on World Trade Center and the Pentagon, symbols of U.S.' economic and military dominance, terrorist organizations of global reach like al Qaeda have identified the world's energy system as a major vulnerability and a certain way to deliver a blow to America's oil dependent economy as well as global economy at large. With attacks against transportation networks, military bases and government installations becoming more difficult to execute due to heightened security, terrorists looking for a big bang might find oil, to quote al Qaeda, the "umbilical cord and lifeline of the crusader community," the object of the next major assault on the west, an assault that could wreak havoc with America's economy and way of life.

Oil supplies 96% of U.S.' transportation energy and is a crucial component in the production and distribution of every commodity from toothpaste to golf balls. Though the U.S consumes a quarter of the world's oil, it has a mere 3% of global reserves. To satisfy its growing energy needs the U.S. imports over 50% of it oil amounting to 10 million barrels per day (mbd). Over the next 20 years this dependency is projected to grow to nearly 70%.

Unfortunately, the world's leading oil producing countries and holders of the lion share of global reserves are either politically unstable and/or, in the words of President George W. Bush, "don't particularly like the U.S." Two thirds of global oil reserves are located in the world's most volatile region, where the U.S. is most disliked: the Middle East. This tremendous oil wealth is shared primarily among six Middle Eastern regimes: Saudi Arabia, Iran, Iraq, United Arab Emirates, Kuwait, and Libya. The Department of Energy predicts that oil imports from the Middle East to the U.S. will increase from 25% today to about 50% by 2020. A quarter of the world's oil reserves are controlled by Saudi Arabia, a country considered by many analysts a powder keg waiting to explode. Some try to underestimate the power of the Kingdom, neglecting the fact that the oil market's only significant excess production capacity, an extra 2.5 mbd that can be pumped at the flick of a switch when other suppliers falter -- as was done in early 2003 to compensate for disruption of flow from Nigeria, Venezuela, and Iraq -- is in Saudi Arabia. This makes Saudi Arabia the world's only guarantor of liquidity in the oil market.

But Saudi Arabia's oil system is target rich and extremely vulnerable to terrorist acts. This is not only due to al Qaeda's strong presence in the kingdom and its ability to carry out coordinated attacks as evidenced by last May's string of suicide bombings in Riyadh - but also because of the structure of the kingdom's oil infrastructure.

Over half of Saudi Arabia's oil reserves are contained in just eight fields, among them the world's largest onshore oil field -- Ghawar, which alone accounts for about half of the country's total oil production capacity -- and Safaniya, the world's largest offshore oilfield. About two-thirds of Saudi Arabia's crude oil is processed in a single enormous facility called Abqaiq, 25 miles inland from the Gulf of Bahrain. On the Persian Gulf, Saudi Arabia has just two primary oil export terminals: Ras Tanura - the world's largest offshore oil loading facility, through which a tenth of global oil supply flows daily - and Ras al-Ju'aymah. On the Red Sea, a terminal called Yanbu is connected to Abqaiq via the 750-mile East–West pipeline. A terrorist attack on each one of these hubs of the Saudi oil complex or a simultaneous attack on few of them is not a fictional scenario. A single terrorist cell hijacking an airplane in Kuwait or Dubai and crashing it into Abqaiq or Ras Tanura, could turn the complex into an inferno. This could take up to 50% of Saudi oil off the market for at least six months and with it most of the world's spare capacity, sending oil prices through the ceiling. "Such an attack would be more economically damaging than a dirty nuclear bomb set off in midtown Manhattan or across from the White House in Lafayette Square," wrote former CIA Middle East field officer Robert Baer. This "would be enough to bring the world's oil-addicted economies to their knees, America's along with them."

Saudi Arabia is not the only major oil producer vulnerable to terror. Many non-Middle Eastern oil producers, primarily in Africa, the former Soviet Union and south Asia, face the threat of Islamist terrorists. Nigeria, half of which is under Islamic Sharia law, is home to the largest part of Africa's oil reserves, and is the fifth largest oil supplier to the U.S.: It was labeled by the Washington Post last year "The Next Hotbed of Islamic Radicalism." Osama bin Laden is known to have sent emissaries to Nigeria in an effort to unite Islamic groups under the umbrella of al Qaeda. U.S. ambassador to Nigeria Howard Jeter warned recently that Nigeria faces real threat of al Qaeda attack because of its close ties with Washington. And indeed, in February 2003, al Jazeera television aired a message allegedly from bin Laden listing Nigeria as one of six countries which needed to be "liberated" from America's "enslavement."

The former Soviet states where more than 10 percent of global oil reserves are concentrated, also face increasing threat of Islamist terror from groups operating in Central Asia and in the Caucasus among them the Islamic Party of Eastern Turkestan, the Islamic Movement of Uzbekistan (IMU), and Chechen and Uighur separatists. Perhaps the most dangerous group is Hizb ut-Tahrir al-Islami -- the Islamic Party of Liberation — a 5,000-10,000 strong group operating in Uzbekistan, Kyrgyzstan, Tajikistan and in the oil-rich Kazakhstan. Hizb seeks to seize power and supplant existing governments with a Sharia-based Caliphate which will carry on jihad against the West. The head of the Kazakh National Security Committee Nartai Dutbayev said that the Hizb has recently increased its clandestine activities in Kazakhstan and poses "a real threat to Kazakhstan's security."

Southeast Asia, the world's fastest growing energy consuming region, is becoming another target for terrorist. In fact, bin Laden's point man in Asia and the leader of the Indonesian terror group Jema'ah Islamiyah, recently arrested Riduan Isamuddin, also known as Hambali, initiated the bombing of the nightclub in Bali in which 200 were killed. Hambali is also known to have plotted to bomb oil depots in the Philippines and is suspected of planning attacks on U.S. oil companies sia. In all of these places Islamic terrorist groups have identified oil as a major vulnerability and oil terrorism as an effective way to weaken the regimes they oppose.

Another reason terrorists groups tend to focus on oil is that oil targets are 'soft' and hardly defensible, therefore relatively easy to hit. Oil targets are so vulnerable that in the past two years, despite intensive counter-terror measures, oil terrorism has almost become a matter of routine. In May 2002, a cell-phone detonated explosive device was attached to a tanker-truck's underside in Israel's central fuel and gas depot north of Tel Aviv. Though the truck caught fire while loading, the fuel was fortunately slow to ignite and the flames did not spread to the fuel drums. Had the attack succeed, a catastrophe of disastrous proportions would most likely have triggered a harsh Israeli response that would have, in turn, changed the landscape of the Middle East. The same summer, a group of Saudis was arrested for involvement in a plot to sabotage Ras Tanura and pipelines connected to it. A slew of other attacks have either taken place or been thwarted in many countries including India, Nigeria, Colombia, Iraq, Pakistan, Russia and Philippines.

There is growing evidence that terrorists find the unpoliced sea to be their preferred domain of operation. Today, over 60% of the world's oil is shipped on 3,500 tankers through a small number of 'chokepoints' – straits and channels narrow enough to be blocked, and vulnerable to piracy and terrorism. The most important chokepoints are the Strait of Hormuz, through which 13 million barrels of oil are moved daily, Bab el-Mandab, which connects the Red Sea to the Gulf of Aden and the Arabian Sea, and the Strait of Malacca, between Indonesia and Malaysia. Thirty percent of the world's trade and 80% of Japan's crude oil passes through the latter, including half of all sea shipments of oil bound for East Asia and two-thirds of global liquefied natural gas shipments. Most of those critical chokepoints are located in areas where Islamic fundamentalism is prevalent. The Strait of Hormuz and its three tiny islands of Abu Musa, Greater Tunb Island and Lesser Tunb Island are controlled by Iran; Bab el-Mandab is controlled by Yemen, the ancestral home of bin Laden. Part of the 500-mile long Strait of Malacca courses through Indonesia's oil rich province Aceh, inhabited by one of the world's most radical Muslim populations.

Many terror experts have expressed concern that al Qaeda might seize a ship or a boat or even a one-man submarine and crash it into a supertanker in one of the chokepoints. Were terrorists to attack such a vessel the resulting explosion and spreading stain of burning oil could shut down the channel for weeks, with a profound impact on global markets and the maritime insurance industry. Tankers are too slow and cumbersome to maneuver away from attackers; they have no protection and they have nowhere to hide. al Qaeda terrorists have demonstrated repeatedly their intent and ability to strike them. In January 2000 al Qaeda attempted to ram a boat loaded with explosives into the USS The Sullivans in Yemen. The attack was aborted when the boat sank under the weight of the explosives. Later, in October, al Qaeda suicide bomber in high-powered speedboat packed with explosives blew a hole in the USS Cole, killing 17 sailors. In June 2002, a group of al Qaeda operatives suspected of plotting raids on British and American tankers passing through the Strait of Gibraltar was arrested by the Moroccan government; and in October that year, the organization badly holed a French supertanker off the coast of Yemen. A statement following this attack warned that it "was not an incidental strike at a passing tanker but...on the international oil-carrying line in the full sense of the word." According to FBI Director Robert Mueller "any number of [terror] attacks on ships…have been thwarted."

To make things worse, there is an increasing signs of collaboration between terrorism and piracy. According to International Maritime Bureau (IMB), pirate attacks on ships have tripled in the last decade. Each year 350-400 piracy attacks take place worldwide. In the first six months of 2003 alone, 234 attacks have been reported, in which 281 seafarers have been killed, assaulted, or kidnapped. The majority of the attacks take place in the Philippines, Indonesia, Bangladesh and Nigeria. The waters off Somalia, a collapsed state and a sanctuary for terrorists, are among the most dangerous in the world. The IMB reported "The risk of attack to vessels staying close to the coastline from Somali armed militias has now increased from one of possibility to certainty." Maritime security experts have repeatedly warned about the collusion between piracy and terror, voicing concerns that Islamist groups operating in these regions could capitalize on the disorder and target strategic chokepoints by placing a bomb on a supertanker or ramming a ship into one. This concern is not unfounded. Most pirates have no ideological tilt. They are petty criminals who would do almost anything for a handful of dollars. Those who create anarchy at sea in so many parts of the globe are the most likely to befriend the successors of Mohammad Atta and lend their hand on the next mega terror assault against the west.

Pipelines, through which about 40% of world's oil flows, are another Achilles heel. They run over thousands of miles and across some of the most volatile areas in the world. In Saudi Arabia alone there are 10,000 miles of pipeline, in Iraq 4,000, much of it above ground and easily sabotaged. A simple explosive device can puncture a pipeline and render it non-operational. Due to their length, pipelines are very difficult to protect adn thus attractive terrorist targets. Beyond the thwarted attack on the Ras Tanura pipeline, there have been numerous pipeline attacks in Nigeria, Colombia and Pakistan. In Iraq, acts of sabotage against pipelines have become the biggest obstacle in bringing Iraqi oil back online.

Pipelines in the U.S. are also vulnerable. The only route to deliver oil from Alaska is the 800-mile-long Trans-Alaska Pipeline System (TAPS). In recent years the pipeline has been sabotaged, bombed twice and shot at more than 50 times. TAPS is not only within terrorists reach but also impossible to repair in the winter. As former CIA Director James Woolsey and energy expert Amory Lovins wrote "If key pumping stations or facilities at either end were disabled, at least the above-ground half of 9 million barrels of hot oil could congeal in one winter week into the world's biggest Chapstik."

An attack on major oil installation, a chokepoint or a pipeline hub would be detrimental to America's economy and likely to affect every aspect of our lives. During the 1973 Arab Oil Embargo, despite the fact that only 28% of U.S. oil was imported, the effect on the U.S. economy was profound. Oil price quadrupled in a matter of weeks; unemployment doubled due to the loss of 500,000 jobs; and the national product declined 6 percent. Today, with more than half of U.S. oil imported, if a chunk of global oil production is disabled, the consequences could be even more severe. While unlike in 1973, the U.S. has today a Strategic Petroleum Reserve, a stockpile created to cover for lost oil for a time, but this amount would only suffice for two months of disruption, hardly enough to offset the loss in case a mega attack takes place.

Many believe today that the U.S. can insulate itself from price spikes and supply disruptions by simply reducing its oil imports from the Middle East. This assumption is misplaced. Since oil is a fungible commodity and its prices and supply levels are determined in the international markets, the U.S. would be adversely affected by oil terrorism even if it does not import a drop of oil from the region. Nor can it remain untouched by the consequences of major disruptions on other economies with which it trades.

To deal with the risks our energy system is facing, the U.S. should assist oil-producing countries to improve security in their main oil installations, to monitor the people who operate them and to employ preventive measures designed to minimize damage in case an attack succeeds. Most importantly, the U.S. should continue to pursue terrorists and disrupt their plans with the greatest vigor.

But the war on terror is a long-term effort and might take many years to win. Throughout the world, major energy consumers and producers are involved in projects designed to ensure safe passage of oil through the chokepoints and at the same time reducing overall demand for oil.

China, the world's fastest growing energy consumer, is currently pursuing an ambitious project to bypass the Strait of Malacca by building a Panama Canal-style passage through Thailand's narrow-necked Kra isthmus. Also in process is a pipeline from the Israeli port of Ashkelon on the Mediterranean coast through which Russian oil from the Black Sea would flow to Eilat on the Red Sea, be loaded onto tankers and shipped to Asia. The route provides a much shorter link between the Mediterranean and Asia, sparing Asian nations the need to transport oil through the dangerous waters of the Persian Gulf.

Without question, the most fundamental way to improve energy security would be through gradually reducing world demand for oil by shifting to next-generation transportation fuels. While the major energy consuming countries lack oil, most are rich in other energy resources. Coal - held in abundance by the U.S., China, and India, among others - can be used to cleanly and cheaply produce methanol (a hydrogen rich fuel used by the Indy 500 and other race tracks because it is less flammable than gasoline.) Energy rich agricultural waste can be used to produce ethanol, municipal waste can be used to produce Department of Energy approved synthetic fuel. Electricity produced from nuclear, wind, solar, hydropower and clean coal technologies can move vehicles with similar performance and less pollution. Such a transition is no pipedream. Millions of flexible fuel vehicles on the road today can run on the first three fuels mentioned. Rechargeable electric vehicles with auxiliary fuel tanks (to overcome the range limit issues of pure electric vehicles) are already in the making. Infrastructure issues can be circumvented and hurdles to getting fuel cell vehicles on the road diminished by focusing on practical solutions as opposed to ideal ones and delivering cheap to produce hydrogen rich liquid fuels such as methanol and ethanol to fueling stations rather than tangling with pure hydrogen.

Such a shift will not only increase energy independence for America and the free world but will also minimize the need to transport oil across the globe and thus reduce our vulnerability to an energy Pearl Harbor.

Gal Luft is executive director of the Institute for the Analysis of Global Security (IAGS). Anne Korin is director of policy and strategic planning at IAGS and editor of Energy Security Biweekly.

Appendix 43

Coordinated Terrorist Attacks on Global Energy Infrastructure: Modeling the RisksBy Ariel Cohen, Ph.D. , David Kreutzer, Ph.D. , William Beach , James Jay Carafano, Ph.D. and John Ligon
March 17, 2011
http://www.heritage.org/research/reports/2011/03/coordinated-terrorist-attacks-on-global-energy-infrastructure-modeling-the-risks

Abstract: The 2010 Heritage Energy Game demonstrated that there are significant vulnerabilities in the domestic and international energy network. Coordinated attacks by terrorists and other violent nonstate actors could cause a massive drop in oil production and price spikes that would seriously harm the U.S. and the global economies. The reality may be even harsher: wide, prolonged instability in the Middle East may threaten Saudi Arabian and other Persian Gulf oil production, including spare capacity. Careful implementation of select policies could limit the economic damage, but implementation of misguided policies could easily make such a crisis even worse. The United States and its allies would need to exercise decisive and effective leadership to deal with the crisis, but this requires the U.S. to develop an assertive international energy policy, preferably before such a crisis.

In June 2010, The Heritage Foundation conducted a simulation exercise to assess the strategic and economic impact of a major energy supply disruption caused by coordinated terrorist attacks on key nodes in the global energy infrastructure. The exercise built on two prior games conducted in 2006 and 2008[1] and included two iterations.

The purpose of the exercise was to examine the international and domestic responses to the crisis, examine the principal actors' interactions, and simulate the effects on world oil supply, demand, and prices. Analysts at The Heritage Foundation's Kathryn and Shelby Cullom Davis Institute for International Studies developed the simulation exercise to assess the long-term and short-term policy implications of the oil disruptions. Analysts in Heritage's Center for Data Analysis measured the effects of these disruptions on the U.S. economy and the international oil price. Under the business-as-usual (baseline) scenario:

Petroleum prices jump from $75 per barrel to $250 per barrel and eventually fall back to $125 per barrel after two years;
Gasoline prices jump to $8 per gallon and remain above $4 per gallon throughout the first year;
Gross domestic product (GDP) losses exceed $300 billion per year for both years of the crisis; and
Employment drops by more than 1.3 million the first year and drops an additional 1.1 million in the second year for a total two-year drop of 2.4 million.

Experts from policymaking circles and academia played individual countries. They identified policy steps that should be taken on the domestic and international levels to mitigate the impact of the terrorist attacks on the price of oil and the global economy and to restore the supply and security of the transportation chain. This includes military, diplomatic, economic, and regulatory measures. Their expertise, insight, and input proved to be invaluable sources of information. Heritage Foundation analysts analyzed these policy recommendations using the same economic model that was used to make the initial baseline estimates and found that the policy recommendations:

Moderate the petroleum price increase by $20 per barrel after three months, but petroleum prices are only $3 per barrel below the baseline by the 24th month; Moderate the gasoline price increase by as much as $0.60 per gallon, but gasoline prices are only $0.10 per gallon below the baseline by the 24th month; Reduce GDP losses by $130 billion in 2011 and by $50 billion in 2012; and Reduce employment losses by 630,000 jobs in 2011 and by 650,000 jobs in 2012.

The purpose of the exercise was to model data on how the United States and other countries would respond to an oil crisis resulting from simultaneous, high-impact terrorist attacks on high-value oil infrastructure targets in the U.S., Saudi Arabia, and the Strait of Malacca. However, lessons learned in this exercise are applicable to the current upheavals in the Arab Middle East, especially concerning oil production and spare capacity disruption. Suffice to say that a one million barrels per day production decline in Libya has already triggered speculative oil spikes to $120 for a barrel of Brent. Continuous social unrest, particularly in the Persian Gulf, including Kuwait, Oman, Bahrain and especially Saudi Arabia, may drive oil prices even higher. If energy prices climb significantly higher, economic repercussions for growth rates in the developed, and especially developing, world are likely to be negative.

In broader terms, the goal of the exercise was to capture the economic impact of a sudden disruption of the petroleum supply. The economic analysis should provide insight into policy decisions that should be made during the energy crisis. In addition, the exercise was intended to test the validity of the economic model used to simulate market responses to policy decisions during an energy crisis.

Why Energy Crisis Simulation Is Important

The demand for oil is growing, driven mostly by China, India, and other developing countries. Producers and consumers are transforming global energy markets through their sheer size and rates of growth. The Persian Gulf, a major energy source and transportation hub, is gaining in importance, making freedom of navigation through the Strait of Hormuz a vital American and global interest. Similarly, the Strait of Malacca, the shortest sea route between Persian Gulf suppliers and East Asian markets, is another critical choke point. An attack on critical energy infrastructure or tankers in any of these regions would be of paramount significance.

Therefore, any evaluation of the potential response to an energy crisis needs to explore the actions of major consumer nations, energy producers, geostrategic powers, and sub-state and transnational nonstate actors that will shape the military and diplomatic agendas and energy policies during and after a crisis.

History shows that the United States has been less than fortunate in formulating policies to respond to energy crises. The oil shocks following the Arab oil embargo in 1973–1974 and the revolution in Iran in 1979 occurred during a period of high inflation and low economic growth. The ill-advised price controls led to fuel shortages and long lines at gas stations, and they compounded the energy-related damage to the overall economy. The escalation in petroleum prices also began a massive wealth transfer from the West to the Middle East. The situation was further exacerbated by newly enacted economic and environmental regulations and new implementing agencies that interfered with domestic energy supplies and limited the private sector's ability to respond to events. The lessons learned from these harmful policy choices should serve as a cautionary tale as America faces similar energy challenges. Bad decisions can make bad situations much worse.

In the face of historical experience, it is critically important to develop tools that will help to evaluate decisions and weigh potential policy options and their consequences before a crisis occurs. With the global markets more competitive and integrated than ever before, any disruption will affect both the U.S. economy and worldwide economy. Thus, in the event of a global energy crisis, it would be valuable to have the tools to evaluate policy decisions and their consequences.

Scenario Description

The crisis scenario was designed to be plausible, to make the results of the game as realistic as possible, and to prevent players from "fighting the scenario." The intent of the attacks was to cause an immediate shock to the global petroleum transportation and processing system, with secondary effects that would reduce petroleum output from producing nations to consuming nations. It was hypothesized that such an oil shock would likely cause an economic downturn of historic proportions, the scope of which would be captured in the scenario.

In the scenario, terrorists affiliated with al-Qaeda attack refineries in Houston along the Houston Shipping Channel and a refinery in Louisiana. Houston is a critically important hub for oil refining and cargo transportation. Terrorists simultaneously attack a large oil processing and loading facility in Saudi Arabia, the world's largest supplier of oil; attack oil tankers transiting the Strait of

Malacca; and mine the strait with EM-52 mines (polymer-coated to reduce the likelihood of detection). The attacks cause a disruption of nearly 1.9 million barrels per day (b/d).[2] An additional attack successfully targets the oil storage hub in Cushing, Oklahoma.

Cushing is the largest crude pipeline facility in North America, one of the world's major oil terminals, and the largest crude transportation hub in the world. More than 70 percent of the petroleum that is shipped in the U.S. flows through Cushing. The Cushing complex is the delivery point for NYMEX West Texas Intermediate crude oil futures contracts. As of August 2009, the Cushing facility held around 47.5 million barrels of oil.

In the Middle Eastern theater, terrorists simultaneously attack the Ras Tanura and Abu Qaiq oil-processing and shipping facilities in Saudi Arabia. Just prior to the attacks, terrorists take hostages in a middle school to distract Saudi security forces. As a result of the destruction of the Ras Tanura and Abu Qaiq facilities, traffic through the Strait of Hormuz is reduced. The terrorists also attack the offices of the Saudi Aramco Company, destroy its Internet facilities, and kill some of its executives.

In the Pacific theater, the terrorist organization Jamaat al-Islamiya attacks oil tankers in the Strait of Malacca and Strait of Sunda. The initial attacks stop all oil traffic through the straits, and insurance agencies stop extending coverage to hydrocarbon cargos. Oil tankers are forced to detour more than 1,000 kilometers to reach the refineries and terminals of Southeast Asian consumers. Transportation delays and costs increase around the globe as producing and consuming nations increase security measures. These events cause a major disruption and a shortage of the refined product in U.S. markets.

As a result of the disruptions:

Six million b/d of oil production goes offline.

Fifteen million b/d can no longer be shipped via the most direct routes. Saudi Aramco insists on being the only contractor for repairs at the damaged oil shipping facilities.

The U.S., U.K., Japan, India, China, and Australia deploy naval and special forces assets to the Strait of Malacca to hunt down al-Qaeda and Jamaat al-Islamiya seaborne and land-based teams and to conduct demining operations. This requires three months.

The U.S. seeks to compensate for gasoline shortages by increasing production in other refineries and increasing imports.

As a result, the world faces a massive oil supply disruption and a moderate refining product shortage, the market is short 6 million barrels of oil, insurance rates skyrocket, and nearly 350,000 b/d of gasoline refining capacity is offline in the United States.

Even in the absence of policy intervention, markets respond to disruptions. After petroleum prices rise, private inventories are drawn down and brought to market, and consumers and consuming industries economize on their use. Further, international agreements govern the use of strategic reserves. Access to these reserves is built into the baseline. (For a description of the responses built into the baseline scenario, see the Appendix.)

The Players

The analysis focused on only some of the primary international actors that are particularly relevant to energy supply and demand. The United States, the European Union (EU), China, India, Russia, Saudi Arabia, Iran, Japan, and al-Qaeda are represented in the game. For research purposes, the United States, which was played by multiple actors (e.g., Congress, National Security Council, the President), was considered a unitary actor. Only decisions approved by the President were used for the final analysis. This provided a finer texture to U.S. decisions, but created more work for the U.S. team and somewhat slowed the process. This same dynamic was applied to the EU, which was played by the same individuals on the level of the institution, the national states, and NATO. The latter functioned in close cooperation and coordination with the United States.

Some important actors, such as Venezuela and Turkey, were not included in the game due to resource limitations. Furthermore, no additional attacks by al-Qaeda were included in the scenario beyond the first day. This made the overall assessment of al-Qaeda's strategy somewhat more complicated because the success rate of any subsequent attacks would be a good indicator of whether the players' strategies were effective over the long term.

The game was conducted in two separate rounds. The first round, conducted on June 5, 2010, enabled the players and organizers to familiarize themselves with the scenario and rules and to improve the performance of the second round of the game, held on June 29, 2010. However, the scenario remained the same, which allowed Heritage analysts to evaluate both rounds as one.

Al-Qaeda

Al-Qaeda is a global Islamic terrorist organization conducting operations against military and civilian targets, including energy infrastructure. Al-Qaeda's security goals are:

Attacks on U.S. political, military, and economic targets;
Attacks on U.S. allies, particularly Saudi Arabia (including toppling the monarchy), Pakistan, Iraq, Jordan, and Israel; and
Reestablishment of the Caliphate.

China

China's energy policy goals are:

Secure supplies of energy;
Safe and reliable energy transit, especially maritime shipping lines, but also a growing number of transnational pipelines; and
Reducing dependence on American goodwill for energy supply.
Another external goal is Chinese geopolitical preeminence in East Asia. All of these are means to achieve the overarching goal of preserving Communist Party rule at home.

European Union

The EU is a status quo power and has a low tolerance for risk. It is not aggressive and seeks to avoid confrontation. Its security goals are:

Avoiding being drawn into a military conflict;
Maintaining reasonable and stable energy prices; and
Ensuring or maintaining reliability of supply.

India

India's security goals, starting with the most immediate, are:

Avoiding being drawn into a military conflict;
Maintaining reasonable and stable energy prices; and
Ensuring or maintaining reliability of energy transit.

Iran

Iran's leadership has messianic characteristics, which gives it a very high tolerance for risk. Iran is opposed to the status quo and is prepared to undertake aggression to accomplish its objectives. Iran's security goals are:

Assumption of a leadership position in the Islamic world;
Establishment of Iranian hegemony in the Persian Gulf;
Greater control of the energy market;
Removal of U.S. influence in the Middle East and broader Muslim regions; and
The destruction of Israel.

Japan

Japan is a status quo power and has a low tolerance for risk. It is not aggressive and seeks to avoid confrontation. Japan's security goals, starting with the most immediate, are:

Avoiding being drawn into a military conflict, particularly as a means for avoiding attacks by either North Korea or China;
A continued U.S. presence in the Asia–Pacific region;
Nuclear disarmament of North Korea;
Blocking regional hegemony by China;
Maintaining reasonable and stable energy prices; and
Ensuring or maintaining reliability of energy supply.

Russia

Russia is the largest hydrocarbon producer and exporter in the world. Russia's security goals are:

Direct involvement in energy and security policies in the Persian Gulf region with a general preference for keeping energy prices high, even at the price of increased political instability;
Increasing the market share of its oil and gas exports;
Expansion of arms sales to the Middle East and around the world; and
Diminishing the U.S. role in the Gulf region and globally.

Saudi Arabia

The Kingdom of Saudi Arabia is a conservative Sunni Muslim power. Saudi Arabia plays the central role in Islam as the "keeper of the two mosques" (Mecca and Medina). It has large energy resources and currency reserves, but is otherwise relatively weak and vulnerable. Traditionally, it has had a close security and economic relationship with the United States because both players have a vital interest in securing the energy resources possessed by the Kingdom. Saudi Arabia's security goals are:

Securing the energy resources it possesses;
Regional stability; and
Defending its leadership of the Muslim world in opposition to Iran.

United States

As a leading world power, the United States prefers the status quo and has a low tolerance for risk. The United States has a vital interest in securing access to energy resources and energy transport within the Persian Gulf and around the world. It is unlikely to resort to the use of force unless provoked. On the other hand, it will likely come to the defense of its allies. The U.S. security goals are:

Deterring or defending against any attack on its homeland;
Deterring attacks against its allies;
Securing access to energy resources and preventing a war that disrupts oil flows;
Maintaining reasonable and stable energy prices;
Ensuring or maintaining reliability of supply;
Limiting the political advantages that would otherwise accrue to other states, particularly adversaries, either as consumers or as producers; and
Continuing its strong presence in the East Asia and Persian Gulf regions.

The Crisis

Policy options to counter the economic impact of the cuts in petroleum throughput are limited, while options to compound the damage are many. The only way to reduce actual—as opposed to apparent—petroleum costs is to increase supply or reduce demand.

In most cases, reducing demand requires limiting economic activity and the accompanying jobs and income. Some opportunities exist for substituting other sources of energy for petroleum. This swap almost always occurs in electric power production. The potential for swapping gas, nuclear, wind, and other energy sources for petroleum is limited in the U.S. because less than 2 percent of petroleum in the U.S. is used in power production, and it generates less than 1 percent of the country's electricity.

Increasing supply means putting more petroleum on the market. In places where oil production is limited by regulation, short-term production increases are possible if there is sufficient capacity to refine and distribute the additional crude. Opening new areas to petroleum production can eventually add to supply, but bringing new production on line typically takes longer than the two-year time horizon of this simulation.

The following policies helped moderate the economic impact:

Additional withdrawals from the Strategic Petroleum Reserve;
Reopening nuclear facilities in Eastern Europe; and
Increased liquefied natural gas (LNG) sales to Japan from Russia.

Policies that had no effect on oil price included:

Selective embargoes. Unless accompanied by a corresponding reduction in petroleum production, selective embargoes may force changes in trading patterns, but will not measurably affect marginal cost of crude in any of the targeted countries.

Low price guarantees. In logic similar to selective embargoes, low price guarantees require an accompanying increase in petroleum production to change the marginal cost. If there is an accompanying increase, the cost of petroleum drops worldwide. In essence, a low price guarantee without a change in oil production is simply a wealth transfer from the oil-producing country to the target beneficiary.

Long-term projects, such as expanding the Strategic Petroleum Reserve or comprehensive energy legislation can help in the longer run. However, they take too long to have an impact within the time frame of this exercise.
Odd-even day sales. Limiting the days on which sets of consumers can purchase gasoline adds extraordinary inconvenience, but has minuscule effect on overall prices because most people would simply plan their purchases more carefully.

Responses to Terrorist Attacks

The following section provides an analysis of short-term (within six months) and long-term (between six months and two years) policies of each of the actors. Countries were given a set of objectives at the beginning of the game as shown above. Policy responses were supposed to be tailored toward achieving these objectives.

Short-Term Responses

The players developed a variety of short-term responses to the energy crisis.

Al-Qaeda.

In the short term, al-Qaeda comprehensively and globally approached tasks at hand. The terrorist organization coupled its successful attacks with an assertive global outreach effort through a sophisticated media campaign. This enabled the organization to survive the period of tightened security measures. It also increased emphasis on intelligence collection and anti-Israeli/anti-U.S. communication strategies. However, al-Qaeda primarily focused on targeting Mecca and Medina. The organization deployed a wide range of strategies to overthrow the "apostate" Saudi regime. Al-Qaeda also reached out to Turkey for support. This should come as no surprise given the recent policy shifts in Ankara and the increasing Islamist orientation of the Turkish government. Al-Qaeda's media strategy was essential and complementary to the successful execution of terrorist operations and to the organization's survival.

China.

China's international and energy policy actions were assertive and backed by ample resources. Beijing not only secured 1 million b/d from the Kingdom of Saudi Arabia in a secret deal, but also gained access to advanced technologies from the International Energy Agency (IEA) in exchange for providing $100 billion in 2010 to help with energy infrastructure reconstruction after the attacks. This was a substantial contribution for an agency with a budget of roughly $33.2 million. Significantly, China used its massive foreign exchange reserves to purchase minority stakes in energy-producing companies worldwide, further expanding its influence and securing its position in the energy markets. Moreover, China invested significant resources to obtain cutting-edge technologies (e.g., information, telecommunications, infrastructure, and bioengineering) by acquiring U.S. companies hit by the crisis.

However, Beijing did not adequately address the friction between maintaining good relations with the United States and pressuring Taiwan to rejoin the mainland. These objectives are at odds with each other. The issue of Taiwan has to be seen in the context of U.S.–Taiwan relations. The United States maintains strong unofficial relations with Taiwan, including sales of military equipment.

An interesting dynamic occurred when the Chinese sought to expand Beijing's presence and influence within Russian borders. In response, Russia reacted by encouraging increases in the Russian population in the Far East.

European Union.

The EU did not take any significant diplomatic steps on the international level. This is likely because the EU's Common Foreign and Security Policy is not developed to the point that the EU can act as efficiently and vigorously as an individual nation-state. Competing national interests inevitably undermine any common action. In the face of high energy prices, EU member states might decide to take a protectionist approach toward their domestic energy markets, effectively stopping any efforts to liberalize them.

The EU decided to call for a 10 percent reduction in short-term oil demand. The mechanism that allows member states to share crude and refined products according to country needs within the framework of IEA would be activated after a certain period of time because IEA member states are required to have oil and gas supplies.

India.

India undertook domestic measures to decrease gas and energy consumption and to increase energy efficiency. Internationally, India focused on cooperation with Russia. It also expanded cooperation with Iran. India concluded a defense supply agreement with Iran. Transfers of advanced military technologies to Iran were particularly troublesome to participants because they would likely have destabilizing effects in the Middle East; complicate the U.S. stabilization efforts in Iraq and Afghanistan, especially given Iranian state sponsorship of terrorism; and present a serious proliferation threat. Both the United States and India have invested significant energy and resources into creating a strategic partnership in recent years, and increasing Indian cooperation with Iran would put this partnership in serious jeopardy.

Iran.

The Islamic Republic of Iran demonstrated tactical flexibility and strategic commitment to hegemony and its nuclear agenda. Iran committed to behaving like a responsible actor in helping to defuse the oil crisis, mitigate its consequences, and maintain the steady supply of oil to its trading partners. Tehran's policy was very assertive and backed by a vital resource, its oil. This allowed Iran to secretly secure important bilateral cooperation and relationships with key players, contrary to U.S. interests. Iran's main objective was to crack the sanctions regime and have sanctions ultimately lifted.

The government of Iran remained committed to building its nuclear program. Tehran presented its moderate front to the world. It skillfully emphasized the threat posed by al-Qaeda and used it as a foil to deceive other countries and buy time to achieve its goals, especially to develop its nuclear weapons program. Iran made temporary and deceptive concessions to the EU and Japan on energy deals.

Japan.

Japan adopted stringent measures to limit domestic energy consumption. It also sought to enhance cooperation to secure energy supplies because Japan is dependent almost exclusively on hydrocarbon energy imports to fill its energy needs. As a result of this dependency, it was one of the countries hardest hit by the crisis. The economic pressure resulting from the rise in the energy prices led to a decision to conclude oil import agreements with Russia and Iran. Such an agreement with Iran would significantly affect the U.S.–Japan relationship, especially considering that the United States provides security guarantees to Japan. Lastly, Japan increased LNG cooperation with other international actors (e.g., Indonesia, Australia, Malaysia, and Brunei), which were not programmed into the game.

Russia.

Russia engaged in active diplomacy both in its "near abroad" and globally. Russia was able to use its national power to influence the EU decision-making process because Germany, France, Italy, Greece, and Spain often discuss policy decisions, especially in the energy sphere, in close collaboration with Moscow. The EU depends heavily on Russia for its energy needs. More than 30 percent of oil and 40 percent of natural gas consumed by member states is imported from Russia.

Moscow successfully took advantage of the crisis to expand cooperation with China and East Asia. The conflict in the Persian Gulf served Russia's interests because it benefits from higher energy prices. The Kremlin's policy toward the Middle East, especially toward Iran, was aimed to ensure that the conflict continues, draining U.S. resources and weakening the United States internationally. Revenues were used to sponsor strategic partnerships (e.g., with Brazil, Mexico, or Indonesia) and massive investments in technology acquisition and military modernization.

Saudi Arabia.

Saudi Arabia did not develop any immediate initiative on either the domestic or international level that could contribute to preventing further attacks. The rapid reconstruction of damaged facilities was slowed by Riyadh's protectionist approach.

Little was done to effectively secure Saudi energy resources. This gave al-Qaeda a better chance and more possibilities to expand its operations. Information operations to combat the influence of al-Qaeda and the Iranian media strategy were limited and insufficient.

United States.

Quite understandably, most decisions taken immediately following the crisis focused on the domestic front. The U.S. strategy was to project confidence in its market-based response. Special emphasis was given to the agencies capable of influencing energy prices, such as the Department of Energy and the Department of the Treasury, and on actions, such as releasing the National Petroleum Reserve and lowering interest rates. The international response was limited to issuing a call for the governments of energy-consuming countries to ask their populations to reduce petroleum use.

Disappointment with U.S. inaction on the international level led to the perception that the United States was unable to secure its interests and protect allies, which resulted in allies seeking assurances elsewhere (e.g., Saudi Arabia reached out to China and Japan reached out to Iran). This would present the United States with significant problems in the long term because the U.S. simply cannot achieve its energy objectives on its own. Real-world policymakers need to develop comprehensive policy responses to address this challenge.

Long-Term Responses

The players also implemented a variety of long-term responses to the crisis.

Al-Qaeda.

Because of the success of al-Qaeda's strategy in the short term, the terrorist organization could definitely pose a threat to the Saudi regime, which was not proactive in combating the threat.

However, al-Qaeda seemed to lack an efficient follow-on strategy. A crackdown by security forces would leave the organization dispersed, decentralized, and vulnerable, if it survived the initial pressure. Global operations would be more difficult to conduct. Al-Qaeda limited its activities to calls for jihad in the United States, Saudi Arabia, and worldwide. The organization did reach out to the Quds Force, a more hard-line element of the Islamic Revolutionary Guard Corps in Iran. However, Iran did not follow up on the offer. Evaluating al-Qaeda's long-term strategy is difficult because no further strikes were "programmed" into the game. The number of subsequent attacks would have been a good indicator of the success or failure of the steps taken to counter the terrorist threat.

China.

Beijing managed to formulate a strategic plan vis-à-vis the United States to take advantage of the crisis. Significantly, this included a major naval expansion. Beijing also invested heavily into expanding its oil refining capabilities. This would eventually challenge the U.S. position as the main global refiner of hydrocarbons. It would also have the side effect of generating more income.

China also pushed opening insurance markets. Such a move not only provides a significant source of intelligence, but would help to influence investment directions in the future. In addition, China fostered an alliance with Iran. The more responsible Iran appeared, the more trading occurred between the two countries. China skillfully used its economic leverage and other levers of power to move Taiwan closer toward unification. Beijing's information messaging toward Taiwan emphasized the inability of the United States to protect a vital interest (oil) and, by implication, a vital ally.

It was surprising that China did not take the opportunity to increase its influence in the Persian Gulf by further expanding its "string of pearls" strategy and its stated objectives to secure reliable transit and reduce dependence on American goodwill for its energy supply. The "string of pearls" is a naval strategy based on the nexus of Chinese geopolitical influence or military presence from the coast of mainland China through the littorals of the South China Sea to the Strait of Malacca across the Indian Ocean to the littorals of the Arabian Sea and the Persian Gulf. Any real-world conflict that would jeopardize China's oil supply from the Gulf would likely result in significant expansion of its string of pearls and the People's Liberation Army Navy.

The European Union.

The EU proposed internal measures, such as accelerating implementation of EU-approved projects for interconnectors in electricity and natural gas projects and implementation of EU unbundling guidelines for ownership of supply and transmission networks. The EU also proposed external measures, such as allocation of EU Structural Adjustment Funds to build oil and gas storage capacity in the EU and reaching out to Central Asian producers to supply oil to the Odessa–Brody pipeline. These measures were designed to reduce the impact of the attacks on the member states. However, its enforcement capacity was very limited, and member states decided for themselves which measures to incorporate.

The EU stated that it will steer away from increased reliance on Russian supplies, but it simultaneously sought to increase commercial engagement to increase production and imports of crude oil and product derivatives from Russia. These two initiatives are in conflict because increased energy commerce would make the EU more, not less, dependent on Russia's supply.

India.

India chose a strategy tailored to avoid military conflict, maintain stable energy prices, and secure energy supplies. The purpose of its policy was to become the center of international attention and benefit as much as possible from the situation. The country sought to expand its influence in Iran and eventually function as a moderating force. India would likely compete with China over influence in Iran because both were interested in Iran's resources.

India has significant counterterrorist capabilities and wants to contribute to global counterterrorist efforts. The U.S. and others should have exploited this willingness more actively. Given that India has the largest Muslim minority in the world (more than 138 million), it is surprising that it did not address the problem of al-Qaeda influence in its territory. Nor did India address China's assertive regional and international policy, even though China is India's main peer competitor. It would be very difficult for New Delhi to counter China's strategic successes.

Iran.

Iran used its appearance of moderation to achieve its objective of lifting the sanctions in the short term. Significant oil reserves gave a major boost to Iranians and their ability to achieve their objectives and reach out to other players.

However, in the long term, Iran chose to encourage terrorist attacks worldwide to keep the prices of oil high. The country also continued to covertly develop weapons of mass destruction. Iran achieved important diplomatic victories and deceived the EU, the United States, and others into lifting the energy sanctions.

Iran was able to secure cooperation with India, China, and Japan, a key U.S. ally.

Regrettably, the United States was not able to see beyond Iran's deception and rewarded what it mistakenly perceived as good behavior. However, Iran did not have a strategy to strengthen its leadership in the Islamic world vis-à-vis Saudi Arabia.

Japan.

Japan chose to prioritize its economy over its long-term strategic and security interests. It concluded a partnership with Iran. Surprisingly, the U.S. welcomed the agreement. In reality, the U.S. would likely exercise considerable diplomatic pressure to prevent such an ad hoc agreement. Both the United States and Japan invested an inordinate amount of energy and resources in sustaining and nurturing the U.S.–Japan relationship. Japan also decided to restart self-defense exercises, which was a welcome contribution to providing for its own security in the face of North Korean and Chinese threats.

Russia.

Russia took advantage of the U.S. "reset" policy to distract the U.S. while it undertook actions that conflicted with American national interests. Moscow's primary focus was on expanding its influence throughout its "sphere of privileged interests" in the Central Asia and Caucasus region rather than in the Middle East. Russia successfully took advantage of the crisis to expand cooperation with China and East Asia writ large. It also exploited the opportunity to exert greater influence and foster cooperation in Central Asia and with the Republic of Korea, the EU, and India. However, Russia's regional focus came at the expense of achieving its objectives in the Middle East. Russia also used its energy windfall to invest heavily in its military and purchase advanced technologies overseas.

Saudi Arabia.

Saudi Arabia decided to conduct reprisals against al-Qaeda while seeking to maintain its religious credibility at the same time. On the domestic side, the Kingdom decided to take measures that would promote stability and gain support among a predominantly conservative public. This included placing blame for the attacks on al-Qaeda and depicting the attacks as aimed against ordinary loyal Saudis. While al-Qaeda was unlikely to succeed in overthrowing the Saudi regime, the attacks challenged the regime's survival, especially with the uncertain transition beyond King Abdullah I. Saudi Arabia added extra capacity in oil production, eventually contributing to a more rapid stabilization of the global energy market.

United States.

Quite understandably, most decisions by the U.S. team focused on the domestic level. The U.S. government decided to liberalize energy market mechanisms and release its Strategic Petroleum Reserves. However, on the international level, the United States limited itself to issuing declarations and public statements, which disappointed U.S. allies and friends, who had expected concrete steps reaffirming the U.S. commitment to their security and stability. The lack of U.S. concrete actions led even traditional U.S. allies and friends to seek assurances from other countries. For example, Japan reached out to Iran and Russia. By focusing the bulk of the attention on the domestic level, the United States gave the impression that the international situation was of secondary importance. This also sent the signal that allies and friends would face no consequences if they acted contrary to U.S. interests (e.g., cooperation between Iran and India, between Saudi Arabia and China, and between Russia and the EU.)

Global Effects of the Crises

The 2010 Heritage Energy Game demonstrated that a transnational, well-organized terrorist organization, such as al-Qaeda, and other violent nonstate actors, such as Jamaa al-Islamiya, are capable of causing a massive decline in oil production by attacking production, shipping, storage facilities, and routes. This demonstrated that there are significant security and diplomatic vulnerabilities throughout the domestic and global oil-producing system. Existing security measures were clearly insufficient to prevent the attacks. It was also evident that the players' responses were belated and slow to materialize and that communication was insufficient and problematic among countries.

Some of the actions taken were predictable. China used its foreign exchange to secure energy supplies for its burgeoning economy. After al-Qaeda's attacks and the resulting diplomatic fallout, U.S. allies showed limited or no interest in supporting the United States. Russia attempted to increase its share of the European and Asian energy markets. Some of the countries (e.g., China, Russia, and Iran) created considerable problems and ultimately prevented the United States from achieving its objectives. The United States failed to seize the opportunity to propose multilateral and bilateral initiatives, including access to Saudi intelligence. Because of the lack of a U.S. response, Saudi Arabia reached out to China and even al-Qaeda to increase cooperation with China and secure the regime against al-Qaeda.

The game showed the lack of communication and policy coordination between the U.S. government and U.S. private energy companies. A major cause of this communication problem was that individuals in private companies could not obtain access to the classified information that they needed to make informed decisions in directing recovery efforts. For the sake of efficiency, it became evident that the government needs to "pre-clear" selected individuals before a crisis occurs rather than develop security clearance mechanisms ad hoc after the crisis begins.

Energy Crisis Outcome Trends

In exploring how crisis decision making occurs in a multiplayer environment, the following practices and trends emerged over the course of the game:

Economic interests apparently heavily influenced the long-term political and security considerations and policy decisions.

Iran was the winner of the game. This was due to a combination of diplomacy, which combined aggression with deception, and ample energy resources that Tehran used as leverage when dealing with other countries. Several non-U.S. players advocated engagement with Iran to fill the supply void. Significantly, the question of Israel did not arise much during the course of the game. This is probably because Israel does not have any significant oil resources, and Iran appeared more interested in global hegemony, rather than regional hegemony, seeing the crisis as a foil. Sanctions against Israel, suggested by Iran, were supported only by India on the condition that they would be initiated by others. The United States did not appear to have efficient strategies at hand to achieve its objectives despite the options available to it and its diplomatic, military, and economic power. The United States lost important allies on the international level and failed to prevent Iran from achieving its objectives. However, the United States had a handicap in the game. "The United States" consisted of multiple actors playing different parts within the U.S. government interagency process. While this consumed additional time in the decision-making process, it simulated the real world experience of the interagency process. Yet important signals from foreign players were often missed or misinterpreted.

The United States needed to develop a coherent, assertive, and proactive international strategy, but did so only partially. U.S. communications with other international actors were lacking. The U.S. team made little effort to use the international momentum due to the crisis to move forward with important international initiatives (e.g., Proliferation Security Initiative and Global Initiative to Combat Nuclear Terrorism). On the other hand, the United States players were able to run a well-structured "Administration" team, accurately simulating the interagency process with its advantages and disadvantages. Saudi Arabia did not develop or implement strategies to protect its leading status in the Islamic world vis-à-vis Iran. Effective counterterrorism and media strategies were lacking. This may be a reflection of organizational paralysis and/or the age of the monarch. Saudi Arabia failed to harden its position toward militant Salafism/Wahhabism. Passing a law stringently regulating and controlling the operation of Islamic charities would have helped to make their funding and expenditures more transparent.

Russia demonstrated its mastery of combining energy geopolitics with an anti-American agenda and by expanding its role in Asia. Russia effectively used the "reset" policy to distract U.S. attention from its actions against the U.S. national interests in the post-Soviet space, especially in the Caucasus. Russia also used the crisis to increase its influence in Europe and Asia. Moscow leveraged the crisis to strengthen its influence around the world.

China did not address the friction between maintaining good relations with the United States and exercising its influence over Taiwan.
China strengthened its presence in areas that are seen as traditionally Russian spheres of influence.

The competing national interests of EU member states prevented the EU from developing a unified and ultimately more efficient international response.
The U.S. mostly avoided policies that could have worsened the crisis. The policy actions worldwide cut petroleum prices by up to $20 per barrel and gasoline prices by $0.60 per gallon. Compared to the business-as-usual scenario, the national income losses were $130 billion lower in 2011 and $50 billion lower in 2012. In comparison to the business-as-usual case, the employment losses were 630,000 jobs lower in 2011 and 650,000 jobs lower in 2012.

Crisis Response

At the end of the game, the participants recommended a number of domestic and foreign policies that the U.S. should implement.

Domestic U.S. Economic Policies

The participants recommended that the U.S.:

Buy $300 billion to $500 billion in new Treasury bonds. This would lower interest rates and stimulate the economy, but it would also reduce the value of the dollar, which increases the dollar cost of petroleum. The effects are assumed to roughly offset.

Tax oil companies' windfall profits. This would negatively affect oil production and increase oil prices, but not in the period covered in this exercise. Further, to the extent the tax failed to recognize the difference between profits from extraction and profits from refining and transportation, the tax could drive down the level of domestic refining even in the short term.

Increase the rate of withdrawals from the Strategic Petroleum Reserve beyond the level in the baseline. This would lower world petroleum prices modestly and increase government revenue.

Implement a variety of initiatives to increase access to resources. Little additional petroleum would be produced within the 24-month horizon.

Foreign and Defense

The participants recommended that the United States should:

Set up an early warning system for terrorist attacks on U.S. and allied energy infrastructure and commerce and shipping lanes; increase their protection; and develop a plan for rapid security response, followed by an economic response based in the private sector.

Increase U.S. intelligence collection and allied intelligence services cooperation to protect energy and shipping infrastructure worldwide, including with energy-consuming and energy-producing countries.

Rely on market forces in the long term and coordinate security and rebuilding activities to restore confidence of markets and consumers faster than a response that relies exclusively on government intervention.

Expand security cooperation between energy companies and government security and intelligence agencies. The existing framework should be expanded to include early warnings and security-related issues (e.g., giving the contractors security clearances before the actual attacks would make effective cooperation easier under difficult post-attack conditions).

Lessons Learned

The 2010 Heritage Energy Game demonstrated that there are significant vulnerabilities in the domestic and international energy network. Terrorists and other violent nonstate actors could cause a massive drop in oil production and price spikes; so can protracted turmoil in principal OPEC and non-OPEC oil producers. The exercise also demonstrated that major producer and consumer nations and the oil and non-energy companies need to cooperate and communicate better to prevent violent disruptions and post-disruption economic downturns. Reliance on markets and security cooperation can do much to restore the confidence of governments, corporations, and consumers. The United States and its allies would need to exercise decisive and effective leadership to deal with the crisis.

Under the business-as-usual baseline scenario (see the Appendix), petroleum prices rose from $75 to $250 per barrel, gasoline prices rose to $8.00 per gallon, GDP fell by $325 billion per year, and employment fell by 2.4 million jobs. All impacts diminished by the end of the 24-month window.

Under policies suggested by Heritage Foundation players, the petroleum price increased $20 less per barrel, gasoline prices increased by $0.65 less per gallon,

GDP fell by $130 billion less per year, and employment dropped by 650,000 fewer jobs.

The Heritage game demonstrated the vulnerabilities of the global system's capacity to produce and deliver sufficient oil supplies in a timely manner after a concerted transnational terrorist threat. This exercise also suggests that the lack of assertive international energy policy of the United States would further weaken the U.S. international position during a crisis. The government and oil companies need to address the U.S. institutional inability to develop proactive, multilayered responses to deal with situations such as those presented in the scenario.

—Ariel Cohen, Ph.D. is Senior Research Fellow in Russian and Eurasian Studies and International Energy Policy in the Douglas and Sarah Allison Center for Foreign Policy Studies, a division of the Kathryn and Shelby Cullom Davis Institute for International Studies, at The Heritage Foundation. David W. Kreutzer, Ph.D., is Research Fellow in Energy Economics and Climate Change in the Center for Data Analysis at The Heritage Foundation. William W. Beach is Director of the Center for Data Analysis at The Heritage Foundation. James Jay Carafano, Ph.D., is Deputy Director of the Kathryn and Shelby Cullom Davis Institute for International Studies and Director of the Douglas and Sarah Allison Center for Foreign Policy Studies, a division of the Davis Institute, at The Heritage Foundation. John L. Ligon is Policy Analyst in the Center for Data Analysis at The Heritage Foundation. The authors are grateful to Owen Graham, Nick Loris, and Michaela Bendikova for their assistance in producing this report.

Appendix 44

Nuclear Terrorism --- How To Prevent It
http://www.nci.org/nci-nt.htm

The attacks of September 11, 2001 have provided a wake-up call for facing the threat of nuclear terrorism. The Nuclear Control Institute, since its inception in 1981, has been analyzing the risks of nuclear terrorism and seeking to alert policymakers and the public to the danger. There was a solid basis for concern long before the attacks of September 11.

Iran threatened attacks against U.S. reactors as early as 1987. Trial testimony has revealed that Osama bin Ladens al Qaeda training camps offered instruction in urban warfare against enemies installations including power plants. It is prudent to assume, especially after the highly coordinated, surprise attacks on the World Trade Center and the Pentagon, that bin Ladens soldiers have done their homework and are fully capable of attacking nuclear plants for maximum effect. It is also clear that bin Laden was seeking nuclear explosive materials (plutonium or highly enriched uranium) and know-how for building atomic bombs, and other dangerous nuclear materials for use in "dirty bombs" to spread radioactive contamination with conventional high explosives.

In 1986, the Nuclear Control Institute, in cooperation with the Institute for Studies in International Terrorism of the State University of New York, convened the International Task Force on Prevention of Nuclear Terrorism, comprised of 26 nuclear scientists and industrialists, current and former government officials, and experts on terrorism from nine countries. The report issued by the Task Force, along with more than 20 commissioned studies, remains the most definitive examination of nuclear terrorism in the unclassified literature. (The report and a number of the studies are reproduced at the end of this section.)

The Task Force warned that the "probability of nuclear terrorism is increasing" because of a number of factors including "the growing incidence, sophistication and lethality of conventional forms of terrorism," as well as the vulnerability of nuclear power and research reactors to sabotage and of weapons-usable nuclear materials to theft. The Task Force's warnings and its recommendations for reducing vulnerabilities, many of which went unheeded, are all the more relevant in today's threat environment of sophisticated and suicidal terrorists dedicated to mass killing and destruction.

Recent Developments

There is now intense national and international attention to the risks of nuclear terrorism. The possibilities that al Qaeda might acquire the materials and the knowledge for building nuclear weapons or "dirty bombs" or might attack commercial nuclear-power facilities to trigger a nuclear meltdown, are of particular concern. The Nuclear Control Institute has been alerting the public and policymakers to these risks, seeking emergency measures to reduce the vulnerabilities, and monitoring and assessing the responses of industry, governments and international agencies.

What follows are some of the key issues pertaining to the risks of nuclear terrorism:

Are reactors adequately protected against attack? For nearly 20 years, the Nuclear Control Institute has pressed the U.S. Nuclear Regulatory Commission to upgrade security at nuclear power plants. In 1994, we and the California-based Committee to Bridge the Gap finally succeeded in getting NRC to require nuclear-power plant operators to install defenses against truck bombs, although we remain concerned that these protective measures are inadequate to defend against the larger bombs used by terrorists since the 1993 truck-bomb attack against the World Trade Center.

Current NRC security regulations do not address the magnitude of threat demonstrated by the September 11 attacks. NRC standards require that nuclear plant operators protect against a much smaller number of attackers than involved in these attacks. Yet, even under the current weak standards, the armed guards at nearly half of the nuclear plants tested in NRC-supervised security exercises have failed to repel mock terrorist attacks or prevent simulated destruction of redundant safety systems that in real attacks could cause severe core damage, meltdown, and catastrophic radioactive releases.

This outcome is all the more worrisome because the NRCs mock terrorist exercises severely limit the tactics, weapons and explosives used by the adversary, do not test plant defenses against attacks from the air or from the water, and do not test whether guards could repel an attack on the spent-fuel pools at plant sites that contain many times more deadly radioactivity than the reactor cores. In addition, in response to industry complaints that the exercises are unfairly severe, the NRC is now preparing to shift responsibility for supervising the exercises to the plant operators themselves. Current events clearly demonstrate that nuclear power plant security is too important to be left to industry self-assessment or to the level of protection that industry is willing to pay for. The heightened security at nuclear plants since 9/11 still falls far short of the military-type protection we have recommended. The NRC is undertaking a "top to bottom" review of plant security with no indication of how long it will take to complete and implement or what additional measures will be required.

Despite nuclear industry claims to the contrary, it is highly unlikely that nuclear-power reactor containment domes are robust enough to withstand a direct hit from a jumbo jetliner. Dr. Edwin Lyman, NCIs scientific director, has calculated that a direct, high-speed hit by a large commercial passenger jet "would in fact have a high likelihood a penetrating a containment building" that houses a power reactor. "Following such an assault," Dr. Lyman said, "the possibility of an unmitigated loss-of-coolant accident and significant release of radiation into the environment is a very real one." Such a release, whether caused by an air strike, or by a ground or water assault, or by insider sabotage could result in tens of thousands of cancer deaths.

Could terrorists build nuclear weapons? A study prepared for Nuclear Control Institute by five former U.S. nuclear weapons designers concluded that a sophisticated terrorist group would be capable of designing and building a workable nuclear bomb from stolen plutonium or highly enriched uranium, with potential yields in the kiloton range. This risk must be taken seriously, particularly in light of documented attempts by al Qaeda to acquire nuclear material and nuclear-weapon design information. Despite claims to the contrary from plutonium-fuel advocates in the nuclear power industry, effective and devastating weapons could be made using "reactor-grade" plutonium, hundreds of tons of which are processed, stored and circulated around the world in civilian nuclear commerce.

Appendix 45

The increasing sophistication of Taliban roadside bombs
By Caroline Gammell and Tom Coghlan
12:16PM BST 18 Jun 2008
http://www.telegraph.co.uk/news/2150789/The-increasing-sophistication-of-Taliban-roadside-bombs.html

The use of roadside bombs against British troops in Afghanistan has become an increasingly popular and sophisticated Taliban weapon in the last year.

The improvised explosive devices (IEDs) have proved a deadly tactic, triggered by remote control when British Forces pass near.

A shortage of coalition helicopters in Afghanistan means much of the military's movement is by road, making them sitting targets for enemy ambushes, roadside bombs and suicide attacks.

The Taliban know that in pitched battles they will lose against coalition forces, so have resorted to increasingly sophisticated terrorist warfare.

While many of the devices use old munitions for the explosive component - such as artillery shells, rockets and even mortar bombs - the method of detonation has become steadily more technical.

There is increasing use of a remote control detonating device called a 'Spider', a specific bomb making component which is thought to have originated in Iran.

It is detonated through a mobile phone, generally by the use of a code number sent by text message.

The Taliban have also used command wire devices and pressure plates, the latter often constructed from the simple but effective use of two saw blades held apart by a piece of wood and encased in a car tyre inner tube.

A vehicle passing over the buried device connects the saw blades and triggers the device.

Officials in Tehran deny supporting Afghanistan or Iraq, but recent intelligence suggested that as much as 90 per cent of the hardware being used by insurgents in southern Iraq originates from Iran.

The Revolutionary Guard is not only accused of helping the Taliban, but giving them the expertise to build powerful explosives which could destroy a tank, let alone an armoured vehicle.

Statistically, only one in five soldiers is expected to survive a tank mine.

The British Army is fighting back with equipment which can disable the IEDs gradually being fitted to armoured vehicles. The technology cannot be explained in detail for operational reasons.

The Electronic Counter Measures (ECM) either jam or scramble the bomb's mechanism, but not every vehicle carries the device.

The Taliban constantly seek new ways around these counter-measures. Western intelligence officials have recently noted a learning curve on the part of the bomb makers and increasingly imaginative devices - some of which use several detonation methods.

For British soldiers, the best defence lies in the armour of heavier vehicles and the discipline and methodical caution of identifying risky areas, particularly choke points that funnel them into the narrow lanes favoured by the bombers.

In this respect, the desert is the best friend of the British solder, while 'close country' and the tracks and villages of Helmand's 'Green Zone', the cultivated land around the Helmand River, represents the greatest threat.

Appendix 46

Roadside bomb kills 3 U.S. soldiers in Afghanistan
Posted 8/12/2007
http://www.usatoday.com/news/world/2007-08-12-afghanistan-violence_N.htm

KABUL, Afghanistan (AP) — A roadside bomb blast killed three U.S. troops in eastern Afghanistan on Sunday, bringing to five the number of international troops killed over the weekend, officials said.

The three troops were engaged in combat operations in Nangarhar province when the roadside bomb hit their vehicle, a statement from the U.S.-led coalition said. A civilian interpreter was also killed.

The coalition did not announce the nationalities of the soldiers, though Noor Agha Zuwak, the spokesman for the Nangarhar governor, identified the troops as American. The majority of troops in eastern Afghanistan are from the U.S.

Elsewhere, one NATO soldier was killed and several others wounded in an attack Saturday in the south, NATO's International Security Assistance Force said in a statement Sunday.

Another NATO soldier was killed and two were wounded when a roadside bomb struck their vehicle during a patrol Saturday in eastern Afghanistan, ISAF said.

ISAF did not give any further details such as the exact locations of the two incidents or the nationalities of the soldiers.

The five deaths brings to at least 127 the number of international troops killed in Afghanistan this year, including at least 61 Americans, according an Associated Press count.

Separately in southern Uruzgan province, Taliban militants attacked a U.S. military base Saturday evening for the third time this week in what the U.S.-led coalition said might be a rehearsal for a future attempt to overrun the outpost.

"Several" suspected Taliban were killed Saturday evening in the latest attack on Firebase Anaconda, in addition to four that were killed in an earlier attack on the base Saturday, the coalition said.

Insurgents first attacked the base in a rare frontal attack on Tuesday. The military had said that 23 were killed in that incident but late Saturday officials raised the number believed killed to 50. Taliban militants usually shun head-on fights, preferring instead to attack foreign forces with suicide blasts and roadside bombs.

Coalition spokeswoman Army Capt. Vanessa R. Bowman said the Taliban attacks are expected "to culminate with a large full-scale attack in the near future."

In Helmand province, Afghan army and NATO forces clashed with Taliban militants on Saturday, and the ensuing battle and airstrikes left seven Taliban dead, said Eizatullah Khan, chief of Sangin district.

Appendix 47

On The Hunt For Roadside Bombs In Afghanistan
by Tom Bowman, October 27, 2009
http://www.npr.org/2009/10/27/114205345/on-the-hunt-for-roadside-bombs-in-afghanistan

The Marines of the 2nd Battalion, 8th Regiment — known as "America's Battalion" — have been fighting the Taliban in southern Afghanistan's Helmand province since July.

They have set up numerous outposts along the dusty roads and cornfields. And now they are moving farther south, looking to extend their area of operation and avoid the deadliest of threats just outside the wire: roadside bombs.

On a recent morning, a platoon of Marines from Fox Company leaves the remote patrol base, a small patch of sandbags, camouflage tents and gravel. Within minutes they're cutting through a cornfield, walking in single file.

It could be any cornfield in Iowa, except for the Taliban radio chatter the Marines are picking up on their radio. The Marines intercept a radio transmission from the Taliban that says the militants are "ready for the guests."

"Guests" is Taliban code for the Marines. On this patrol, the Marines are searching for roadside bombs, commonly known as IEDs.

"We're lucky if we find them. Better than when they find us, I guess," says Lance Cpl. Dan Leary, from Boston.

Leary will be going back to the United States in just a few weeks, and he's worried his luck will run out.

'They're Always Watching Us'

"We had like one week where we found like 21, 22 of them. They were everywhere. We went back two days later. They were everywhere again. They were putting them — like everywhere they put them were places that we had stopped and taken cover," Leary says. "They're watching. They're always watching us."

The Taliban plant bombs everywhere — along dirt paths, in the fields and especially along the main roads. The insurgents are brazen, placing the explosives in the middle of the day.

They have either intimidated the local population, or they have support among them.

The Marines walk on patrol for about two hours, cutting through cornfields, hopping over irrigation canals and trudging along dirt paths.

At the front of the patrol, a Marine sweeps the ground with a hand-held minesweeper, a flat green, angular version of what people use on a beach to find coins.

Before long, he finds a bomb at a dirt-road intersection just outside a compound of mud houses. It's a perfect example of why they call these devices improvised. It is a 5-gallon yellow jug stuffed with a mix of fertilizer, diesel fuel and metal.

The Marines set some plastic explosives to detonate the IED. They call out a 10-second warning, and the Marines take cover in a ditch beside the dirt road. The explosion propels a wave of dirt over the squad.

The Marines talk about the unsettling feeling of walking along the trails and fields, slopping through canals, just waiting for an explosion.

'A Morale Killer'

"People would rather deal with firefights than IEDs. Like, IEDs are just a — it's a morale killer, definitely," says Lance Cpl. Raymond Grabau, from Minnesota.

Since July, 40 Marines in Helmand province have been killed, and more than 160 have been seriously wounded, most by IEDs.

But four months into their mission, the Marines are getting better at finding these crude and hidden bombs.

Another hour goes by, and the patrol detects two more IEDs. One is found by a Marine combat engineer, Pfc. Brad Sexton. But not with his metal detector.

"Yeah, I found it. Stepped on it, actually," he says.

The IED was rigged with a trigger known as a pressure plate. Just enough pressure, from a foot or a truck tire, and it detonates the buried explosive charge. Luckily for Sexton, this one had no batteries.

"Yeah, I'd probably [have] lost a leg or maybe even more. It was a metal cylinder, so I'd have had a lot of shrapnel. It would have been bad. I feel extremely lucky right now," he says.

A Marine lifts the pressure plate from the ground. It looks like a poorly wrapped Christmas present, a long rectangle covered in plastic and heavily taped.

'Everywhere You Go, It's Dangerous'

The Marines stuff the pressure plate into a backpack. It will be shipped to Bagram Air Field, where a special forensics team will look for clues — fingerprints or materials that could help identify the bomb maker. The Marines suspect that in their area, IEDs are manufactured and set by three or perhaps four insurgents.

Many Marines say they could do a better job going after the bomb makers if there weren't so many restrictions on the use of force. Some Marines say they have identified insurgents but had to wait for approval from higher-ups to call in artillery or other firepower.

Lt. Sam Oliver recalled an incident involving a man on a motorcycle who had a hand-held radio. The Marines intercepted his conversations with the insurgents.

"By the time we passed all the information, made sure [that] no, there's no civilians around — by the time that all goes through, he was gone," Oliver says.

But the battalion commander, Lt. Col. Christian Cabaniss, says the Marines have to take care not to kill innocent civilians in their pursuit of the Taliban. It makes their job more dangerous, he says, but in the long run the cautious approach will do more to gain the support of Afghan civilians.

"There is a little bit more risk upfront. Everywhere you go, it's dangerous," he says. "The reality is to be, you know, in an environment where we're completely safe. As we move, we would be destroying buildings and tree lines everywhere we went. We're not going to win the consent of the people that way, and the fight is actually going to get worse over time."

Some Marines still grumble about having to keep going out to search for IEDs. They were a lot more willing when they first arrived in Helmand province in July.

'The Unknown Is Real'

"Well, now they know that the unknown is real," says 1st Sgt. Derrick Mays, the top enlisted man in Fox Company. "And that the possibility of you getting shot or blown up could be the minute you step out on your next patrol."

But some of the Marines wonder if the patrols to find IEDs are reckless.

"You're going to have the ones that are going to probably ask that question, 'Why are we still doing this?' " says Mays. "Because we still have a job to do. And it'd be unfair to those individuals that are coming behind us to not do our job."

Fresh Marines are already arriving in Helmand, and some are following along on patrols to learn what they can from Fox Company's veterans.

Near a mud compound, Afghan adults and children squat on the ground shucking corn and glance at the advancing Marines on patrol.

Outside a small mosque, a Marine questions the local mullah about who is making the bombs.

The mullah says he knows nothing — about the bombs or the Taliban.

"How are we supposed to keep your mosque safe if you don't let us know what's going on out here?" the Marine asks, using a translator.

More than five hours after they started their foot patrol, the Marines get the signal to head back to their camp.

They peel off their helmets and gear, and grab some food. Inside their headquarters, a Marine sticks red pins on a large map, representing the IEDs found on the patrol.

And in a day or two, the Marines of the 2/8 will head out again in search of bombs and the insurgents who plant them.

Appendix 48

16, 2009 10:53 AM PrintText
Roadside Bomb In Iraq Kills 3 Americans
http://www.cbsnews.com/stories/2009/05/26/iraq/main5039228.shtml

(CBS/AP) Three Americans, including a State Department employee, were killed by a roadside bomb that struck a convoy in Iraq's western Anbar province, the U.S. military said Tuesday.

The blast killed a U.S. soldier, a State Department official and a civilian contractor working for the Defense Department as their convoy headed through Fallujah to a nearby construction site on Monday, the military said. Two others were wounded.

The Associated Press reports that Terry Barnich, deputy director for the Iraq Transition Assistance Office, was the State Department official killed.

Barnich, 56, was a former Illinois Commerce Commission chairman and also had worked as chief counsel to former Gov. Jim Thompson.

Barnich's sister, Rochelle Barnich, described her brother as a person with a great sense of humor who had great pride in his country and had been interesting in politics since they were children.

Like many cities in Iraq, there are a number of U.S.-funded or backed reconstruction projects, many of them aimed at improving essential services as well as promoting businesses.

American military and government officials see the projects as essential to helping maintain security gains in the region. Some of the projects are overseen by provisional reconstruction teams, a joint U.S. civil-military office, and others are overseen by the State Department's U.S. Agency for International Development.

Insurgents once held sway over Anbar, which was the scene of some of the deadliest fighting of the war. But violence fell off dramatically after Sunni fighters turned on al Qaeda in Iraq and joined U.S. forces in what has become known in Iraq as "the Awakening."

Insurgents, though, have continued to sporadically target American and Iraqi security forces in Fallujah, where four Blackwater employees were ambushed in 2004 by insurgents and their remains strung from a bridge.

The U.S. military has withdrawn from most of the cities in the vast Anbar province, including Fallujah.

The military said the identities were being withheld pending notification of next of kin.

As of Monday, May 25, 2009, at least 4,301 members of the U.S. military had died in the Iraq war since it began in March 2003, according to an Associated Press count.

The figure includes eight military civilians killed in action. At least 3,443 military personnel died as a result of hostile action, according to the military's numbers.

Appendix 49

Blast Injuries
Author: Andre Pennardt, MD, FACEP, FAAEM, FAWM
http://emedicine.medscape.com/article/822587-overview

Explosions have the capability to cause multisystem, life-threatening injuries in single or multiple victims simultaneously. These types of events present complex triage, diagnostic, and management challenges for the health care provider. Explosions can produce classic injury patterns from blunt and penetrating mechanisms to several organ systems, but they can also result in unique injury patterns to specific organs including the lungs and the central nervous system. Understanding these crucial differences is critical to managing these situations.

The extent and pattern of injuries produced by an explosion are a direct result of several factors including the amount and composition of the explosive material (eg, the presence of shrapnel or loose material that can be propelled, radiological or biological contamination), the surrounding environment (eg, the presence of intervening protective barriers), the distance between the victim and the blast, the delivery method if a bomb is involved, and any other environmental hazards. No two events are identical, and the spectrum and extent of injuries produced varies widely.

Between 1991 and 2000, 93 terrorist attacks worldwide produced more than 30 casualties, with 885 of these incidents involving explosions. The 2005 London subway bombings, the 1995 bombing of the Murrah Federal Building in Oklahoma City, and the catastrophic explosions of aircraft into 3 buildings on September 11, 2001 in New York City and Washington DC reminded health care workers of the magnitude of injuries and death that can result from a blast mechanism. Internationally, explosive devices directed against both civilian and military targets are frequently used in war or acts of terrorism. Approximately 25,000 US and coalition forces and 100,000 Iraqis were estimated to have been injured or killed by explosions in the Global War on Terrorism as of early 2009.[1] Although the United States has been spared the majority of these events, the potential exists for use of explosive weapons in the United States in the future.

As the risk of terrorist bombings in the United States increases, emergency physicians and Emergency Medical Services (EMS) personnel should be especially concerned about radiation and/or chemical contamination of explosion victims. Careful observation for signs and symptoms of exposure to poisonous chemicals, screening for radiation contamination, and decontamination of patients as needed are important steps in the management of victims of nonaccidental explosions. In addition to deliberately set explosions, incidents also occur as a result of industrial accidents (eg, factory and mining operations, fuel transportation and storage, grain elevator explosions).

In many parts of the world, undetonated military incendiary devices such as land mines and hand grenades contaminate the sites of abandoned battlefields. Such devices cause significant numbers of civilian casualties years and even decades after local hostilities cease. During wartime, injuries arising from explosions frequently outnumber those from gunshots with many innocent civilians becoming victims.

Much of the challenge facing the care providers is the potential for the sudden creation of large numbers of patients who require extensive medical resources. This scenario can overwhelm local EMS and hospital resources. Emergency physicians must remain attentive to the possibility and consequences of blast injuries.

Once notified of a possible bombing or explosion, hospital-based physicians should consider immediately activating hospital disaster and contingency plans, including preparations to care for anywhere from a handful to hundreds of victims.

Appendix 50

Wars and Battles, 1944-1945 Japan's Suicide Pilots of World War II
http://www.u-s-history.com/pages/h1740.html

Transcend life and death. When you eliminate all thoughts about life and death, you will be able to totally disregard your earthly life. This will also enable you to concentrate your attention on eradicating the enemy with unwavering determination, meanwhile reinforcing your excellence in flight skills.

- A paragraph from the Kamikaze pilot's manual, located in their cockpits.

In the year 1281, Japan was under attack by a Mongol invasion — led by the powerful Kublai Khan. However, just as it appeared that the invading Mongols were about to overwhelm the Japanese, a catastrophic typhoon swept through the land, eliminating the entire Mongol army. From that point on, the typhoon that saved Japan became known as the Kamikaze or Divine Wind.

Background

After the defeat at the Battle of Midway, and the fall of Saipan in July 1944, the Japanese revived the name Kamikaze and ascribed it to the suicide missions of their air force.

Japanese Vice Admiral Takashiro Ohnishi, commander of the First Air Fleet in the Philippines, had noted that the most effective way to inflict damage upon Allied warships was to crash planes into them. He noted that one accidental crash could do more damage than 10 planes firing machine guns. It was decided then that pilots would purposely crash their planes — with half a ton of explosives — into American warships.

The Kamikaze pilot

Generally, Kamikaze pilots were university students motivated by obligation, and loyalty to family and country. A typical pilot was a science student in his twenties. He prepared for his fiery destiny by writing farewell letters and poems to loved ones, receiving a "thousand-stitch sash*," and by holding a ceremony — a drink of water that gave him a "spiritual lifting" before wedging himself between 550-pound bombs.

It was adamantly believed that, because they were fighting for their Emperor God, the Kamikaze would bring them deliverance at the darkest hour, just as it had in the 13th century. In fact, the call for Kamikaze pilots drew a staggering response. Three times as many applied for suicide flights as the number of planes available. Experienced pilots were turned down. They were needed to train the younger men how to fly to their deaths.

The fact that they were to go on suicide missions was accepted without question by the Japanese pilots. All inductees into the Japanese armed forces were indoctrinated with the following five-point oath:

A soldier must make loyalty his obligation.

A soldier must make propriety his way of life.

A soldier must highly esteem military valor.

A soldier must have a high regard for righteousness.

A soldier must live a simple life.

The Mitsubishi A6M2

Nicknamed the "Zero," the Mitsubishi A6M2 was the Kamikaze pilot's personal "flying coffin." It had a maximum speed of 332 mph and a range of 1,930 miles. The A6M2 was 29 feet nine inches long, with a wingspan of about 39 feet. The aircraft was armed with two machine guns and could carry 264 pounds of bombs; however, the Japanese modified its structure to accommodate a heavier arsenal. The Zero was the main strike aircraft used at Pearl Harbor — dominating the skies during the early stages of World War II. A large number were shot down during the Battle of Midway, and it eventually became outperformed by the latest allied aircraft, such as the P-51 Mustang.

First attacks

Beginning with the Pearl Harbor Attack, Japanese suicide bombers sporadically crashed their planes into the enemy as a spur-of-the-moment decision.

On October 21, 1944, the flagship of the Royal Australian Navy, the heavy cruiser HMAS Australia, was hit by a Japanese plane carrying a 441-pound bomb, off Leyte Island. Although the bomb did not explode, the damage was devastating — killing at least 30 crew members.

On October 25, the Australia was hit again and was forced to retire to the New Hebrides for repairs. That same day, five Zeros attacked a U.S. escort carrier, the USS St. Lo off the Philippines coast, although only one Kamikaze actually hit the ship. Its bomb caused massive fires that resulted in the ship's bomb magazine exploding, sinking the carrier. Japanese pilots also hit and damaged several other Allied ships.

The initial successes of those attacks sparked an immediate expansion of the program. During the next few months, more than 2,000 planes staged such attacks. Those included new types of suicide attacks and explosives, including purpose-built Yokosuka MXY7 Ohka rocket-bombs, small boats packed with explosives, and manned torpedoes (equipped with a 3000-pound warhead) called the Kaiten.

Iwo Jima and Okinawa

On February 19th, 1945, the USS Enterprise and other carriers took up stations off Iwo Jima, attacking nearby enemy airfields, and providing close air support for the Marines that landed. By the time the marines unfurled the U.S. flag on Iwo Jima's summit, Kamikaze attacks had sunk the escort flattop Bismarck Sea CVE-95, knocked the USS Saratoga CV 3 out of the war for good, and temporarily halted the Enterprise — all while regularly harassing amphibious forces at the beachhead.

The day of April 6th, 1945, proved to be most telling for the use of Kamikazes in the battle for Okinawa. More than 350 aircraft at a time dove at the Allied fleet. Just the anticipation of Kamikaze attacks drove some American sailors literally insane. The destroyer Laffey was attacked by 20 aircraft at once. Her gunners stopped nine Kamikazes, but six others rammed into the ship. As on the similarly damaged USS Franklin, ineffable courage, and intensive training in firefighting, kept the Laffey afloat.

On the 7th of April, Kamikazes were still attacking in great numbers off the coast of Okinawa, severely damaging the carrier Hancock. By April 16th, suicide bombers desperately, but effectively damaged the USS Enterprise yet again, as well as the flattop USS Intrepid, and numerous picket destroyers were sunk or damaged. Admiral Marc A. Mitscher led Task Force 58 from his flagship, the carrier Bunker Hill CV-17. On May 11th, 1945, the flagship was hit by a Kamikaze pilot that killed 350 of his men.

The final Japanese defense of Okinawa was hard fought. For the Americans, victory brought a heavy price. The capture of Okinawa cost the Americans 49,000 in casualties, of whom 12,520 died. More than 110,000 Japanese were killed on the island. When it was clear that he had been defeated, General Mitsuru Ushijima committed ritual suicide (hara-kiri).

War's end

From October 25, 1944, to January 25, 1945, Kamikazes managed to sink two escort carriers and three destroyers. They also damaged 23 carriers, five battleships, nine cruisers, 23 destroyers and 27 other ships. American casualties amounted to 738 killed and another 1,300 wounded as the result of those attacks.

Several thousand Kamikaze planes had been set aside for an invasion of the Japanese mainland that never happened. Kamikaze pilots were one of the reasons President Harry S. Truman decided to drop the atomic bombs.

On the eve of the Japanese surrender, Takijiro Onishi ended his own life, leaving a note of apology to his dead pilots — their sacrifice had been in vain.

Appendix 51

Method Without Madness?
Suicide bombers are not deranged, psychiatrists say. Under group pressure, they see logic and a 'higher purpose' in their actions.
Los Angeles Times/July 30, 2002
By Benedict Carey
http://www.rickross.com/reference/brainwashing/brainwashing22.html

The list includes architects and drifters, engineers and poets, teenagers and middle-aged men, a 30-year-old woman, an 18-year-old girl, and, every week it seems, someone else, someone different.

"You hear people say that these are all desperate people, or poor people whose families need the money," said Rohan Gunaratna, a terrorism specialist at the University of St. Andrews in Scotland. "This is nonsense."

Long before the recent rash of suicide bombings in Israel, psychiatrists, terrorism specialists and others were searching for clues to what prompts people to strap on explosives and annihilate themselves in a crowded street or cafe.

Experts examined psychological profiles. They interviewed Sri Lankan separatists and imprisoned Palestinian militants. They studied the mass suicide at Jonestown, Guyana, in 1978 and the Japanese kamikaze missions of World War II.

Their emerging understanding contradicts the notion that suicide bombers are deranged fanatics. The evidence is just the opposite: They tend to be free of obvious mental illness. Many are competent, successful, even loving and loved.

What, then, triggers their awful acts?

Most have fallen under the influence of an extreme group, whether it be Al Qaeda, Hamas or the Tamil Tigers of Sri Lanka, experts say. Like a cult, the group demands absolute obedience and promises immortality to the most devoted.

Conditions of chronic conflict and bloodshed endow suicide with a sinister logic. When death seems pervasive and unavoidable, whether in Sri Lanka or a refugee camp in the Gaza Strip, members of the group come to value its survival above their own. They become willing, even eager, to sacrifice their lives for a greater cause--a psychological response found not just in terrorist cells, experts note, but among soldiers in wartime.

In the end, the suicide terrorist sees his mission as acceptable, logical, even noble. "It can be perceived as a very idealistic act," said psychiatrist Robert Jay Lifton, a visiting professor at Harvard Medical School and an author who has studied cults and suicide.

"They believe there's a higher purpose, that in some way they are bringing about a purification, a perfection. They are destroying the world to save it."

A common trait of nonpolitical suicides--people who take their own lives without harming others--is a feeling of isolation or disconnectedness from the world.

Suicide terrorists are anything but isolated. Often, they have connected with others deeply, and it's this affiliation that helps prepare them to take their own lives, said Clark McCauley, a psychologist at the University of Pennsylvania who studies terrorism.

"It's the group that's abnormal and extreme," McCauley said. "The bombers themselves are psychologically as normal as you and I."

A Wake-Up Call

Americans confronted the horror of suicide attacks on April 18, 1983, when a Shiite Muslim truck bomber attacked the U.S. Embassy in Beirut, killing 63 people. Six months later, another truck bomber killed 241 Marines on a peacekeeping mission in Lebanon.

Since then, more than 300 men, women and children have blown themselves to pieces in suicide attacks around the world. Those carried out by Palestinians in Israel have received the most publicity, but two-thirds of the attacks occurred in Sri Lanka, where Hindu separatists have been waging a guerrilla war for 20 years.

The best evidence that these terrorists are mentally competent is the planning and patience required for many of their missions.

The Sri Lankan woman known as Dhanu who killed former Indian Prime Minister Rajiv Gandhi in 1991 prepared for months, performing several practice runs, according to Gunaratna, the terrorism expert.

Dhanu, a member of the Tamil Tigers separatist group, got so close to Gandhi that she was able to reach out and touch him before pulling a cord beneath her dress and ending both their lives, witnesses said.

Another Tamil bomber, Babu, worked for many months to infiltrate the household of Sri Lankan President Ranasinghe Premadasa before killing him in a 1993 suicide attack.

Wafa Idris, a Palestinian woman who blew herself up in Jerusalem in January, killing an 81-year-old man, was a volunteer paramedic who had founded a women's relief group to assist victims of the conflict with Israel. She was not known as an Islamic extremist.

The 19 hijackers who carried out the Sept. 11 attacks on the U.S. stayed in touch and under cover for many months before executing their well-coordinated plan.

Some attended flight schools and spent hours practicing on flight simulators.

Their leader, Mohamed Atta, grew up in a middle-class Egyptian family and appeared to have a promising career ahead of him as an architect and urban planner. Ziad Jarrah, another of the suicide pilots, was educated, well-off and said by his Lebanese family to be planning to get married.

These did not appear to be mentally unbalanced people, researchers say. Indeed, crazed loners are not likely to be selected for suicide missions.

"The crucial quality that recruiters look for is mental stability," said Jerrold Post, a psychiatrist at George Washington University who recently completed a study of 35 Palestinian militants in Israeli jails, several of whom had recruited suicide attackers.

In addition to levelheadedness, terrorist organizations look for a willingness to conform and obey.

Those qualities are not hard to find, research shows. Regardless of education or background, most people have a tendency to follow instructions, especially when given by an authority figure who promotes a larger cause.

In a series of now-famous experiments during the early 1960s, psychologist Stanley Milgram showed how this instinctive obedience can lead people to cross an ethical line. The authority in this case was a scientist; the larger cause, a learning experiment in which electric shocks would be used to "teach" word associations to a middle-aged man (an associate of Milgram's who was not actually being shocked).

The participants began by delivering mild shocks, then gradually increased the voltage. By the end, 60% were delivering 450-volt blasts--even when the "victim" screamed for them to stop.

This is the same principle on which many terrorist groups operate. They begin by asking members to take small risks and gradually up the ante, said the University of Pennsylvania's McCauley.

The Baader-Meinhof gang in Germany, the Marxist Red Brigades in Italy and the Symbionese Liberation Army of California included middle-class, well-educated people who graduated from protest to murder under the sway of impassioned leaders.

Such groups demand total commitment and fealty. "Commanders in Hamas"--the Islamic resistance movement in Gaza and the West Bank--"are commanders in every way," an imprisoned terrorist told researchers working with Post, the George Washington University psychiatrist. "A commander's orders are absolutely binding and must not be questioned in substance."

In the case of the Tamil Tigers, Post said, "there's almost a chemical connection that seems to develop between the personality of the leader"--the reclusive Velupillai Prabhakaran--"and those of the followers. It's as if the followers merge with each other and with what the leader says."

In an eerie echo of Jonestown, Prabhakaran's acolytes are said to wear cyanide containers around their necks in case of capture.

Suicide as a Statement
The latter 20th century offers many examples of suicide as a political or religious statement, however eccentric or inscrutable. In Northern Ireland in 1981, 10 prisoners starved themselves to death to protest British rule. In 1978, more than 900 American followers of People's Temple leader Jim Jones poisoned themselves on his orders at the Jonestown compound in Guyana.

Five years ago, Marshall Applewhite and 38 of his followers in the Heaven's Gate cult killed themselves in Rancho Santa Fe, Calif.

They expected to shed their earthly bonds and travel to a "next level" of existence on a spacecraft they believed was shadowing the Hale-Bopp comet.

Many commentators have cited Christianity's taboo against suicide as a protection against such extremism. In Christian teaching, to kill oneself is to sinfully reject God's gift of life. Yet the ban was imposed in the 5th century partly to halt an epidemic of suicide among early Christians, according to Jaroslav Pelikan, a Yale University expert on the history of the faith.

In those early centuries of the church's history, many believers saw suicide as a means to prove their faith, cleanse themselves of sin and leave the pain of this life for the bliss of the next. The popularity of suicide among some groups prompted St. Augustine to remark that "to kill themselves out of respect for martyrdom is their daily sport."

In Islam, too, strong prohibitions against suicide coexist with a rich history of martyrdom. The Persian Assassins of the 11th century, sometimes called the Muslim Hashshashin, were said to smoke hashish before carrying out suicide assassinations. In the Iran-Iraq war of the 1980s, Iranian children as young as 14 and unarmed were sent into battle. Some reportedly had "keys to paradise" hanging from their necks.

Groups that sponsor suicide attacks invoke both the future world and the ancient one to recruit and inspire. After Sept. 11, investigators found letters in Arabic believed to have been written by Atta, the presumed ringleader. The letters emphasize the importance of "obeying 100%"; instruct the attackers to be courageous, "as our predecessors [were] when they came to the battle"; and promise that "paradise has been decorated for you with the best of its decorations and ornaments."

"It's hard to accept for outsiders, but from the bombers' point of view, they don't actually die in a suicide attack--they become immortal," said Gunaratna, whose recent book, "Inside Al Qaeda," details the ideological indoctrination that occurred at Osama bin Laden's training camps. "It's not the end, but the beginning. You are surviving in a way; you are being granted an eternal life."

Bonding as Soldiers

In their willingness to sacrifice all for their group, suicide bombers have something in common with traditional soldiers, say researchers who have studied heroism in combat.

If a war becomes sufficiently destructive and prolonged, troops lose faith that they will survive, said David Marlowe, former chief of military psychiatry at the Walter Reed Army Institute of Research in Silver Spring, Md. The question becomes not whether one will die, but how. Under these conditions, small groups of soldiers forge an often-unspoken pact to do anything for the good of their comrades.

"It creates a kind of bonding between members, a love that transcends anything you've ever known," Marlowe said. "You come to the absolute belief that the noblest and most important thing you can do is die for the others."

Perhaps the most vivid example of suicide attacks committed for comrades and country was those by Japan's kamikaze squads in World War II. In their oral history, "Japan at War," Haruko Taya Cook and her husband, Theodore Cook, interviewed several former members of Japan's "special attack corps," who survived because their missions were canceled or foiled.

One of them, Yokota Yutaka, recalled the words his Naval Academy commander used to recruit suicide attackers: "If there be any among you who burn with a passion to die gloriously for the sake of their country, let them step forward."

Yutaka said that all but 120 of the 2,000 young men in his academy volunteered. On April 20, 1945, Yutaka climbed aboard a motorized suicide torpedo, said goodbye to his comrades in arms and awaited the order to launch. It never came.

"I was ordered to come back in," he said. "That was the moment I really wanted to die."

Post, the George Washington University researcher, found a similar yearning among the Palestinian militants he studied. One of them is serving 26 life terms for his role in several suicide bombings. In a prison interview, the man recalled learning from a confederate that another suicide attack was in the works:

"I asked him what it was all about, and he told me that he had been on the wanted list for a long time and did not want to get caught without realizing his dream of being a suicide bomber.... I remember that besides the tremendous respect I had for him and the fact that I was jealous of him, I also felt slighted that he had not asked me [to join him]."

People who have witnessed or been subjected to violence are particularly susceptible to this call to immortality, researchers say. The families of Palestinian suicide bombers often cite motives of revenge for a father or brother killed or beaten by Israeli soldiers.

In Sri Lanka's contested territory, the 19-year civil war has left very few people untouched by violence. The tragedy and nearness of death are such that even children become fatalistic, according to Margaret Trawick, an anthropologist at Massey University in New Zealand who lived in Sri Lanka during the late 1990s.

Based on conversations with a dozen girls and young women who belonged to the Tamil Tigers, Trawick concluded that joining the group is itself a kind of suicide gesture: "They have no ideology but for the words 'I want to fight.' ... Most expect to die in battle, and many will die in just that way. They think their lives are unimportant, and they think the same of their deaths. They seek no fame, they ask no voice. They do wish to be remembered."

So, for that matter, does the person who jumps off a bridge, psychiatrists say. If there's a common thread connecting all suicides, perhaps it is that desire: to have done something memorable, whether for an audience of one or two or for the entire world.

In his 1990 book, "The Savage God," the British poet and literary critic A. Alvarez, a failed suicide himself, writes that suicide is "a closed world with its own irresistible logic. Once a man decides to take his own life, he enters a shut-off, impregnable but wholly convincing world where every detail fits and each incident reinforces his decision."

Once a member of Hamas or the Tamil Tigers has begun to consider a suicide attack, the same kind of hermetic logic applies, experts say. Only by destruction can the world be renewed; only by killing can the group live; only by leaving the world can you leave a mark on it.

"I think in this sense," said Lifton, the Harvard psychiatrist, "all suicide has to do with making a lasting statement one could not make in life."

Appendix 52

Sheik Muhammad Husayn Fadlallah
From Professor Raymond Tanter's Political Science course 353 & 498, at the University of Michigan 13-Mar-96
http://almashriq.hiof.no/lebanon/300/320/324/324.2/hizballah/Fadlallah-Muhammad.html

Fadlallah Role Profile
Name: Sheik Muhammad Husayn Fadlallah
Role: Spiritual Leader of the Lebanese Hizbullah (Party of God)
Born: 1935

Quotation: "What martyrdom is greater than making yourself a human bomb detonating it among the enemy? What spiritualism is greater than this spiritualism in which a person loses all feeling of his body and life for the sake of his cause and mission?"

Narrative section:

I was born in 1935 in Najaf, Iraq, to a Shi'i Muslim family from Aynata in southern Lebanon. My father, Ayatollah Abd-al Rauf Fadlallah, was an alim (religious scholar) in Najaf, a shrine and university city. I underwent all of my schooling in Najaf, where Muhammad Baqir al-Sadr also studied. Baqir al-Sadr became my friend and mentor, and it was he who encouraged me to combine my religious convictions with political and social participation. Consequently, when the ulama (community of religious scholars) appointed me, in 1966, to Nab'ah, an impoverished suburb of Beirut, I began opening community centers and cultural clubs for our youth, as well as free clinics.

When the Maronites, a Lebanese Christian sect, destroyed Nab'ah, in 1976, I went to southern Lebanon with fellow Shi'i Muslim refugees. Several years later, when the Ayatollah Ruhollah Khomeini launched his successful revolution in Iran, I began to recognize the necessity for an Islamic revolution in Lebanon.

Since 1985, I have been president of the Lebanese council of Hizbullah. In that capacity, I helped draft the Lebanese Islamic Constitution, which was inspired by the model cast by my friend Baqir al-Sadr in Najaf in 1979. In addition to drafting the constitution, I provide authoritative opinions, advice, and decisions for Hizbullah members and Islamists everywhere, as we prepare for a full Islamic revolution. Such a revolution will lead to an Islamic economy and social structure. Despite my influence, however, I do not participate directly with political or military affairs any longer. Instead, I have assumed the unofficial role of spiritual leader for the party, serving as a highly influential beacon of Islamic truth for all the oppressed peoples of the world.

Politically, my primary objective is to see the Islamic revolution in Lebanon brought to fruition. The newly dissolved and recreated Lebanese government, led by men like Hrawi, Berrih, and Jumblatt, is clearly an obstacle in the path to revolution, and I believe that this government has been put together by imperialist Americans hoping to achieve their own ends in the Middle East. The United States and Israel are full partners in a war against the people of the Middle East. Therefore, we must secure their departure from Lebanon as a precursor to Israel's obliteration from existence, and as the first step towards liberating our people from the talons of Western imperialism. Only then may we begin to construct a political system favored by the people based upon the teachings of the holy Quran.

All those who seek peace with Israel are traitors to our cause, including the treasonous Yasir Arafat. We reject the accords signed between Israel and the PLO, just as we have rejected Camp David, the Fahd, Fez, Reagan, Brezhnev, and French-Egyptian plans, and any other plan that offers even tacit recognition of the Zionist entity.

"Land for Peace" is a betrayal of Palestinian blood and of the sacred cause of Palestine. Arafat, just like Israel, America, and the rest of the Western world stand in our way of revolution. So too, the secular government in Lebanon stands in our way. So too the Amal with its Syrian ties and secular orientation. The latter two have gone so far as to combat their kin, the Palestinian refugees in Beirut, during the camp wars of the mid-80's. We stood up for our people then, as we do now, while traitors like the Syrians strive for accords with the Zionists and imperialists.

Only Iran stands firmly by the Palestinian cause. Khomeini provided inspiration with the Iranian revolution, and then military and financial support in later years. Since Khomeini's death, Iran under Khamenai and Rafsanjani has continued to support us, although to a lesser degree. Still, they remain allies against the Zionist/Imperialist menace.

The Hizbullah has also cultivated allies from a wide array of groups, including the Islamic Resistance Movement, Jund Allah, the Hussein Suicide Squad, al Dawa, Holy Warriors for Freedom, The Organization of the Oppressed of the Earth, Islamic Amal, and Revolutionary Justice Organization. Together, we fight for an Islamic nation.

In addition, as articulated in the Hizbullah's covenant, also known as the open letter, we consider all the downtrodden people of the world to be our allies. Whether they are Muslim or not, we believe that they will discover a path to freedom through Islamic principles.

Thus far, we have celebrated one major achievement, namely the military defeat of the Israeli occupation forces in Lebanon. February 18, 1985 stands as a triumphant day as Sidon was freed from Zionist clutches. Yet, that was but a small step towards the ultimate goal: Our finest hour will arrive when the revolution is complete and Lebanon is reconstructed along Islamic lines.

For the most part, my political ideologies are shaped by theological convictions. I write commentaries on the Quran, as well as spiritual poetry. However, I also try to include historical and psycho- sociological perspectives in my speeches and sermons. I am not an active policy-maker; my influence is manifested through speeches and sermons. I welcome cooperation with non-Muslims, and I am willing to leave margin for compromise, provided no interference arises hindering the creation of an Islamic state. I do not believe that conditions are right yet for an Islamic state in Lebanon due to the significant non-Muslim minority, but the time will come soon for revolution--that is our primary objective.

Here are some excerpts from my writings, speeches, and interviews:

- "The Zionist occupation continues to usurp the lands of the Muslims"
- "Israel poses a great danger to our future generations and to the destiny of our modern nation, especially since it embraces a settlement-oriented and expansionist idea that it has already begun to apply in occupied Palestne and it is extending and expanding to build Greater Israel, from the Euphrates to the Nile"
- "I believe that there is an attempt to cause something similar to a political tremor in the region through the world arrogance of the United States, whose changes in loyalties according to changes in economic and strategic interests are familiar to us."
- "Iran is standing alone in the world with the Palestinian people and supporting their struggle."
- "All Palestine is a war zone and every Jew who unlawfully occupies a house or land belonging to a Palestinian is a legitimate target."
- "There are no innocent Jews in Palestine. The area is a war zone. They kill many of our women, children, and elderly people. They destory our homes. They confiscate our water and freedom."

Appendix 53

THE TERROR CONSPIRACY: THE CHARGES;A Gamble Pays Off as the Prosecution Uses an Obscure 19th-Century Law
By RICHARD PEREZ-PENA
Published: October 02, 1995
http://www.nytimes.com/1995/10/02/nyregion/terror-conspiracy-charges-gamble-pays-off-prosecution-uses-obscure-19th-century.html

At the outset of its seditious-conspiracy case against a blind Muslim cleric and 11 of his followers, the Government was thought to be taking quite a gamble in pinning its hopes on an obscure 19th-century law that makes it a crime to "conspire to overthrow, or put down, or destroy by force the Government of the United States."

Before yesterday, Federal prosecutors said, the last time seditious-conspiracy charges had been brought successfully was in 1987, against a group of Puerto Rican nationalists in Chicago. In two seditious-conspiracy cases in the late 1980's, one in Arkansas and one in Massachusetts, jurors acquitted all the defendants.

A person can be convicted of seditious conspiracy without the Government showing that the defendant committed any specific act to further the conspiracy. This is a departure from other conspiracy laws, like the racketeering statutes that are often used against organized-crime figures.

The law's broadness can work against the prosecution. It gives the defense room to tell the jury -- as it did in this case -- that the defendants are being prosecuted for nothing more than their political or religious beliefs, and for offhand statements that reflect no real criminal intent.

But in the case of Sheik Omar Abdel Rahman and his nine co-defendants (two others pleaded guilty shortly after the trial began), the prosecution may have calculated that it would help to cast their case in political terms, linking the defendants to Middle East terrorism.

The sedition law presented other advantages for the United States Attorney for the Southern District of New York, Mary Jo White, and her aides. It allowed them to charge defendants, like the Sheik, who did little more than talk about the plot with others. According to Federal law enforcement officials, until the defendants' indictment in August 1993, many prosecutors and F.B.I. officials said that the Sheik could not be charged unless he could be tied to a specific criminal act, but that Ms. White was determined to include him in the case and saw the seditious-conspiracy law as the way to do it.

And with a maximum penalty of 20 years and a $250,000 fine, the law allowed prosecutors to seek much stiffer penalties than were available for most of the crimes, like explosives charges, that were included as pieces of the conspiracy.

The law has historically been used against groups with unpopular views. It was enacted after the Civil War, intended for use against Southerners who rejected the authority of the Federal Government, and amended in 1918, with Socialists and anarchists in mind.

The law has been assailed by defense lawyers as overly broad and an infringement of the right of free speech, an argument that legal experts say can give grounds for appeal after a conviction.

Appendix 54

Haganah
Encyclopedia of the Modern Middle East and North Africa, 2004
http://www.encyclopedia.com/topic/Haganah.aspx

HAGANAH

Underground military defense organization for Jewish community in Palestine, 1920–1948.

The Haganah ("defense") was founded in June 1920 by the Labor Zionist Party Ahdut ha-Avodah in response to Arab riots in April. Its military and organizational complexity increased as the conflict with the Palestinian Arabs intensified during the Mandate era. By the time full scale Arab–Jewish warfare erupted in Palestine following the November 1947 United Nations partition resolution, the Haganah was well positioned to serve as the Yishuv's main armed force and to become the core element of the Israel Defense Force (IDF).

In December 1920 the Haganah was placed under the direct control of the newly created Histadrut, headed by David Ben-Gurion. After the 1929 riots, the Haganah expanded into a Yishuv-wide defense force, and a six-member civilian National Command council was established, led by Eliyahu Golomb. The 1936–1939 Arab Revolt was a watershed event in the development of the Haganah. In the process of responding to the rebellion it developed new doctrines and structures and became an army capable of taking offensive military actions. The Haganah mobilized Jewish youth for military training, established officers' courses, and set up arms depots and underground small arms factories. Elite units were formed under the command of Yitzhak Sadeh, who would also become a major figure in the Palmah and the IDF.

The military doctrine of the Haganah during the 1920s and 1930s was based on self-restraint (havlagah). As the Arab Revolt intensified, those most opposed to havlagah split off and in 1937 formed the Irgun Zva'i Le'umi, which committed retaliatory acts of terrorism against Arab civilians. In 1940 some Irgun members, led by Abraham Stern, rejected the Irgun's wartime truce with Britain and founded the "Stern Gang," also known as LEHI.

In 1938 the British created a Jewish military unit for counterinsurgency missions against the Arabs, the Special Night Squads. They were trained and commanded by Orde Wingate and drew volunteers from the Haganah, even though the Haganah was technically illegal according to the Mandatory government. Wingate's commando tactics greatly influenced the Haganah and later the IDF. Yigal Allon (Palmah commander) and Moshe Dayan were Wingate protégés.

In 1939 control over the Haganah was transferred to the MAPAI-dominated Jewish Agency, which was headed by Ben-Gurion. A professional Military General Staff was established and Ya'akov Dori became the Haganah's first chief of staff. The Haganah ran illegal immigration operations (Aliyah Bet) during and after World War II to circumvent the 1939 White Paper restrictions. At the same time, Britain supported the creation of an elite strike force, the Palmah (Plugot Mahatz, or "shock companies") in May 1941, and Haganah members enlisted in the British Army's Jewish Brigade. When Britain refused to lift the White Paper restrictions after the war, the Haganah and Palmah joined with the Irgun and LEHI to form the Hebrew Resistance Movement (1945–1946). The undergrounds coordinated military operations against British targets in Palestine. The harsh British crackdown on the Yishuv in June 1946 convinced Ben-Gurion to end the Haganah's participation.

By 1947 the Haganah had evolved into a cohesive military organization with British Army professionalism and combat experience. The original Palmah battalions had expanded to three full brigades, and the Haganah grew to twelve brigades. On the eve of the first Arab–Israel war, the Haganah had a nascent air force, medical and signal corps, and intelligence units, with membership totaling 60,000. The bulk of Jewish fighters during the Arab–Israel War of 1948 came from Haganah ranks.

On 28 May 1948 Order Number 4 of the Provisional Government declared the establishment of a single national army with a unified national command, to be called the Israel Defense Force (Zva Haganah le-Yisrael, or ZAHAL). All independent military organizations were to be dismantled and absorbed into the IDF. The Haganah's personnel and command structure became the main elements of the new Israeli army and Dori became the IDF's first chief of staff. Many Haganah veterans would later become generals in the IDF, including Dayan, Yigael Yadin, Mordechai Gur, and Ariel Sharon.

See also irgun zva'i le'umi (izl); lohamei herut yisrael; white papers on palestine; yishuv.

Bibliography

Ben-Eliezer, Uri. The Making of Israeli Militarism. Bloomington: Indiana University Press, 1998.

Herzog, Chaim. The Arab–Israeli Wars: War and Peace in the Middle East from the War of Independence through Lebanon, revised and updated. New York: Vintage Books, 1982.

Jewish Agency for Israel. "Israel and Zionism: The Haganah." Available from <http://www.jafi.org.il/education/>.

Peri, Yoram. Between Battles and Ballots: Israel Military in Politics. New York and Cambridge, U.K.: Cambridge University Press, 1983.

Van Creveld, Martin. The Sword and the Olive: A Critical History of the Israeli Defense Force. New York: Public Affairs, 1998

Appendix 55

From the Irv Rubin Bust To
The Stern Gang -The Rich
History Of Jewish Terrorism
By Jason Vest
VillageVoice.com
12-21-1
http://www.rense.com/general18/fromtheIrvRubin.htm

WASHINGTON, DC - At a moment when the popular mind-set once again links the words "Arab" and "Islamic" with all things retrograde and threatening¬óincluding terrorism--cue the new Charlie Daniels anthem and revel in the poetry:

"This ain't no rag, it's a flag
And we don't wear it on our heads. . . .
We're gonna hunt you down like a mad dog hound"

it came as a surprise to some that the latest malefactors accorded POW status in the "War on Terrorism" turned out to be Jewish.

Arrested and charged last week with intriguing to do explosive little actions on a Culver City, California, mosque and the offices of Lebanese American U.S. Representative Darrell Issa, Jewish Defense League chief Irving David Rubin and JDL member Earl Leslie Krugel were, according to FBI wiretap transcripts, anything but circumspect about their devices and desires: Though Rubin lamented the wanting state of technology in the JDL's possession (not good enough to "blow up an entire building"), Krugel was adamant that "Arabs need a wake-up call" and that the JDL needs to do something to one of their "filthy mosques" - which may explain the five pounds of gunpowder and pipe-bomb materiel found at his house. "If the people responsible for September 11 are the quintessence of evil genius, these guys are at the Keystone Kops end of the spectrum," says Hussein Ibish, communications director for the American Arab Anti-Discrimination Committee. "The only reassuring thing about them is their absolute ineptitude and the fact that they were arrested."

Mainstream Jewish groups were quick to condemn the JDL as well: Characterizing the activities of the organization - founded in 1968 by Brooklyn's own, now deceased Rabbi Meir Kahane - as "contemptible," the Anti-Defamation League's regional director issued a statement "abhor[ing] and condemn[ing] the potential terrorist plot." The American Jewish Committee said it "categorically condemns in the strongest possible terms the alleged JDL plot," and went so far as to follow up with a personal letter to Republican representative Issa, decrying "such wanton lawlessness," which is "so clearly contrary to the fundamental tenets of our faith, and to the basic principles of justice and liberty that brought our parents and grandparents to America's shores and that form the bedrock of our national values."

Yet some observers of the current Middle East crisis see more than a bit of disingenuousness and historical irony here. While both the ADL and the AJC have condemned the JDL, they've unequivocally backed Israeli prime minister Ariel Sharon's indiscriminate use of force against the Palestinians and the cutting of ties with Palestinian Authority president Yasir Arafat—neither of which is universally seen as a particularly constructive way to slow the cycles of violence across Israel and the Occupied Territories.

But what's even more vexing to others is the apparent inability or unwillingness to discern similarities between the current Palestinian milieu and Israeli operations of 50-plus years ago, which secured statehood from colonialist occupiers—as well as similarities between violent, internecine struggles among disparate underground groups. "It's peculiar, it's paradoxical, that Sharon and Likud should be the ones who are trying to equate any authentic resistance in Palestine with some of the terrorist activities, as terrorism in Israel really started with Begin and Shamir and later Sharon," says Clovis Maksoud, the former Arab League ambassador to the United Nations. "It's a very valid question as to why they see no similarities between themselves under the British and the Palestinians under their occupation." Especially, he adds, as the Israeli government supports museums that honor assassins and terrorists—including one located on a street named for a terrorist.

The thoroughfare in question runs between Florentine and Emeq-Yisrael, and bears the name Stern Street—in honor of Avraham Stern, a 1920s Zionist and charter member of the Haganah, then a loose-knit Jewish militia organized as a self-defense mechanism against Arab violence. Finding the Haganah insufficiently proactive in realizing the goal of a Jewish state that would encompass "both sides of the River Jordan," erstwhile Mussolini follower and early-day ultra-nationalist Ze'ev Jabotinsky broke with the militia and formed the Irgun, which devoted itself to terrorist operations against the British. Once an enthusiastic Irgunist, Stern was appalled when the Irgun decided to make common cause with the British against the Nazis, and created the even more underground and more violent Lehi (Lohamei Herut Yisrael, or Fighters for the Freedom of Israel), also known as the Stern Gang, which held there was no greater threat to the Jews of Palestine than the mandate's British administrators.

To this end, Stern actually made overtures to the Axis powers; September 1940 found him in dialogue with an emissary from Il Duce in Jerusalem, and in January 1941 he dispatched an agent to Vichy-controlled Beirut with instructions to convey a letter to representatives of the Reich. In it, Stern held that the "establishment of the historical Jewish state on a national and totalitarian basis, and bound by a treaty with the German Reich, would be in the interest of a maintained and strengthened future German position of power in the Near East. Proceeding from these considerations, [the Lehi] in Palestine, under the condition [that] the above-mentioned national aspirations of the Israeli freedom movement are recognized on the side of the German Reich, offers to actively take part in the war on Germany's side."

The Germans declined to take Stern up on the offer, but Stern held out hope as his organization continued to engage in terrorism against the British. After Stern died in a shoot-out with British police in 1942, his mantle was picked up by future Israeli prime minister Yitzhak Shamir. Still, the Israeli underground focused on the British as the greatest of all evils, and on November 6, 1944, Lord Moyne, the British minister for Middle East affairs, was assassinated in Cairo by Eliyahu Beit-Tzuri and Eliyahu Hakim—both members of the Lehi, who were later arrested, convicted, and hanged. After the state of Israel was established, the Lehi, displeased with what it considered the too pro-Arab views of the Swedish UN-appointed mediator for Palestine, assassinated him; on September 17, 1948, Count Folke Bernadotte—who, as a neutral diplomat in World War II, had saved thousands of Jews from Nazi death camps—was shot and killed by Lehi assassins, along with French colonel Andre Serot, the senior UN military observer, whose wife's life had been saved by Bernadotte.

The Bernadotte assassination was so outrageous that the nascent government of David Ben-Gurion had little problem disbanding the Lehi (though none of the assassins were ever brought to justice). Yet, despite this history of terror, the Israeli Ministry of Defense underwrites museums commemorating the Stern Gang and the Irgun—which, under Menachem Begin, bombed the British headquarters at the King David Hotel in 1946, leaving 90 dead and 45 wounded (with 15 Jews among the casualties). Like Lehi, it wasn't until 1948 that the Irgun was forced out of existence, after its arms-transport ship, the Altalena, was blown up by the provisional Israeli government—a point analysts like Ibish say bears remembering.

"There are streets named after the assassins of Moyne and Bernadotte. They are historical figures not disavowed by the rhetoric of the state of Israel, nor is there any reflection on the fact that two terrorist leaders later became distinguished leaders of the republic," Ibish says. "And now people are saying that Arafat must have his Altalena." Ibish adds that Israel's first prime minister, David Ben-Gurion, "never moved against the Irgun and the Stern Gang until after the state was established and secured, which is definitely not true in the case of the Palestinian Authority. Essentially, the Israelis are asking the Palestinians to do something they themselves refused to do."

Appendix 56

US Counterinsurgency and Terrorism Policy
Posted September 26th, 2010.
http://alexgaynor.net/2010/sep/26/us-counterinsurgency-and-terrorism-policy/

Over the course of the last nine years the United States has attempted to implement a number of policies to combat terrorism, and to engage in a counter insurgency, the formal on a global scale, and the latter primarily in Iraq and Afghanistan. However, viewed in a broader historical context current policies represent a nearly 180 degree shift.

In the wake of 9/11 there was a potential for a passive jurisdictional fight: the FBI has jurisdiction in domestic terrorism cases, NYPD had jurisdiction under local murder statutes, the National Transportation Safety Board has jurisdiction in the event of an accident, and while the Department of Defense and intelligence apparatus formally have no jurisdiction any international response is within their purview. The myriad of government agencies with jurisdiction is broadly representative of US policy with respect to terrorism in the pre-9/11 world, with the typical result being other agencies acting as support to the FBI (as in the Oklahoma City bombing). Though this may seem disorganized, in practice there is one clear trend: any organization with statutory jurisdiction is a civilian organization. This is indicative of a fundamental view point that combating terrorism is fundamentally an operation for police. Indeed as a result of these jurisdiction the United States military is barred from performing any functions, with US borders, as it would constitute law enforcement functionality which is strictly prohibited under the Posse Comitatus Act (1878).

However, the last nine years have seen a radical shift in these policies. The most striking evidence for this is in the name given to these operations, "War on Terror", designating these operations as a war is already a violent change in direction. The Central Intelligence Agency has largely been re-purposed to the point where it's primary function is obtaining and processing evidence on terrorism. The greatest change, however, has been a deployment of US military personnel around the world, most notably in Iraq and Afghanistan. This is clear evidence of the change in US policy towards treating terrorism as a military conflict.

With US military deployments in Iraq and Afghanistan the principle question has become whether to handle local combatants as insurgents or terrorists (somewhat ironic given the characteristic aspect of the colonial strategy during the revolutionary war as to act as guerrillas). However, the the mere fact that the US is deploying troops answers this question, it's to be treated as a counterinsurgency. This is, practically speaking an impossible strategy, short of killing (or converting) anyone who would oppose US rebuilding interests, local insurgents can always wait out a military, foreign occupiers are unlikely to maintain a local force indefinitely (US military presence in Japan and Germany following World War II notwithstanding). US counterinsurgency efforts have, however, largely been following a "clear-hold-build" strategy, in the hopes of building a foundation that can persevere in the face of the inevitable opposition once US forces cease holding.

Appendix 57

Counterterrorism and Counterinsurgency
by Jason Rineheart
http://www.terrorismanalysts.com/pt/index.php/pot/article/view/122/html

Abstract

This article focuses on current counterterrorism and counterinsurgency doctrines. It argues that the more traditional frameworks for analyzing counterterrorism campaigns, which structure debates around a military (or war) model or a criminal justice model, need to be updated in the light of the current state of terrorism. As a potential new framework, the author restructures the debate around hard and soft power tactics. He also describes how the existing counterinsurgency literature primarily focuses on two frameworks: classical and modern (or global) counterinsurgency. Using the war in Afghanistan as an example, he compares and contrasts the strengths, weaknesses, and potential offsetting effects of modern counterterrorism and counterinsurgency strategies, arguing that in order for the United States to be successful in its battle against Al-Qaeda's brand of international terrorism, it must take its struggle from the open battlefields of counterinsurgency into the shadowy world of counterterrorism.

Introduction

Nine years after 9/11, the struggle against international terrorism is at a crossroads. Policy debates on whether to adopt a counterterrorism or counterinsurgency strategy in Afghanistan continue to drive contemporary security discourse in the United States and NATO.[1] However, these debates provide little strategic clarity on how to counter international terrorism. While Al-Qaeda's strategy is adaptive, the war in Afghanistan has become much more complicated than one would surmise from America's stated goal to "disrupt, dismantle, and defeat Al-Qaeda in Pakistan and Afghanistan, and to prevent their return to either country in the future."[2] Counterterrorism and counterinsurgency debates on Afghanistan are somewhat shortsighted – focusing too much on the strengths and weaknesses of short and long-term commitments while avoiding critical discussions about what a sustainable counterterrorism strategy should consist of at the international level. The line between counterterrorism and counterinsurgency strategy has become increasingly blurred, yet they are two rather distinct doctrines.

The American-led invasion of Iraq not only diverted attention away from the perpetrators of the 9/11 attacks, it also gave rise to a new wave of research and analysis on insurgency and counterinsurgency warfare. While the Al-Qaeda terrorism threat was not entirely ignored, research on terrorism tended to aggregate America's terrorism and insurgency threats and frame counterterrorism within the context of counterinsurgency warfare, leading to the misleading conclusion that both strategies where mutually reinforcing. There were at least three perceptions of the problem at hand. The first focused on how Al-Qaeda was exploiting the largely nationalist insurgencies in Iraq and Afghanistan in order to play the role of strategic spoiler. The second focused on the resilient and adaptive nature of Al-Qaeda as a global organization and its ability to project its ideology worldwide in order to gain more recruits and encourage new attacks. The third focused on the need to change the facts on the ground and address the root causes of terrorism.

This gave rise to several theoretical approaches to counter the threat posed to the U.S. forces on the ground in Iraq and Afghanistan: including enhanced policing, better intelligence and information operations, increased international cooperation, counter-radicalization programs, and the need for good governance and economic development – all in an attempt to address the ill-understood underlying causes of terrorism. Such prescriptions tended to misunderstand the nature of the terrorism and overplay causal linkages.

In the following I shall try to address five questions: What is counterterrorism? How has counterterrorism evolved over the past four decades? What is the nature of counterinsurgency? How are counterterrorism and counterinsurgency doctrines similar and how are they different? And, finally, to what extent has the increased focus on counterinsurgency warfare after 9/11 affected how we view the current nature of counterterrorism?

What is Counterterrorism?

Counterterrorism is a difficult concept to define, especially for western democracies. Paul Wilkinson writes that: "There is no universally applicable counter-terrorism policy for democracies. Every conflict involving terrorism has its own unique characteristics."[3] Both Paul Wilkinson and Louise Richardson argue, and they are not alone, that Western democracies must make respect for civil liberties and the rule of law a staple in their counterterrorism strategies.[4] While this advice to liberal democracies is admirable and complies with championed democratic principles, it does not amount to a counterterrorism strategy – these are simply highly valued principles meant to guide counterterrorism.

Counterterrorism is defined in the U.S. Army Field Manual as "Operations that include the offensive measures taken to prevent, deter, preempt, and respond to terrorism."[5]. This definition is more concrete but has its strengths and weaknesses. First, it correctly states that counterterrorism is an all-inclusive doctrine including prevention, deterrence, preemption, and responses, which would require bringing to bare all aspects of a nation's power both domestically and internationally. Second, this definition includes everything but essentially differentiates nothing, which is a problem. If an effective counterterrorism doctrine means 'whatever we need, whenever we need it,' then this could create problems with developing effective counter strategies, allocating resources, and determining accountability – it might make the concept of counterterrorism rather worthless. There are, however, advantages to an all-encompassing approach to counterterrorism. It allows a government such as the United States to recognize the complexities of responding to terrorism; it also provides a rhetorical tool that reinforces the notion that there is no simple fix to America's terrorism problem – but that does little to help our understanding of counterterrorism.

Counterterrorism operations are subject to change according to the nature of the terrorism threat. Indeed, international terrorism, particularly Al-Qaeda terrorism, is and remains persistent and adaptive. While terrorism is a tactic that cannot be entirely eradicated, steps can be taken to disrupt, dismantle, and ultimately defeat organizations that use terrorism. As such, policy prescriptions for addressing threats emanating from 'corrigible' groups like Hamas and Hezbollah will look entirely different according to the political context, the current threat environment, and, of course, the government conducting the counterterrorism operations. For instance, American would probably shy away from conducting Predator and Reaper drone strikes in southern Lebanon; this might not be a productive strategy in the long-term if the objective is to encourage Hezbollah to renounce terrorism, disarm, and fully blend its political and military forces into the existing Lebanese system. By the same token, while Israel may continue to carry out targeted assassination strikes against Hamas leaders, it would not be in the interest of American foreign policy or its counterterrorism policy to conduct U.S. strikes in Gaza and the West Bank. Al-Qaeda, on the other hand, is considered an 'incorrigible' terrorist organization with ambitious socio-political objectives which no government could realistically accommodate when trying to negotiate a political settlement and bring about an end to Al-Qaeda's terrorism. Therefore, America has chosen a clearly enemy-centric approach to combating Al-Qaeda in order to achieve its objectives, which, as President Obama has recently stated, is to disrupt, dismantle, and defeat Al-Qaeda.

In order to effectively frame current American counterterrorism efforts, it is important to appreciate the difference between counterterrorism policy and counterterrorism operations, and to fully understand the competing objectives and mandates within the American government. The U.S. Department of State has had a long-term no concessions counterterrorism policy, which continues today.[6] This position was defined early on during its struggle against international terrorism. In 1973, Palestinian terrorists seized six diplomats (including the American ambassador to Sudan) in Khartoum and demanded the release of over 60 terrorists jailed in Israel, Jordan, West Germany, and the United States. Richard Nixon's response was direct: "As far as the United States as a government giving in to blackmail demands, we cannot do so and will not do so."[7] However, after 9/11, while America's no concessions policy remains intact, counterterrorism operations carried out by the Department of Defense and CIA highlight that counterterrorism had evolved into a more lethal form of asymmetric warfare, which further blurred the line between policy and operations and reinforced the notion that counterterrorism has become an all-encompassing approach.

American counterterrorism policy and operations worldwide have, at times, appeared to present contradictions. But this is largely a problem of understanding the American bureaucracy and the competing efforts of the U.S. State Department, Department of Defense, and its intelligence agencies, rather than proving or disproving any contradictions in American counterterrorism policy. For example, Mark Perry has recently argued that America must talk to terrorists or risk losing the so-called war on terrorism. Perry argues that America violated its 'no concessions' counterterrorism policy in Iraq when it chose to negotiate a settlement with the loose network of Iraqi tribal militias in the al-Anbar province. By this logic, he argues, the U.S. must engage with other terrorist organizations like Hamas and Hezbollah because they are completely rational organizations with realistic political and social goals.[8] But within the fog of war in Iraq, it is important to understand how the negotiations unfolded. The American military engaged in talks with an insurgent enemy in order to quell violence within the broader context of an ongoing war. On the other hand, future negotiations with Hamas or Hezbollah, if they were to ever take place, would be handled by the Department of State within a non-war context.

Daniel Byman argues that despite America's attempts to isolate and weaken Hamas, the group has emerged stronger than ever and that direct engagement is the only option for resolving the conflict.[9] The same can be said for Hezbollah in Lebanon. However, practically no responsible analyst has argued that direct engagement with Al-Qaeda is an option for ending Al-Qaeda's terrorism. This highlights the fact that different counterterrorism strategies are needed for different terrorist organizations and that different departments within the same government have different approaches. In short, America's ability to successfully isolate and weaken terrorist organizations is subject to debates.

We also have to look how counterterrorism has evolved over the past four decades in order to fully appreciate the current state of affairs and the widening gap between policies and operations.

The Evolution of Counterterrorism

Counterterrorism has changed over the past four decades; unsurprisingly, this evolution has mirrored changes in the nature of terrorism. The current wave of international terrorism began arguably on July 22, 1968, when three members of the Popular Front for the Liberation of Palestine (PFLP) hijacked a commercial passenger flight from Rome to Tel Aviv.[10] This represented at least three novelties. First, it was one of the first hijackings where the objective was primarily political, and the target was specifically chosen for its symbolism. Instead of hijacking any airplane, three Palestinian terrorists took control of an El Al plane from Israel's national airline. Second, the hijacking was intended to influence a wider audience, rather than for personal criminal gain or for escape by simply redirecting a flight for transport. Rather, the terrorists were intending to trade hostages for imprisoned Palestinian terrorists in Israel. In addition, it was the first time a terrorist organization began operating regularly at the international level, leaving its home turf to attack citizens of a foreign country who, in many cases, had nothing to do with their struggle in order to promote their political cause before an international audience.[11] This encouraged other non-Palestinian groups – such as the ethno-nationalist/separatist ASALA (the Armenian Army for the Secret Liberation of Armenia), the JCAG (Justice Commandos of the Armenian Genocide), militant elements within the Free South Moluccan Youth organization, and left-wing groups such as the German Red Army Faction (a.k.a the Baader-Meinhof Group) – to "internationalize" their political struggles. These groups, Bruce Hoffman observed, learned from the PFLP that they could promote their cause worldwide by simply taking a plane, its crew, and its passengers hostage. "When we hijack a plane it has more effect than if we killed a hundred Israelis in battle," said George Habbash, the founding leader of the PFLP in a 1970 interview. "For decades world opinion has been neither for nor against the Palestinians. It simply ignored us," he said. "At least the world is talking about us now."[12]

International terrorism became a serious problem in 1968 for two reasons. First the loss of the 1967 Six-Day War, and subsequent Israeli occupation of the Golan Heights, West Bank, and the Sinai Peninsula, was a devastating defeat for the Palestinians and the Arab countries bordering Israel. This inspired groups like the PFLP to begin operating internationally to promote their cause because there was no chance that it could defeat Israel on the battlefield. Second, Latin American guerrilla fighters, frustrated with their battlefield failures in the countryside, began an urban terrorism campaign, which involved at first mainly the kidnapping of foreign diplomats. The primary tactics used by all of these groups were hijackings, kidnappings, and embassy raids, and the intention was, in addition to obtaining publicity, gaining ransoms and having imprisoned comrades exchanged for hostages and/or a safe passage away from the crime scene.[13] Such terrorist blackmail forced governments to respond accordingly. While acts of terrorism at this time killed relatively few people, such publicity stunts put tremendous pressure on governments to respond responsibly since a wrong decision during a hostage crisis could have disastrous consequences and the blame was likely to land in the court of the government. An example of this was the German response to the attack on Israeli athletes at the Olympic Games in Munich on September 5, 1972: eleven Israeli athletes (and eight members of the Palestinian Black September) were killed after a hostage standoff that ended in a shootout. While the West German government was not the primary target of the attack, the scene of crime was on German soil and the government was forced to act and bungled in its rescue attempt. This was an eye-opener as not only Germany but many other governments realized how insufficient their response capabilities were. As a consequence, several countries developed elite rapid-reaction hostage rescue teams. In short, during this period, governments' counterterrorism efforts consisted mainly in improving responses to groups hijacking international flights, taking hostages, and raiding embassies. At that time, the terrorists' primary intention was not to kill, but rather to raise attention for their cause by playing to the media and blackmailing governments into acceding to their political demands before worldwide television audiences.

Over time the nature of international terrorism changed and so too did counterterrorism.[14] It appeared that terrorists were no longer taking people hostage or hijacking airplanes as the primary tactic to achieve their goals. These tactics offered diminishing returns and no success in achieving the terrorists' primary political objectives. Palestinian militants quickly realized that hostage takings and hijackings were little more than a nuisance to governments. New groups, such as Hamas, introduced more lethal tactics like suicide bombings with the intention of achieving at least the same level of limited strategic success that Hezbollah and the Tamil Tigers had reached by using suicide strategies.[15] Al-Qaeda also started attacking the United States, aiming at mass-casualty terrorism from the 1990s onward, which culminated with the theatrically orchestrated 9/11 attacks. In 1995, the Japanese religious cult Aum-Shinrikyo carried out a Sarin gas attack on a Tokyo subway system, apparently with the intention of causing mass casualties. Terrorism had evolved into a more lethal and indiscriminate form of warfare that appeared to be more religiously motivated. This once again put governments in a predicament to respond forcefully to an enemy that it did not entirely understand.

The evolution of counterterrorism over the past forty years was a slow process that involved adapting to the nature of international terrorism, as well as taking advantage of new advancements in military technology. The Revolution in Military Affairs (RMA) played a significant role in this evolution. The RMA is associated with new advancements in military technologies. It began in the 1970s during the nuclear stalemate between America and the Soviet Union when it was becoming clear that possession of nuclear weapons offered little strategic or political advantage over the other since using them would have drastic consequences. The answer, for America, was to develop more conventional weapons capabilities that the USSR did not have or could not afford to develop. This, it was assumed, would ultimately give them the upper hand in the event of a conventional war.[16] Yet the new weapons had to be politically and morally acceptable, i.e. they had to be precise, minimize collateral damage, and reduce the risk of death by the military personnel delivering them.[17] They had to make war "bloodless, risk-free and precise as possible."[18] These military capabilities, combined with modern advancements in computer technology, were the kicker in the RMA, because if linked into precision-guided weaponry, military commanders could, in theory, orchestrate the battlefield in real-time from a safe distance. These advancements in military technologies are what Michael Ignatieff dubbed "virtual war," meaning "a war without death – to our side – is a war that ceases to be fully real to us."[19]

After 9/11 the evolution of counterterrorism became more apparent. Michael Boyle argues "the development of counterterrorism as a model of warfare is new to the post-September 11 era."[20] Peter Bergen dubs counterterrorism in the post-9/11 world as "The Drone War"; some have even characterized the Obama administration's over-reliance on drones as the "Obama Doctrine." Indeed, the use of unmanned aerial Predator and Reaper drones by the US military and CIA has revolutionized how America combats terrorism; it can be seen as a new tactic in counterterrorism warfare. But using unmanned drones is not the first attempt by America to use the benefits of the RMA to respond to international terrorism. Before 9/11, President Bill Clinton ordered a one-off, precision-guided cruise missile attack aimed at Al-Qaeda bases in Afghanistan in response to the 1998 bombings of the American embassies in Kenya and Tanzania. The use of unmanned drones has had interesting implications on the development of counterterrorism strategies not only in the unpopular Bush administration, but as highlighted above, the Obama administration has considered drone warfare to be "the only game in town".

"President Obama has not only continued the drone program," writes Peter Bergen, "he has ratcheted it up further." He goes on to say that in 2007 "there were three drone strikes in Pakistan; in 2008, there were 34; and, in the first months of 2009, the Obama administration has already authorized 16."[21] At the time of writing, in 2010 alone, the Obama administration has authorized over one-hundred drone strikes worldwide. The large majority of them have occurred in the border regions between Afghanistan and Pakistan.[22] Regardless of the controversy surrounding these operations, American drone strikes have been successful to a certain extent. Mohammed Atef, AQ's top military strategist, was killed in November 2001 in a drone strike near Kabul, two months after the 9/11 attacks. In 2002, Abu Ali Al Harethi, a suspected mastermind of the 2000 attack on the USS Cole, was killed in Yemen - the first drone operation outside of Afghanistan. Kamal Derwish, an American citizen, was also killed in the attack - the first American citizen to be killed by a CIA-orchestrated drone strike.[23] Drone strikes have also been seen as successful. Since 2008, according to Bergen, "U.S. drones have killed dozens of lower-ranking militants and at least ten mid-and upper-level leaders within Al Qaeda or the Taliban."[24]

However, it is debatable whether the drone strikes will prove strategically successful in the long-term, due to their often-unintended consequences. Killing AQ leaders and rank-and-file members might be considered a 'success' in the short-term, but they can be replaced relatively quickly. Drone strikes can also lead to collateral damage, killing innocent bystanders who are presumably not affiliated with AQ or its leaders, which could alienate the local population or blunt the effectiveness of more population-centric strategies such as state-building and counterinsurgency, which focuses on winning the legitimacy of the local population and promoting good governance. Yet it remains to be seen if drone attacks alone are sustainable. In order to identify, locate, and target AQ and its affiliates from the air in regions like Pakistan, Afghanistan, Somalia, and Yemen, America needs effective and timely human intelligence. Drone strikes are also questionable from an ethical and international law perspective because operations are deadly – capitulation to a drone is not possible. Such strikes may well violate the sovereignty of a state like Pakistan, which allows America to carry out attacks in the Federally Administered Tribal Areas (FATA), which has historically been an autonomous region outside the authority of the Pakistani government. Yet the Pakistani government has yet to authorize strikes in Baluchistan which is a hotbed for Islamic extremism in Pakistan proper. At the end of the day, an advanced drone program is an operational tool, and a campaign of targeted strikes can provide a counterterrorism strategy with some innovative and timely successes. Yet drone operations are a tactic, not an overarching strategy. Moreover, the changes in the nature of counterterrorism raise a larger question of the nature of power in modern counterterrorism operations. If counterterrorism is indeed an all-encompassing approach requiring all aspects of a nation's power, then it is important to understand both the hard and soft power options of counterterrorism.

Hard and Soft Power in Counterterrorism

Existing research on counterterrorism tends to structure debates around two approaches: the war (or military) model and the criminal justice model.[25] The war model tends to frame the struggle against terrorism in military terms of an enemy-centric war where the armed forces of a state are primarily in charge of developing counterterrorism strategy. On the other hand, the criminal justice model champions the rule of law and democratic values which prevail in Western democracies. Doing so puts restrictions on the government and thereby risks reducing the effectiveness of counterterrorism measures. However, as Ami Pedahzur and Magnus Ranstorp have argued, both models rarely function according to academic theory during an actual counterterrorism campaign. While democracies tend to champion democratic ideals and the preservation of civil liberties, their attempts to combat terrorism forcefully have continually tested the boundaries of the criminal justice model.[26]

There is a need to view counterterrorism from other angles. It is becoming increasingly clear that a new framework is needed in order to develop and measure successful counterterrorism strategies.[27] Considering the evolution of counterterrorism, it could be more useful to view counterterrorism in terms of "hard" and "soft" power. This would require restructuring the debate around a direct and indirect approach to counterterrorism.[28] The direct approach would be an enemy-centric doctrine consisting of primarily offensive, hard power tactics such as Predator and Reaper drone strikes, special forces operations, increased policing and intelligence operations. These are useful tools if the goal is to isolate and destroy groups like Al-Qaeda. The indirect soft power approach would consist of population-centric methods, and would contain features such as capacity building, economic development, and counter-radicalization focusing on the underlying causes that allow terrorism to thrive.

The direct approach to counterterrorism is straightforward but it raises serious questions regarding the ethical and legal use of force – on top of the issue of collection of intelligence and the protection of civil liberties within a democratic society. On the other hand, it remains to be seen if soft power alternatives such as democracy promotion, economic development, and counter-radicalization effectively address the ill-defined "root causes" of terrorism. Robert Jervis argues that even if political oppression, weak states, poverty, and economic inequality were the real root causes, "there is little reason to think that we could deal with them effectively". He concludes that "we cannot point to solid evidence that doing so would make much difference."[29] This is not to say that American involvement internationally would not include some form of economic and development assistance in weak and failing nations. But it is difficult to give aid to weak states like Afghanistan, Pakistan, and Yemen and expect to be able to determine effectiveness in terms of countering Al-Qaeda's terrorism. Moreover, providing development aid to increase capacity building is questionable from a counterterrorism perspective since a causal link between weak states and terrorism cannot be proven. Aid may well increase the standard of living, level of education and general quality of life in some countries. Yet it is difficult to argue that locals would turn to terrorism or political violence without it. Furthermore, such root cause theories would have to address the fact that homegrown terrorists do indeed radicalize and carry out attacks in democratic countries as well as weak and failing nations – and that while poverty and economic inequality are prevalent throughout the world, terrorism is not.[30] It may be more useful from a counterterrorism perspective to view terrorists as rational actors who adopt the tactic of terrorism as a strategic choice to pursue political objectives, not as passive observers who are susceptible to what the supposed underlying causes forces them to do.[31]

Then there is the issue of counter-radicalization and de-radicalization in counterterrorism. Some argue that terrorist radicalization and de-radicalization should be viewed as a complex process consisting of a variety of interdependent push- and pull-factors and triggering events that drive people into and out of terrorism.[32] Others contend that social networks and group dynamics better explain how individuals are violently radicalized.[33] So far theories of radicalization have had difficulties in explaining why individuals take up or leave terrorism behind. This is mainly due to the fact that terrorists come from a wide variety of backgrounds and there exists no single individual terrorist profile.[34] Despite the absence of a single terrorist phenotype, some view counter-radicalization programs as a critical part of counterterrorism. Lorenzo Vidino argues that attempts to dismantle terrorist networks is similar to playing a game of "whack-a-mole" and that governments should take steps to prevent radicalization in order to stop people from becoming terrorists. He goes on to argue that anti-radicalization programs would vary from "convening interfaith meetings to creating government-funded Muslim magazines and TV channels, from promoting lectures of Muslim clerics exposing the theological flaws of al Qaeda's ideology to mentoring projects and professional development seminars."[35] Theories of counter-radicalization also have trouble measuring success from a counterterrorism perspective, because such programs essentially amount to increased community engagement that requires community leaders to target and mentor individuals who are presumably susceptible to terrorism recruitment. Yet it is difficult to prove that they would have turned to terrorism in the first place, and, more importantly, that they will not engage in terrorism afterwards.

Some go a step further and look at ways soft power can facilitate an exit for individuals from terrorist groups, arguing that government counterterrorism programs should offer terrorists a pathway out of terrorism by facilitating disengagement and rehabilitation.[36] While research on disengagement, de-radicalization, and rehabilitation is in the early stages, it is realistic that (local) government can play a crucial role in facilitate pathways out of terrorism for groups and individuals who want to leave terrorism behind.[37] In Lebanon, soft approaches such as political engagement and increased capacity building might have some influence on bringing about Hezbollah's disarmament and its full integration into the Lebanese political system. Yet the fact remains that Hezbollah already chose to join the political process in Lebanon many years ago and has yet to decommission its militia.[38] Similarly, attempts to weaken and isolate Hamas have proved questionable from a hard power perspective. Hamas showed in 2006 that it could use democracy to its benefit without having to moderate its political aims or renounce violence. The FMLN in Central America, on the other hand, decommissioned its militia and joined a democratic system in the early 1990; it is now one of the largest political parties in El Salvador. So the record is mixed on whether democracy can offer groups a pathway out of terrorism. Yet it is reasonable to assume that some soft power measures could indeed offer certain individuals and groups some sort of pathway out of terrorism.

While both hard and soft power measures in counterterrorism do not necessarily provide a magical way to defeat terrorism, such a framework can be a useful way to characterize and analyze counterterrorism initiatives. In the context of countering Al-Qaeda terrorism, however, it seems America prefers hard power to soft power. One of Al-Qaeda's primary goals is to reverse American foreign policy and its influence in the Middle East while overthrowing corrupt Arab regimes it supports.[39] But it is clear, and rightfully so, that American government has little appetite for addressing the root causes of Al-Qaeda's terrorism since it has just approved $60 billion in military sales to Saudi Arabia - the largest military sales package ever for an Arab state[40]. According to Bob

Woodward's new book Obama's Wars, the CIA has Presidential and Congressional approval to carry out covert, lethal counterterrorism operations in over sixty countries. It also manages a 3,000-man team of Afghans known as Counterterrorism Pursuit Teams (CTPT). Its purpose is to take the fight to Al-Qaeda in Afghanistan and Pakistan. In short, it appears that for the time being aerial drone strikes and other hard power tools will drive American counterterrorism strategy.[41]

Nevertheless, America should be mindful that counterterrorism operations that cause high civilian casualties rates allow terrorists to exploit its actions and to strengthen their own position from a propaganda perspective. There is a fine line between effectively responding to terrorism and strategic overreach. John Brennan, President Obama's top counterterrorism advisor, recently commented on the need to resist using the "hammer" in counterterrorism. He went on to argue that America must use the "scalpel" and prepare for a long struggle against Al-Qaeda, a struggle that would take the fight from the battlegrounds of counterinsurgency into the shadows of more covert counter terrorist operations.[42] However, this does not mean that more precise is necessarily less lethal. While post-modern terrorists may want a lot of people watching and a lot of people dead, covert counterterrorism forces now want few people watching and a lot of terrorists dead.

Counterinsurgency Theory

How does counterinsurgency differ from counterterrorism? Counterinsurgency has been defined as "those military, paramilitary, political, economic, psychological and civic actions taken by a government to defeat an insurgency."[43] Based on this definition, counterinsurgency is an all-encompassing approach to countering irregular insurgent warfare – an approach which recognizes that a military solution to a conflict is not feasible; only a combined military, political, and civilian solution is possible. Seth Jones of the RAND Corporation has argued that, based on his analysis of 90 insurgencies, defeating an insurgency is a long process that lasts on average 14 years.[44] T. E. Lawrence has been quoted as saying "to make war upon rebellion is messy and slow, like eating soup with a knife."[45]

There are several studies that highlight the best practices of waging counterinsurgency warfare. David Galula, a former Lieutenant Colonel in the French army, is considered the intellectual God Father of counterinsurgency studies. In his famous book Counterinsurgency Warfare: Theory and Practice (1964), Galula argued that, in order to counter an insurgency, it was essential for the counterinsurgent to win the support and legitimacy of the local population, promote good governance, and keep a sufficient amount of troops in an area to provide security after the governments forces have taken it over. He also argues that is important to "destroy or expel the main body of armed insurgents" or, if that is not possible, to "win over or suppress the last insurgent remnants."[46]

These principles provided the intellectual framework for countries like America and Britain to further develop and implement their respective counterinsurgency doctrines at both the theoretical and practical level. They are also the foundation of General Petraeus's "clear, hold, and build" strategy.

John Nagl, building on Galula's work, argues that there are two approaches to counterinsurgency: the direct and indirect approach. The direct approach focuses primarily on defeating the enemy with military force. The indirect approach, on the other hand, involving a "battle for the hearts and minds," focuses on a more population-centric strategy. It involves denying the insurgency the support of the local population while at the same time attacking the insurgency with military force.[47] The primary goal of both the insurgent and the counterinsurgent is promoting good governance and winning legitimacy in the eyes of the local population. This framework for victory has been the primary focus of American counterinsurgency operations in Iraq and Afghanistan. As a consequence, General Petraeus's declaratory strategy has revolved around denying the insurgency its sanctuary within the population and training the local security services to hold the territory so the insurgents do not return, while building infrastructure, promoting good governance, and eliminating political corruption – thereby wining the population's "hearts and minds."

Counterinsurgency theory can be seen within a classical and modern framework. Classical counterinsurgency theory is similar to both the Nagl and Petraeus approaches. Since a classical insurgency is generally associated with a struggle within one state, with a possible safe haven in a bordering state, a classical counterinsurgency is confined within the borders of a single state. Seth Jones, in his analysis of 90 insurgencies, identified three key variables that are, in theory, critical to a successful classical counterinsurgency: 1) training the local police and security forces to combat the insurgency; 2) improving the quality of local governance; and, 3) denying the insurgency any external support and outside sanctuary.[48] Jones goes on to argue that America is not likely to commit itself to a 14-year long counterinsurgency in Iraq, Afghanistan, or Pakistan. Thus, in his view, training and supporting the host government's security forces to defeat the insurgency is critical. Locals have more legitimacy and are more familiar with the local geography, language, culture, political landscape, and history. They are simply more capable of gathering intelligence from the local population and thus should take the lead in any long-term counterinsurgency effort.

Modern counterinsurgency theory, on the other hand, takes a more international approach. After 9/11, Al-Qaeda's network across national borders was characterized by many as a global insurgency.[49] This new insurgency threat was not only local, it was international, which as some argue, requires a re-thinking of how such irregular warfare should be combated.[50] Many counterinsurgency experts acknowledge that as the nature of an insurgency evolves so too does the counterinsurgency strategy[51] Indeed, Kilcullen's observation that "a globalized insurgency demands a rethink of traditional counterinsurgency" appears to make sense if one subscribes to the argument that Al-Qaeda is a global Islamist insurgency.[52] Bruce Hoffman recently framed the global Al-Qaeda threat in a similar way, and argued that while AQ does not enjoy the operational safe-haven it did before 9/11, it has "nevertheless been able to reconstitute its global terrorist reach."[53] As such, Hoffman argues that a new Global Counterinsurgency (GCOIN) strategy is needed to combat this international terrorist threat. This approach would include: vital information operations to counter the radical narratives; separating the enemy from its support base to deny it sanctuaries and freedom of movement; continuing to detect and defuse the enemy domestically and internationally; and a commitment to build legitimate civil governance which could counter the underlying causes of terrorism and insurgency.[54] This modern approach is basically a classical counterinsurgency theory of winning the "hearts and minds," which denies the enemy sanctuary, seeking to promote good governance and engaging in information operations - but on a global scale. It is a much more ambitious undertaking than conducting classical counterinsurgency within a single state. However, it also remains to be seen whether AQ merits this type of attention and whether it really amounts to a global Islamist insurgency.

If we consider Al-Qaeda a serious global insurgency threat that has the resources and support to overthrow multiples governments worldwide, then it is certainly reasonable to adopt both Kilcullen and Hoffman's approaches. However, if we do so it blurs even further the line between counterterrorism and counterinsurgency because it not only inhibits our understanding of both doctrines, it requires us to develop a new form of hybrid warfare. Just because an organization such as Al-Qaeda may use terrorism on an international scale and dabble in domestic insurgencies does not make it subject to the same respective counter strategies. Furthermore, to a certain extent, labeling Al-Qaeda as a globalized insurgency threat legitimizes Al-Qaeda's cause and gives this organization or network too much credit. "The Al-Qaeda organization is neither an insurgency against a US hegemonic order nor the vanguard of a global Islamic resistance to globalization and westernization," Michael Boyle has argued. "It is a resilient and highly lethal terrorist organization with a fanciful political programme and relatively little popular support in the Muslim world."[55]

Counterterrorism and Counterinsurgency

Counterterrorism and counterinsurgency are two fundamentally different doctrines and it is important to understand the strengths and weaknesses of each in order to fully appreciate the offsetting effects they might have. Michael Boyle has recently asked the question whether counterterrorism and counterinsurgency go together, and concluded that there is no reason to think that both strategies are fully compatible or mutually reinforcing, and despite the recent conflation of the two doctrines, that a counterinsurgency strategy should not be seen as a counterterrorism strategy and vice-versa.[56] Counterinsurgency can provide a clear framework for success if the situation is ripe for this type of warfare. The main tenet of counterinsurgency recognizes that a sole military solution is not feasible, making it essential for a dual military-political solution that adopts a population-centric approach. Additionally, counterinsurgency doctrine rests on a few key pillars of protecting the local population, promoting good governance, eliminating enemy safe-havens, and training the locals to take the fight to the insurgency. Classical counterinsurgency seeks to combat an insurgency confined within the borders a nation-state, while modern counterinsurgency theory takes these classical principles and applies them at the international level, or what Bruce Hoffman calls Global Counterinsurgency (GCOIN), which ultimately seeks to combat international terrorism while addressing the underlying socio-economic conditions that supposedly allow terrorism to thrive.

Counterterrorism, on the other hand, provides a less clear framework for success but is equally complex. Counterterrorism has evolved over the past four decades into a more lethal form of unconventional warfare. Not surprisingly, this evolution has mirrored the trends in international terrorism. Since international terrorists from the late 1960s to roughly the end of the Cold War were primarily hijacking airplanes, raiding embassies, and taking hostages to promote their causes, counterterrorism forces adjusted to meet these threats. Yet over the past few decades terrorism has become bloodier and more indiscriminate, which forced governments to adjust their counter tactics. With the RMA developing unmanned, precision-guided weaponry that drastically decreases the risk of one's own soldiers dying in conflict on the ground, counterterrorism was able to evolve into a form of irregular warfare that is, as Michael Ignatieff described the RMA, as "bloodless, risk-free and precise as possible."[57] Instead of hostage negotiators being called to deal with a terrorist's demands, now a soldier operates unmanned aerial Predator and Reaper drones with Hellfire missiles to seek and destroy Al-Qaeda terrorists. Counterterrorism today is indeed a complex, multifaceted phenomenon. In the context of combating Al-Qaeda, counterterrorism is a sharp, quick, and lethal form of warfare focused on isolating, boxing in, and destroying the organization and its members. However, counterterrorism is something entirely different when thinking in terms of dealing with the complexities of Hamas and Hezbollah, as well as the hard and soft power alternatives that an all-encompassing strategy can bring to bear.

Recently the debate between counterterrorism and counterinsurgency advocates has gained traction within the Obama administration. Some argue that a long-term counterinsurgency is the only way to achieve America's goals in Afghanistan, while others argue that it does little to address the global threat posed by Al-Qaeda. For this a number of reasons can be cited. First, Afghanistan has been a "nightmare, a graveyard of empires," ranging from the

Brits to the Soviets and now, potentially also to the Americans.[58] No one has ever effectively ruled Afghanistan. The country is so diverse in terms of its tribal structures that no unified state has ever been formed. Second, based on the counterinsurgency principles, success in Afghanistan requires certain underlying conditions that America currently does not have and cannot create. For example, having a legitimate host government is the bedrock of any successful counterinsurgency strategy. However, the current Karzai regime has been criticized for being extremely corrupt and for having made little progress in development.[59]

A recent poll of 6,500 Afghans conducted in 34 of the 36 provinces put the police and judiciary as the most corrupt departments in the Afghan government. These are the very entities responsible for implementing the rule of law.[60] Different U.S. governmental agencies in Afghanistan also appear to be working at cross-purposes. For example, the CIA has been funding Hamid Karzai's corrupt brother, Ahmed Wali Karzai, who is essentially the governor of Kandahar City, to provide security, collect intelligence, and combat the Taliban using his local militias. But the military, at the same time, is working to promote legitimate governance and win the "hearts and minds" of the locals. Major General Michael Flynn was quoted as saying: "If we are going to conduct a population-centric strategy in Afghanistan and we are perceived as backing thugs, then we are just undermining ourselves."[61] Furthermore, CIA drone operations used for counterterrorism purposes are not only highly lethal but also have a tendency to cause unintended civilian causalities. Therefore, while targeted drone strikes that have relatively high levels of collateral damage may be seen as a necessary evil for a successful counterterrorism strategy, it essentially blunts the effectiveness of the nearby counterinsurgency operation since it has the potential to further alienate the local population.[62]

Third, the costs of a long-term commitment to counterinsurgency in Afghanistan are astronomic. As Kalev Sepp has argued, "If – as in Iraq – counterinsurgency means a campaign that will cost $2 trillion, engage 150,000 troops, see the deaths of some 5,000 of those soldiers, and last for at least six years with an indeterminate end, then only the United States can do it, and probably only once in a generation."[63] According to Bob Woodward's new book on the Obama administration, President Obama has been quoted as saying, in relation to the war in Afghanistan: "I'm not doing long-term nation-building. I am not spending a trillion dollars."[64] Due to the costs of counterinsurgency warfare, as the argument goes, the United States is not likely to sustain an international coalition or the international legitimacy required that some argue is critical to succeeding in Afghanistan. Fourth, counterinsurgency is "clearly not working" writes Richard Haass, President of the Council on Foreign Relations.[65] Haass goes on to argue that America must stop thinking that the Taliban and Al-Qaeda represent the same security threat to Afghanistan and to its national security interests in the region, and that the Taliban is not likely to harbor Al-Qaeda again because of the enormous consequences.

Above all, counterterrorism and counterinsurgency strategies must keep in mind the current threat that Al-Qaeda poses. CIA Director Leon Panetta estimated that Al-Qaeda has only "60 to 100, maybe less" members in Afghanistan.[66] And a recent estimate put its size in both Afghanistan and Pakistan at fewer than 500.[67] So if the mission in Afghanistan is to disrupt, dismantle, and defeat Al-Qaeda, as President Obama has stated, then a strategy focusing on this threat seems to be more feasible and have a higher likelihood of success. However, some have argued that the size of Al-Qaeda's membership in Afghanistan and Pakistan is not necessary a productive method to measure its strength. Al-Qaeda has never had more than a few hundred core members and it continues to use affiliate organizations to project its terrorist brand internationally.[68] Whatever its size, as America's battle against Al-Qaeda continues worldwide, it seems counterinsurgency warfare will be marginalized for a more enemy-centric counterterrorism strategy which will utilize a variety of hard and soft power tactics to disrupt, dismantle, and destroy Al-Qaeda.

Conclusion

The line between counterterrorism and counterinsurgency strategy has become increasingly blurred, yet as we have seen, both concepts represent two different strategic doctrines. However, the increased focus on counterinsurgency warfare after 9/11 has affected how we view current counterterrorism efforts. At the heart of any counterinsurgency strategy is a "hearts and minds" approach of promoting good governance and gaining legitimacy in the eyes of the local population. This way of thinking appears to have had a certain impact on the development of more soft power counterterrorism measures, which now seek to promote legitimate governance and capacity building to address the somewhat unclear underlying causes of terrorism. Indeed, Daniel Benjamin, the U.S. State Department's Coordinator of Counterterrorism, writes that America must address the complex factors of radicalization and "confront the political, social, and economic conditions that our enemies exploit to win over recruits and funders" by increasing "foreign assistance to nations and communities where violent extremism has made inroads, such as Pakistan and Yemen."[69] This view reinforces the notion that American can effectively address its terrorism problems by changing the facts on the ground. Yet, in reality, this only highlights the State Department's strategy for countering Al-Qaeda terrorism, which at the end of the day assumes a dubious causal linkage between socio-economic and political conditions and terrorism, and appears to be at odds with the more hard power approaches used by the CIA and American military.

However, critical questions remain regarding American counterterrorism strategy. Will the hard power counterterrorism tactics such as Predator drone strikes used by the CIA blunt the effectiveness of the State Department's soft approach to counterterrorism? In contrast to counterinsurgency doctrine, does America really need the support and legitimacy of a local population in order to be successful in counterterrorism?[70] If so, can America and its allies develop a realistic framework to counter extremism and violent radicalization? If not, to what extent can hard power tactics prove strategically successful? Can both hard and soft power in counterterrorism be fully compatible and mutually reinforcing, or will both always operate at cross-purposes? And, more importantly, just because local populations in regions like Afghanistan, Pakistan, Yemen, and Somalia may have extremist views or despise American foreign policy, does that necessarily mean they will join Al-Qaeda and resort to international terrorism? In short, the larger task for America and its allies will be to find adequate answers to such questions and determine what the long, perhaps multigenerational struggle against international terrorism will look like after the war in Afghanistan, and, in this way, move beyond the current debate surrounding counterterrorism and counterinsurgency.

About the Author: Jason Rineheart is a Freelance Writer specializing in counterterrorism and Middle East security and a Research Assistant at the Terrorism Research Initiative. He holds a B.A. from the University of Oklahoma and an M.Litt from the University of St Andrews.

Notes

[1] Robert Haddick. "This Week at War: Obama vs. Team Surge". Foreign Policy, 24 Sept. 2010.

[2] Quoted in Austin Long. "Small is Beautiful: The Counterterrorism Option in Afghanistan". Published by Elsevier Ltd on behalf of the Foreign Policy Research Institute, 2010.

[3] Paul Wilkinson. Terrorism Versus Democracy: The Liberal State Response. New York: Routledge, 2006, p. 203.

[4] Paul Wilkinson. Terrorism and the Liberal State. Basingstoke: Macmillan, 1977, 1986; Louise Richardson. What Terrorists Want: Understanding the Enemy, Containing the Threat. New York: Random House, 2006.

[5] Quoted in the US Army Field Manual, 2006, p. 4.

[6] See Morris Busby. "U.S. counterterrorism policy in the 1980s and the priorities for the 1990s". Studies in Conflict and Terrorism, 13:1, 2005, pp. 7-13; Paul Bremer. "The West's Counter-terrorist Strategy". Terrorism and Political Violence, 4: 4, 1992, pp. 255-262.

[7] Quoted in Bruce Hoffman. "Is Europe Soft on Terrorism?". Foreign Policy, 1999.

[8] Mark Perry. How to Lose the War on Terror. London: Hurst & Company, 2010.

[9] Daniel Byman. "How to Handle Hamas: The Perils of Ignoring Gaza's Leadership". Foreign Affairs, Sept/Oct., 2010.

[10] Bruce Hoffman. Inside Terrorism. New York: Columbia University Press, 2006,

   pp. 63-80.

[11] Ibid.

[12] Quoted in Ibid, p. 66.

[13] Richard Clutterbuck. Negotiating with Terrorists. In: Alex P. Schmid and Ronald Crelinsten (Eds.). Western Responses to Terrorism. Frank Cass: London, 1993.

[14] Bruce Hoffman (1999). Terrorism Trends and Prospects. In: I.O. Lesser, B. Hoffman, J. Arquilla, et al. (Eds.) Countering the New Terrorism., Santa Monica: The RAND Corporation, 1999, pp. 7-35; Walter Laqueur. "Postmodern Terrorism". Foreign Affairs, 75: 5, 1996, pp. 24-36; p. 26.

[15] See Mia Bloom. Dying to Kill: The Allure of Suicide Terrorism. New York: Columbia University Press, 2005; Robert Pape. Dying to Win: The Strategic Logic of Suicide Terrorism. New York: Random House, 2005.

[16] Michael Ignatieff. Virtual War. London: Vintage Random House, 2001.

[17] David Lonsdale. Strategy. In: David Jordan and James Kiras et al. "Understanding Modern Warfare." New York: Cambridge University Press, 2008.

[18] M. Ignatieff, op. cit., p. 164.

[19] Ibid, p. 5.

[20] Michael Boyle. "Do counterterrorism and counterinsurgency go together?",

International Affairs,86:2, 2010, 333-353, p. 342.

[21] Peter Bergen and Katherine Tiedemann. "The Drone War". The New Republic, 3 June 2009.

[22] For more information on drone strikes and statistics, see the Counterterrorism Strategy Initiative at the New American Foundation: http://counterterrorism.newamerica.net/drones .

[23] P. Bergen and K. Tiedemann, op.cit.

[24] Ibid.

[25] P. Wilkinson, 2006; A. P. Schmid. "Frameworks for Conceptualizing Terrorism", Terrorism and Political Violence, 16: 2, 2004, pp. 197-221.

[26] Ami Pedahzur and Magnus Ranstorp. "A Tertiary Model for Counter Terrorism in Liberal Democracies: The Case of Israel". Terrorism and Political Violence, 13: 2, 2001, pp. 1-26.

[27] Alex P. Schmid and Rashmi Singh. Measuring Success and Failure in Terrorism and Counter-Terrorism: US Government Metrics of the Global War on Terror. In: Alex P. Schmid and Garry Hindle (Eds.).After the War on Terror: Regional and Multilateral Perspectives on Counter-Terrorism Strategy. London: RUSI Books, 2009.

[28] John Nagl discusses a similar direct and indirect approach to counterinsurgency.

[29] Robert Jervis. American Foreign Policy in a New Era, New York: Routledge, 2005, p. 43.

[30] Michael Boyle. "The War on Terror in American Grand Strategy". International

Affairs, 84: 2, 2008, pp. 191-209.

[31] For a discussion on root causes, see Tore Bjorgo (Ed.). The Root Causes of Terrorism: Myths, Reality, and Ways Forward. New York: Routledge, 2005.

[32] John Horgan. Walking Away From Terrorism. New York: Routledge, 2009.

[33] Marc Sageman. Understanding Terror Networks. Philadelphia: University of

Pennsylvania Press, 2004.

[34] John Horgan. The Psychology of Terrorism. New York: Routledge, 2005.

[35] Lorenzo Vidino. "Europe's New Security Dilemma". The Washington Quarterly, 32: 4, 2009, pp. 61-75.

[36] J. Horgan, op. cit.

[37] Jennifer Windsor. "Promoting Democracy Can Combat Terrorism". The Washington Quarterly, 26: 3, 2003, pp. 43-58.

[38] For more information on Hezbollah and its history, see: Augustus Richard Norton. Hezbollah: A Short History. Princeton: Princeton University Press, 2007.

[39] Michael Scheuer. Imperial Hubris: Why the West is Losing the War on Terror. United States: Potomac Books, 2004.

[40] Thom Shanker and David E. Sanger. "Obama Is Said to Seek Approval on Saudi Arms Sale". New York Times, 17 Sept. 2010.

[41] Mark Mazzetti and Eric Schmitt. "CIA Steps Up Drone Attacks in Pakistan to Thwart Taliban". New York Times, 27 Sept. 2010.

[42] Scott Shane et al. "Secret Assault on Terrorism Widens on Two Continents". New York Times, 14 Aug. 2010.

[43] Quoted in Michael Boyle. Terrorism and Insurgency. In: Snyder, C. (Ed.) Contemporary Security and Strategy, Palgrave Macmillan, 2008, p. 186.

[44] Seth Jones. Counterinsurgency in Afghanistan. Santa Monica: The RAND Corporation, 2008.

[45] Quoted in John Nagl. Learning to Eat Soup with a Knife. Chicago: University of Chicago Press, 2005.

[46] David Galula. Counterinsurgency Warfare: Theory and Practice. United States: Praeger Security International, 1964; 2006, pp. 55-56.

[47] J. Nagl, op. cit.

[48] S. Jones, op. cit.

[49] See Kim Fishel. "Challenging the Hegemon: Al Qaeda's Elevation of Asymmetric Insurgent Warfare Onto the Global Arena". Low Intensity Conflict and Law Enforcement, 11: 2&3, 2002, pp. 285-298;and David Kilcullen. "Counterinsurgency Redux". Survival, 48: 4, 2006, pp. 111-130.

[50] D. Kilcullen, op. cit.

[51] Ibid.

[52] D. Kilcullen, op.cit., p. 608.

[53] Bruce Hoffman. "A Counterterrorism Strategy for the Obama Administration". Terrorism and Political Violence, 21, 2009, pp. 359-377, p. 362.

[54] Ibid, pp. 372-373.

[55] M. Boyle, 2010, p. 338. For more on the current Al-Qaeda threat and its "Americanization" trend, see: Kim Cragin, "Understanding Terrorist Motivations", Congressional Testimony. Santa Monica: The RAND Corporation, 2009; Peter Bergen and Bruce Hoffman. "Assessing the Terrorist Threat". A Report of the Bipartisan Policy Center's National Security Preparedness Group, 2010; and Brian Jenkins. "Would-be Warriors: Incidents of Jihadist Terrorist Radicalization in the United States Since September 11, 2001". Santa Monica: The RAND Corporation, 2010.

[56] M. Boyle, op. cit.

[57] M. Ignatieff, op. cit., p. 164.

[58] Christoph Schwennicke. "Why NATO Should Withdrawal from Afghanistan". Spiegel Online, 28 July 2010.

[59] Ahmed Rashid. "Save Whatever We Can". The New Republic, 26 July 2010.

[60] Ernesto Londono. "Survey of Afghans points to rampant corruption in government". Washington Post, 8 July 2010.

[61] Mark Sappenfield. "Ahmed Wali Karzai and the CIA: America's conundrum in Afghanistan". Christian Science Monitor, 29 Oct. 2010.

[62] M. Boyle, op. cit..

[63] Kalev I. Sepp. Special Forces. In: Thomas Rid and Thomas Keaney. Understanding Counterinsurgency: Doctrine, operations, and challenges. New York: Routledge, 2010, p. 138.

[64] Bob Woodward. Obama's Wars. New York: Simon and Schuster, 2010, p. 251.

[65] Richard N. Haass. "We're not winning. It's not worth it". Newsweek, 18 July, 2010.

[66] Ibid.

[67] David Sanger and Mark Mazzetti. "New Estimate of Strength of Al Qaeda is Offered". New York Times, 30 June, 2010.

[68] Brian Fishman. "Counting Al-Qaeda". Foreign Policy AFPAK Channel, 1 July, 2010.

[69] Daniel Benjamin. Quoted in Foreword, Country Reports on Terrorism 2009, U.S. State Department, p. 9.

[70] This question was raised by Michael Boyle at a counterterrorism workshop in St Andrews, United Kingdom, 2010.

Appendix 58

The Muslim Brotherhood: The rise of a political movement
by Storrey Rider, Created on: May 22, 2007   Last Updated: May 25, 2007
http://www.helium.com/items/348044-the-muslim-brotherhood-the-rise-of-a-political-movement

Terrorist attacks in recent years have reached an all-time high. The fallout from the most recent attacks-from 9/11 and the UK subway bombing to other transnational operations-have struck fear into people in many countries around the globe. One little-known fact is that many terrorist organizations performing these atrocities have all been influenced by a single terrorist group: the Muslim Brotherhood.

Though many can agree on the Brotherhood's influential impact, some are uncertain of its exact origins. Others fail to differentiate between whether it is a terrorist or revolutionary group. To create a concise analysis that clearly defines the Muslim Brotherhood, one must identify the definition of a terrorist, clarify dimensions of terrorism, and research trends in evolution, based upon methods of operation, changes in ideology, and other impacts which lead to its final transformation.

Paradoxically, the term terrorism' currently enjoys no universally agreed definition. The media uses the term loosely, and even counter-terrorism agencies use different definitions based on their mission-specific operating parameters. The result is that, with so many definitions and information sources, to arrive at a definition of terrorism can create confusion and blur the distinction between terrorism and criminality.

Co-authors Howard and Sawyer give a solid definition in their book titled Terrorism and Counterterrorism. They explain that, to differentiate between terrorism and other forms of criminal activity, one must recognize the five distinct characteristics of what constitutes a terrorist as well as the five elements that comprise terrorism itself. The characteristics shared in common through the actions and ideologies of all terrorists are embraced in the following: political aims and motives; violence or threats of violence; acts designed to have far-reaching psychological repercussions beyond the immediate victim or target; actions conducted by an organization with an identifiable chain of command or conspiratorial cell structure (whose members wear no uniform or identifying insignia); and actions perpetrated by a sub-national group or non-state entity.

The five elements that mark terrorism itself, strikingly similar to the definition of a terrorist, begins first with premeditation, or what can be termed as the "intent and prior decision to commit an act." The second element is political motivation, which "excludes criminal violence motivated by monetary gain or personal vengeance." The third element is marked by any act that targets non-combatants or "people who cannot defend themselves with violence in return." The fourth element encompasses those acts perpetrated by "either sub-national groups or clandestine agents." The last and fifth element is a recognition not only of clear incidents of terrorism, but also threats either posed or the potential for further threatening actions in the future.

Appendix 59

9/11 Rescue Workers Face Increased Multiple Myeloma Risk
http://www.benzeneleukemialawblog.com/leukemia/acute-myelogenous-leukemia/911-rescue-workers-face-increased-multiple-myeloma-risk/

USnews.com reports that 9/11 responders may face increased risk of the hematological disease multiple myeloma.

The brave and selfless heroes who worked at Ground Zero in the wake of the World Trade Center bombings have in many cases sacrificed their health for the good of the country. Most of them probably would have been there even if the EPA had not deliberately downplayed the risks posed by massive exposure to the carcinogenic dust and smoke. Perhaps if the EPA had taken the threat more seriously, more precautions could have been taken to protect the health and futures of those who risked it all to help others in our country's hour of need.

Countless photos show responders wearing SARS style dust masks, which in this case were the breathing protection equivalent of a sugar pill, not up to the task of filtering carcinogens from heavily chemical laden smoke.

The recent upswing of multiple myeloma in ground zero workers is being seen as the beginning of a "third wave" of debilitating ground zero related illness. The first wave was coughing and acute respiratory distress and the "second wave" was chronic lung diseases. Dr. Robin Herbert, co-director of the World Trade Center Medical Monitoring Program fears that this "third wave" could last for decades as most workers can safely be said to have inhaled large quantities of carcinogens, and many cancers take years to develop.

Alarmingly, though multiple myeloma is almost always a disease of the the elderly, with only 1% of cases found in patients under 40, half of the cases diagnosed in 9/11 rescue workers were identified among law enforcement officers under the age of 45.

Appendix 60

Seven Signs of Terrorist Activity
http://www.scnus.org/page.aspx?id=101218

The following information was obtained from the ASIS public website. These seven signs of terrorist activity were developed by the Metropolitan Transportation Authority of New York. The Michigan State Police have created a video presentation of the seven signs of terrorist activity. To view the video, click here.

Surveillance
Elicitation
Test of Security
Acquiring Supplies
Suspicious People Who Don't Belong
Dry Runs
Deploying Assets/Getting Into Position

Surveillance

If terrorists have chosen a specific target, that target area will most likely be observed during the planning phase of the operation. They do this in order to determine the strengths, weaknesses and number of personnel that may respond to an incident. Routes to and from the target are usually established during the surveillance phase. It is therefore important to take note of such things as someone recording or monitoring activities, drawing diagrams on or annotating maps, using vision-enhancing devices and/or having in one's possession floor plans or blue prints of places such as high-tech firms, financial institutions or government/military facilities. Any of these surveillance-type acts may be an indicator that something just is not right. Nothing is too trivial and should not be discarded as such.

Elicitation

The second sign or signal is elicitation. What this means is anyone attempting to gain information about a place, person or operation. An example is someone attempting to gain knowledge about a critical infrastructure like a power plant, water reservoir or maritime port.

Terrorists may attempt to research bridge and tunnel usage, make unusual inquiries concerning shipments or inquire as to how a military base operates. They may also attempt to place "key" people in sensitive work locations.

Tests of Security

Tests of security is another area in which terrorists would attempt to gather data. This is usually conducted by driving by the target, moving into sensitive areas and observing security or law enforcement response. Terrorists would be interested in the time in which it takes to respond to an incident and/or the routes taken to a specific location. They may also try to penetrate physical security barriers or procedures in order to assess strengths and weaknesses. They often gain legitimate employment at key locations in order to monitor day-to-day activities. In any event, they may try to gain this knowledge in order to make their mission or scheme more effective.

Acquiring Supplies

Another area to be cognizant of is anyone acquiring supplies. This may be a case where someone is purchasing or stealing explosives, weapons or ammunition. It could also be someone storing harmful chemicals or chemical equipment. Terrorists would also find it useful to have in their possession law enforcement equipment and identification, military uniforms and decals, flight passes, badges or even flight manuals. If they can't find the opportunity to steal these types of things, they may try to photocopy IDs or attempt to make passports or other forms of identification by counterfeiting. Possessing any of these would make it easier for one to gain entrance into secured or usually prohibited areas.

Suspicious People Who Don't Belong

A fifth pre-incident indicator is observing suspicious people who just "don't belong." This does not mean we should profile individuals; rather, it means we should profile behaviors. These include suspicious border crossings, stowaways aboard a ship or people jumping ship in a port. It may mean having someone in a workplace, building, neighborhood or business establishment that does not fit in because of their demeanor, their language usage or unusual questions they are asking. As an officer you may respond to a complaint that may appear to be a routine investigation but results in something much larger in significance.

Dry Runs

Another sign to watch for is "dry runs." Before execution of the final operation or plan, a practice session will be run to work out the flaws and unanticipated problems. A dry run may very well be the heart of a planning stage of a terrorist act. If you find someone monitoring a police radio frequency and recording emergency response times, you may very well be observing a "dry run." Another element of this activity could include mapping out routes and determining the timing of traffic lights and flow. This stage is actually our best chance to intercept and stop an attack. Multiple dry runs are normally conducted at or near the target area.

Deploying Assets/Getting Into Position

The seventh and final sign or signal to look for is someone deploying assets or getting into position. This is a person's last chance to alert authorities before the terrorist act occurs. It is also important to remember that pre-incident indicators may come months or even years apart. It is threfore extremely important to document every fragment of information no matter how insignificant it may appear and forward this information.

Appendix 61

Osama bin Laden dead, killed by US in Pak; buried at sea
Peter Baker, Helene Cooper, Mark Mazzetti, The New York Times, Updated: May 02, 2011 20:10
http://www.ndtv.com/article/world/osama-bin-laden-dead-killed-by-us-in-pak-shot-in-the-head-102859

In a dramatic late-night appearance in the East Room of the White House, Mr. Obama declared that "justice has been done" as he disclosed that American military and C.I.A. operatives had finally cornered bin Laden, the Al Qaeda leader who had eluded them for nearly a decade. American officials said bin Laden resisted and was shot in the head. He was later buried at sea.

The news touched off an extraordinary outpouring of emotion as crowds gathered outside the White House, in Times Square and at the Ground Zero site, waving American flags, cheering, shouting, laughing and chanting, "USA, USA!" In New York City, crowds sang the Star-Spangled Banner. Throughout downtown Washington, drivers honked horns deep into the night.

"For over two decades, bin Laden has been Al Qaeda's leader and symbol," the president said in a statement televised around the world. "The death of bin Laden marks the most significant achievement to date in our nation's effort to defeat Al Qaeda. But his death does not mark the end of our effort. There's no doubt that Al Qaeda will continue to pursue attacks against us. We must and we will remain vigilant at home and abroad." (Watch: The raid that located, killed Osama)

Bin Laden's demise is a defining moment in the American-led war on terrorism, a symbolic stroke affirming the relentlessness of the pursuit of those who attacked New York and Washington on Sept. 11, 2001. What remains to be seen, however, is whether it galvanizes his followers by turning him into a martyr or serves as a turning of the page in the war in Afghanistan and gives further impetus to Mr. Obama to bring American troops home. How much his death will affect Al Qaeda itself remains unclear. For years, as they failed to find him, American leaders have said he was more symbolically important than operationally significant because he was on the run and hindered in any meaningful leadership role. And yet, he remained the most potent face of terrorism around the world and some of those who downplayed his role in recent years nonetheless celebrated his death. (Read: US embassies on high alert)

Given Bin Laden's status among radicals, the American government braced for possible retaliation. A senior Pentagon official said late Sunday that military bases in the United States and around the world were ordered to a higher state of readiness. The State Department issued a worldwide travel warning, urging

Americans in volatile areas "to limit their travel outside of their homes and hotels and avoid mass gatherings and demonstrations."

The strike could exacerbate deep tensions with Pakistan, which has periodically bristled at American efforts even as Bin Laden evidently found safe refuge on its territory for nearly a decade. Since taking office, Mr. Obama has ordered significantly more unmanned drone strikes on suspected terrorist targets in Pakistan, stirring public anger and prompting the Pakistani government to protest. (Read: Pak distances itself from Osama raid, killing)

When the end came for bin Laden, he was found not in the remote tribal areas along the Pakistani-Afghan border where he has long been presumed to be sheltered, but in a massive compound about an hour's drive north from the Pakistani capital of Islamabad. He was hiding in the medium-sized city of Abbottabad, home to a large Pakistani military base and a military academy of the Pakistani army. (Read: Osama was 800 yards from Pakistan Military Academy)

The house at the end of a narrow dirt road was roughly eight times larger than other homes in the area, but had no telephone or television connections. When American operatives converged on the house on Sunday, bin Laden "resisted the assault force" and was killed in the middle of an intense gun battle, a senior administration official said, but details were still sketchy early Monday morning. (Read: Osama bin Laden - World's most-wanted man)

The fate of Ayman al-Zawahiri, the Al Qaeda second-in-command, was unclear Sunday night.

The official said that military and intelligence officials first learned last summer that a "high-value target" was being protected in the compound and began working on a plan for going in to get him. Beginning in March, Mr. Obama presided over five national security meetings at the White House to go over plans for the operation and on Friday morning, just before leaving Washington to tour tornado damage in Alabama, gave the final order for special forces and C.I.A. operatives to strike.

Mr. Obama called it a "targeted operation," and added: "No Americans were harmed. They took care to avoid civilian casualties. After a firefight, they killed Osama bin Laden and took custody of his body."

Bin Laden's death came nearly 10 years after Al Qaeda terrorists hijacked four American passenger jets, crashing three of them into the World Trade Center in New York and the Pentagon outside Washington. The fourth hijacked jet, United Flight 93, crashed into the Pennsylvania countryside after passengers fought the militants.

"This is important news for us, and for the world," said Gordon Felt, president of the group Families of Flight 93. "It cannot ease our pain, or bring back our loved ones. It does bring a measure of comfort that the mastermind of the September 11th tragedy and the face of global terror can no longer spread his evil."

The mostly young people who celebrated in the streets of New York and Washington saw it as a historic moment, one that for many of them culminated a worldwide manhunt that started when they were children.

Some climbed trees and lampposts directly in front of the White House to cheer and wave flags. Cigars and noisemakers were common. One group started singing, "Osama, Osama, hey, hey, hey, good bye."

Maureen Hasson, 22, a recent college graduate working for the Justice Department, came down to Lafayette Square in a fushia party dress and flip-flops. "This is full circle for our generation," she said. "Just look around at the average age here. We were all in middle school when the terrorists struck. We all vividly remember 9/11 and this is the close of that chapter."

Sam Sherman, 18, a freshman at George Washington University originally from New York, also rushed down to the White House. "The feeling you can't even imagine, the feeling in the air. "It's crazy," he said. "I have friends with parents dead because of Osama bin Laden's plan, okay? So when I heard this news, I was coming down to celebrate."

Mr. Obama said Pakistan had helped develop the intelligence that led to Bin Laden, but an American official said Islamabad was not informed about the strike in advance. "We shared our intelligence on this compound with no other country, including Pakistan," the official said.

Mr. Obama recalled his statements in the 2008 presidential campaign when he vowed to order American forces to strike inside Pakistan if necessary even without Islamabad's permission. "That is what we've done," he said. "But it's important to note that our counterterrorism cooperation with Pakistan helped lead us to bin Laden and the compound where he was hiding."

Relations with Pakistan had fallen in recent weeks to their lowest point in years. Adm. Mike Mullen, the chairman of the Joint Chiefs of Staff, publicly criticized the Pakistani military two weeks ago for failing to act against extremists allied to Al Qaeda who shelter in the tribal areas of North Waziristan. Last week, Gen. Ashfaq Pervez Kayani, head of the Pakistani army, said Pakistan had broken the back of terrorism on its territory, prompting skepticism in Washington.

Mr. Obama called President Asif Ali Zardari of Pakistan to tell him about the strike after it was underway and his advisers called their Pakistani counterparts.

"They agree that this is a good and historic day for both of our nations," Mr. Obama said.

The city of Abbottabad where Bin Laden was found has had other known Al Qaeda presence in the past. A senior Indonesian militant, Umar Patek, was arrested there earlier this year. Mr. Patek was protected by a Qaeda operative, a postal clerk who worked under cover at the main post office, a signal that Al Qaeda may have had other operations in the area.

As the operation's start approached, many American officials posted at the United States consulate in Peshawar, the capital of the north west area of Pakistan, were told suddenly to depart last Friday, leaving behind only a core group of essential staff. The American officials said they had been told to leave because of fears of kidnapping but were not tipped off to the operation.

Analysts said Bin Laden's death amounted to a double blow for Al Qaeda, after its sermons of anti-Western violence seemed to be rendered irrelevant by the wave of political upheaval rolling through the Arab world.

"It comes at a time when Al Qaeda's narrative is already very much in doubt in the Arab world," said Martin S. Indyk, vice president and director of foreign policy at the Brookings Institution. "Its narrative was that violence was the way to redeem Arab honor and dignity. But Osama bin Laden and his violence didn't succeed in unseating anybody."

Al Qaeda sympathizers reacted with disbelief, anger and in some cases talk of retribution. On a web site considered an outlet for Al Qaeda messages, forum administrators deleted posts by users announcing Bin Laden's death and demanded that members wait until the news was confirmed by Al Qaeda sources, according to the SITE Intelligence Group, an organization that monitors radicals.

Even so, SITE said, sympathizers on the forum posted messages calling Bin Laden a martyr and suggesting retaliation. "America will reap the same if the news is true and false," said one message. "The lions will remain lions and will continue moving in the footsteps of Usama," said another, using an alternate spelling of Bin Laden's name.

In the United States, the Council on American-Islamic Relations, an advocacy organization, said it welcomed Bin Laden's death. "As we have stated repeatedly since the 9/11 terror attacks, Bin Laden never represented Muslims or Islam," the group said in a statement. "In fact, in addition to the killing of thousands of Americans, he and Al Qaeda caused the deaths of countless Muslims worldwide."

"This momentous achievement marks a victory for America, for people who seek peace around the world, and for all those who lost loved ones on September 11, 2001," former President George W. Bush, who launched the war against Al Qaeda after Sept. 11 and called for Bin Laden to be caught "dead or alive," said in a statement. "The fight against terror goes on, but tonight America has sent an unmistakable message: No matter how long it takes, justice will be done."

Mr. Obama used similar language and warned that the war against terrorists has not ended. "We will be relentless in defense of our citizens and our friends and allies. We will be true to the values that make us who we are. And on nights like this one, we can say to those families who have lost loved ones to Al Qaeda's terror, justice has been done."

The president was careful to add that, as Mr. Bush did during his presidency, the United States is not at war with Islam. "Bin Laden was not a Muslim leader; he was a mass murderer of Muslims," Mr. Obama said. "Indeed, Al Qaeda has slaughtered scores of Muslims in many countries, including our own. So his demise should be welcomed by all who believe in peace and human dignity."

Appendix 62

21st THEATER SUPPORT COMMAND
Deputy G2 (Intelligence)
http://c21.maxwell.af.mil/terrorism/protective_measures.htm

PERSONAL PROTECTIVE MEASURES
AGAINST TERRORISM

General. Any member of the Department of Defense--not just senior leaders--can become a target for terrorists. The purpose of this memorandum is to provide general guidance to DOD members and their families on how to avoid acts of terrorism, as well as to provide basic instructions in the event DOD personnel become victims of a terrorist attack.

Precautions. Attitude toward security is most important. Although some of these precautions are applicable overseas, you can decrease your chances of becoming a terrorist target, as well as those of your family members, by taking the precautions listed in this appendix. Therefore, it is highly recommended you share this information with every member of your family. It is also suggested that you and your family review these precautions on a regular basis.

a. At All Times

(1) Encourage security awareness in your family and discuss what to do if there is a security threat.

(2) Be alert for surveillance attempts or suspicious persons or activities, and report them to the proper authorities. Trust your gut feelings.

(3) Vary personal routines whenever possible.

(4) Get into the habit of checking in to let your friends and family know where you are or when to expect you.

(5) Know how to use the local phone system. Always carry telephone change. Know the emergency numbers for local police, fire, ambulance, and hospital.

(6) Know the locations of civilian police, military police, government agencies, US Embassy, and other safe locations where you can find refuge or assistance.

(7) Avoid public disputes or confrontations. Report any trouble to the proper authorities.

Know certain key phrases in the native language such as "I need a policeman," "Take me to a doctor," "Where is the hospital?," and "Where is the police station?"

(9) Set up simple signal systems to alert family members or associates that there is a danger. Do not share this information with anyone not involved in your signal system.

(10) Carry identification showing your blood type and any special medical conditions. Keep a minimum of a 1-week supply of essential medication on hand at all times.

(11) Keep a low profile. Shun publicity. Do not flash large sums of money.

(12) Do not unnecessarily divulge your home address, phone number, or family information.

(13) Watch for unexplained absences of local citizens as an early warning of possible terrorist actions.

(14) Keep your personal affairs in good order. Keep wills current, have powers of attorney drawn up, take measures to ensure family's financial security, and develop a plan for family actions in the event you are taken hostage.

(15) Do not carry sensitive or potentially embarrassing items.

b. At Home

(1) Have a clear view of approaches to your home.

(2) Install strong doors and locks.

(3) Change locks when you move in or when a key is lost.

(4) Install windows that do not allow easy access.

(5) Never leave house or trunk keys with your ignition key while your car is being serviced.

(6) Have adequate lighting outside your house.

(7) Create the appearance that the house is occupied by using timers to control lights and radios while you are away.

(8) Install one-way viewing devices in doors.

(9) Install intrusion detection alarms and smoke and fire alarms.

(10) Do not hide keys or give them to very young children.

(11) Never leave young children at home alone.

(12) Never admit strangers to your home without proper identification.

(13) Use off street parking at your residence, if at all possible.

(14) Teach children how to call the police, and ensure that they know what to tell the police (name, address, etc.).

(15) Avoid living in residences that are located in isolated areas, on one-way streets, dead-end streets, or cul-de-sacs.

(16) Avoid residences that are on the ground floor, adjacent to vacant lots, or on steep hills.

(17) Carefully screen all potential domestic help.

(18) Do not place your name on exterior walls of residences.

(19) Do not answer the telephone with your name and rank.

(20) Personally destroy all envelopes and other items that reflect personal information.

(21) Close draperies during periods of darkness. Draperies should be opaque and made of heavy material.

(22) Avoid frequent exposure on balconies and in windows.

(23) Consider owning a dog to discourage intruders.

(24) Never accept unexpected package deliveries.

(25) Don't let your trash become a source of information.

c. While Traveling

(1) Vary times and routes.

(2) Be alert for suspicious-looking vehicles.

(3) Check for suspicious activity or objects around your car before getting into or out of it. Do not touch your vehicle until you have thoroughly checked it (look inside it, walk around it, and look under it).

(4) Know your driver.

(5) Equip your car with an inside hood latch and a locking gas cap.

(6) Drive with windows closed and doors locked.

(7) Travel with a group of people--there is safety in numbers.

(8) Travel on busy routes; avoid isolated and dangerous areas.

(9) Park your car off the street in a secure area.

(10) Lock your car when it is unattended.

(11) Do not routinely use the same taxi or bus stop. NOTE: Buses are preferred over taxis.

(12) If you think you are being followed, move as quickly as possible to a safe place such as a police or fire station.

(13) If your car breaks down, raise the hood then get back inside the car and remain there with the doors locked and the windows up. If anyone offers to assist, ask the person to call the police.

(14) Do not pick up hitchhikers.

(15) Drive on well-lit streets.

(16) Prearrange a signal with your driver to indicate that it is safe to get into the vehicle. Share this information only with persons having a need to know.

(17) Have the driver open the door for you.

(18) If the driver is absent, do not get into the car.

(19) If possible, tell your driver your destination only after the car has started.

(20) Keep your vehicle's gas tank at least half full.

d. In Hotels

(1) Keep your room key on your person at all times.

(2) Be observant for suspicious persons loitering in the area.

(3) Do not give your room number to strangers.

(4) Keep your room and personal effects neat and orderly so you will recognize tampering or strange out-of-place objects.

(5) Know the location of emergency exits and fire extinguishers.

(6) Do not admit strangers to your room.

(7) Know how to locate hotel security guards.

e. Ground Transportation Security

(1) Use a plain car that is common in the area to minimize the rich American look.

(2) Do not be predictable in your daily travel behavior; vary your travel times, your routes, and your mode of transportation whenever possible.

(3) Check the area around the vehicle, the exterior of the vehicle, and then the interior of the vehicle before starting the engine.

(4) Travel with companions or in convoy whenever possible.

(5) Know the locations of safe havens (e.g., police and fire stations) along your travel routes.

(6) Install appropriate mirrors, locks, and other devices to secure your car against tampering.

(7) Safeguard car keys at all times.

(8) Screen chauffeurs or permanently assigned drivers. Develop a simple system for the driver to alert you to danger when you are picked up. Share this information only with persons having a need to know.

(9) Lock your car, especially at night, and check and lock your garage when you park there overnight.

(10) Park in well-lighted areas if you must park on the street.

(11) Always fasten seat belts, lock doors, and close windows when driving or riding in a car.

(12) Be alert for surveillance and be aware of possible danger when driving or riding in a car.

(13) Drive immediately to a "safe haven" when surveillance is suspected; do not drive home.

f. Air Travel Security

(1) Use military aircraft whenever possible.

(2) Avoid travel through high-risk areas; use foreign flag airlines and/or indirect routes to avoid such areas.

(3) Do not use rank or military addresses on tickets, travel documents, hotel reservations, or luggage.

(4) Select a window seat on aircraft because they offer more protection and are less accessible to hijackers than are aisle seats.

(5) Select a seat in the midsection of the aircraft because it is not one of the two usual areas of terrorist activity.

(6) Do not discuss your US Government affiliation with any other passengers.

(7) Consider using a tourist passport when traveling in high-risk areas; if you use a tourist passport, store your official passport, identification card, travel orders, and other official documents in your carry-on bags. Also, if you normally wear a military ring; e.g., Service or academy, consider leaving it at home or pack it in your checked baggage.

(8) Do not carry classified material unless it is mission-essential.

(9) Use plain civilian luggage; avoid using B-4 bags, duffel bags, and other military-looking bags. Remove all indications of your rank and any military patches, logos, and decals from your luggage and briefcase.

(10) Do not carry official papers in your briefcase.

(11) Travel in conservative civilian clothing. Do not wear military-oriented organizational shirts or caps or military-issue shoes or glasses. Also, avoid obvious American clothing such as cowboy boots and hats as well as American-logo T-shirts. Cover visible US-affiliated tattoos with a long-sleeved shirt.

(12) If possible, check your baggage with the airport's curb service.

(13) Adjust your arrival at the airport to minimize waiting time, be alert for any suspicious activity in the waiting area, and proceed immediately to the departure gate.

3. Hostage Defense Measures

a. Survive with honor--this is the mission of any American hostage.

b. If your duties may expose you to being taken hostage, make sure your family's affairs are in order to ensure their financial security. Make an up-to-date will and give appropriate powers of attorney to your spouse or to a trusted friend. Concern for the family is a major source of stress for persons in kidnap or hostage situations.

c. If you are taken hostage and decide not to resist, assure your captors of your intention to cooperate, especially during the abduction phase.

d. Regain your composure as quickly as possible after capture, face your fears, and try to master your emotions.

e. Take mental note of the direction, time in transit, noise, and other environmental factors that may help you identify your location.

f. Note the numbers, names, physical characteristics, accents, personal habits, and rank structure of your captors.

g. Anticipate isolation and terrorist efforts to confuse you.

h. Try to mentally prepare yourself for the situation ahead as much as possible. Stay mentally active.

i. Do not aggravate your abductors; instead, attempt to establish a positive relationship with them. Do not be fooled by a friendly approach--it may be used to get information from you.

j. Avoid political or ideological discussions with your captors; comply with their instructions, but maintain your dignity.

k. Do not discuss or divulge any classified information that you may possess.

l. Exercise daily.

m. Read anything you can find to keep your mind active.

n. Eat whatever food is offered to you to maintain your strength.

o. Establish a slow, methodical routine for every task.

p. When being interrogated, take a simple, tenable position and stick to it. Be polite and maintain your temper. Give short answers, talk freely about nonessential matters, but be guarded when the conversation turns to substantial matters.

q. If forced to present terrorist demands to authorities, in writing or on tape, do only what you are told to do. Avoid making a plea on your own behalf.

r. Be proud of your heritage, government, and military affiliation, but be careful that your behavior does not antagonize your captors. Affirm your faith in basic democratic principles.

s. In the event of a rescue attempt:

(1) Drop to the floor.

(2) Be quiet and do not attract your captors' attention.

(3) Wait for instructions.

(4) Rescue forces will initially treat you as one of the terrorists until you are positively identified as friend or foe. This is for your security. Cooperate, even if you are initially handcuffed.

(5) Once released, avoid making comments to the news media until you have been debriefed by the proper US authorities.

www.ingramcontent.com/pod-product-compliance
Lightning Source LLC
Chambersburg PA
CBHW081058290526
45795CB00006B/1902